CULTURE**SHOCK**!
A Survival Guide to Customs and Etiquette

GERMANY

Richard Lord

GRAPHIC ARTS
BOOKS
Portland, Oregon

Marshall Cavendish
Editions

Photo Credits:
Archiv fúr Kunst und Geschichte: pages 33, 35, 45 ▪ Bundesbildstille: pages
6, 10, 76, 88, 138, 140, 145, 182, 238, 271 ▪ Inter Nationes: 16, 54, 79,
115, 117, 165, 187, 205, 207, 211, 213, 226, 227, 263, 282 ▪ Masterfile/
Larry Fisher: cover

All illustrations by TRIGG

First published in 1996.
Copyright © 2005 Marshall Cavendish International (Asia) Private Limited

This edition published in 2005 by:

Marshall Cavendish Editions
An imprint of Marshall Cavendish International (Asia) Pte Ltd
1 New Industrial Road, Singapore 536196
Tel: (65) 6213 9300, fax: (65) 6285 4871.
Email: te@sg.marshallcavendish.com
Online bookstore: www.marshallcavendish.com/genref

and

Graphic Arts Center Publishing Company
P.O. Box 10306, Portland, Oregon 97296-0306
United States of America
Tel: (503) 226 2402
Website: www.gacpc.com

Please contact Graphic Arts Center Publishing Company for the Library of
Congress catalogue number

ISBN 981-261-122-3 (Asia & Rest of World)
ISBN 1-55868-936-3 (USA & Canada)
ISBN 1-904879-83-7 (Europe)

Printed in Singapore by Times Graphics

ABOUT THE SERIES

Culture shock is a state of disorientation that can come over anyone who has been thrust into unknown surroundings, away from one's comfort zone. *CultureShock!* is a series of trusted and reputed guides which has, for decades, been helping expatriates and long-term visitors to cushion the impact of culture shock whenever they move to a new country.

Written by people who have lived in the country and experienced culture shock themselves, the authors share all the information necessary for anyone to cope with these feelings of disorientation more effectively. The guides are written in a style that is easy to read and covers a range of topics that will arm readers with enough advice, hints and tips to make their lives as normal as possible again.

Each book is structured in the same manner. It begins with the first impressions that visitors will have of that city or country. To understand a culture, one must first understand the people—where they came from, who they are, the values and traditions they live by, as well as their customs and etiquette. This is covered in the first half of the book

Then on with the practical aspects—how to settle in with the greatest of ease. Authors walk readers through how to find accommodation, get the utilities and telecommunications up and running, enrol the children in school and keep in the pink of health. But that's not all. Once the essentials are out of the way, venture out and try the food, enjoy more of the culture and travel to other areas. Then be immersed in the language of the country before discovering more about the business side of things.

To round off, snippets of basic information are offered before readers are 'tested' on customs and etiquette of the country. Useful words and phrases, a comprehensive resource guide and list of books for further research are also included for easy reference.

CONTENTS

INTRODUCTION

How to describe Germany to someone coming from another culture and planning to live here?

When I first set out to write this book, I somehow thought it would all come flowing out in a rush. After all, the advantages, disadvantages, obstacles and benefits of living as a foreigner in Germany confronted me almost every day, and served as major topics of conversation whenever I got together with foreign friends and associates. But in attempting to pour all this into a book that could serve other foreigners just coming to Germany, I found the task more daunting than I had at first imagined.

After talking to many foreign residents of Germany, this assignment began to remind me more and more of that old tale of the three blind men sent out by a ruler to describe an elephant. You know the story: the first blind man returns to inform his ruler that an elephant is a long, thin animal; the second reports that it's a huge, flat, hairless creature; while the last describes the behemoth as a long, thick cylindrical beast with a butterfly mouth that makes a strange, tooting sound.

The moral of this story is clear—each of the blind men was honest and accurately described what he had experienced. But the first blind man had only experienced the tail, the second the broad torso, and the third the trunk. Well, writing about a massive, complex country like Germany is a similar task. No one can fully experience and describe all of it, not even someone who had spent his or her whole life here. (Plus, a native German would probably miss certain features that just leap out and grab newcomers by the throat.)

We all have our little blind spots, some of us may even have an axe or two stashed away, ready for grinding. I readily admit that I have a few of the former, and maybe even one or two of the latter. I also accept that this book would be somewhat different, would possibly have a different focus had it been written by someone else—someone with her or his own particular blind spots, a different axe to grind. For instance, I found that friends or acquaintances I've had long discussions with recently were obsessed with their own parts of the elephant. I've tried to incorporate all of these perspectives into the overall view presented here, even when they were in some cases wildly contradictory.

But then, German society itself is wildly contradictory in so many ways. It embodies great wealth and depressing poverty; an obsession with order along with a taste for measured chaos; a great concern for the threatened natural environment and a careless disregard for obvious restrictions that might better protect that beloved environment.

Many of the cliches you've heard about Germany are still readily observable here; others presumably were some time ago, but no more; while other cliches are not only no longer operable, they're positively harmful.

I admit that even after you've travelled through this whole book, you still won't know every inch of the elephant, but at least you'll have a good idea of what kind of beast this elephant is, and how you might begin to deal with it.

ACKNOWLEDGEMENTS

This book would have been a much slimmer and poorer volume if not for the input, support and assistance of a good many people and institutions. I can't possibly fit in everyone who helped me in some way, but I must thank the following:

ADAC
Amt für Multikulturelle Angelegenheiten, Frankfurt
Archiv für Kunst und Geschichte, Berlin
Bundesbildestelle, Bonn
Deutsche Bibliothek
Financial Times (Europe)
Industrie-und Handelskammer, Frankfurt am Main
Inter Nationes, Bonn
Wolfgang Huhn and the Polizeiladen, Frankfurt am Main
Landesverband des Hessischen Einzelhandels e.V.

And an even deeper debt of gratitude goes out to:

Bernd Basten
Martin Harrison
Brigid Ibell
Sally Lamm
George McIlhenney
Robert Rodger
Inge Schlaile
Robert Stevenson
Susan Stern

Dr Peter Linder
Heinz Frey and Rita Da Silva-Frey
Alessandra Helm
Doris Linda Jones
Gudrun Lord
James G. Neuger
Orly Selinger
Helmut and Hedwig Stein
Ulla and Marylane Silundika

For Gudrun,
the main reason that I stayed in Germany.

MAP OF GERMANY

NORTH SEA

DENMARK

BALTIC SEA

NETHERLANDS

BERLIN ●

POLAND

GERMANY

BELGIUM

CZECH REPUBLIC

LUXEMBOURG

FRANCE

AUSTRIA

SWITZERLAND

ITALY

FIRST IMPRESSIONS

CHAPTER 1

'If you inquire what the people are like here,
I must answer, "The same as everywhere. '
—JWF Goethe, *The Sorrows of Young Werther*

'Every man takes the limits of his own field
of vision for the limits of the world.'
—Arthur Schopenhauer (1851)

ALMOST EVERYONE WHO ARRIVES IN GERMANY brings along a sack of prepackaged conceptions about the country and its people. Most of these should be handed over at Customs— because they're of no value. Unless you've been unusually well informed about the country before you arrive, you are sure to run into some major surprises.

You will probably fly into the country, arriving at one of the major airports, possibly Frankfurt, the largest and busiest. The airports are bustling with activity, aglitter with shops and stands, and commendably clean. Right; this is Germany as you always imagined it.

First Impressions

Emerging from the airport or train station, you head for the taxi rank and are struck by the fact that almost all taxis are Mercedes. You knew this was a prosperous country, but this well-wheeled? Somebody will tell you before long that the government gives big tax write-offs for the purchase of these luxury cabs, which are well-built to take all sorts of wear and tear. And don't forget that Mercedes is a proud German product. Still, it is impressive.

Driving or walking through town, you start looking for Germans—the Germans you've always seen in picture books. You know, men in cute *Lederhose* shorts, ruffled shirts and those funny hats favoured by Robin Hood and his merry men or women decked out like grown-up Heidis in *dirndl* skirts, even more ruffled shirts and precariously pointed shoes. And of course, everyone with at least one fist wrapped around a huge beer stein.

Don't strain your neck looking too hard. You will find that you can live for decades in Germany and never see these sights in the flesh. Sure, if you go to the right parts of the country, during the right festivals, you'll see lots of 'Hansis' and 'Lottis' like that. Otherwise, Germans don't dress a lot like 'Germans.'

Nor do they talk a lot like Germans—"Zee Yermans don't reellee talk like ziss, you zee." It's true, most Germans speak English with an obvious accent, but the accents you're apt to hear wouldn't pass muster on *Hogan's Heroes*. In fact, many non-Britons take them for wobbly British accents. I once knew a German actor in London who told the sad tale of how he lost a role as a German soldier in a British television film because he didn't sound enough like a German. Most of them don't.

But you continue your search for the typical German. What is confusing is that a lot of these Germans look like Turks or Croatians or Italians or Arabs or Asians or Africans or Greeks. The fact is, that's just what many of these folks you see are. Before long you'll realise that in many big cities, there are almost as many foreigners as Germans on the streets and in

the shops. In fact, if you enter through Frankfurt, you should be aware that at least 30 per cent of Frankfurt's residents are non-Germans.

Where Am I?

So what is German then, and what is Germany? Well, you had always heard how clean this place was, that the Germans were almost compulsive about public cleanliness. Could it be that you somehow landed in the wrong country? I mean, look at all these papers thrown on the ground, some of them within a leaping slam dunk of a trash receptacle. And in many places, cigarette butts are scattered like so many wildflowers growing out of the sidewalks, or clinging to the curbs. This is what they call a compulsion for cleanliness and order?

Or what may grab you as you move about the centre of town is the lack of a distinct German personality to the place. Maybe one of your first impressions will echo the crumpled disappointment of one world-weary American visitor: "I was pretty much used to the fact that in today's world, every place looks like every place else. But Germany looks more like every place else than any place else."

Not quite, not quite. Before long, your first wave of first impressions will be overtaken by a second wave of first impressions. Look, this must be Germany after all—lots of stands with people eating *wursts* with toothpicks or their fingers, without the benefit of buns. And, as you make your way down any main thoroughfare, you're caught up in the anxious bustle of people sweeping by with clear, Teutonic seriousness of purpose stamped on their faces. This is more like the Germany you've heard and read about.

Even more of what you thought was typically German may be tucked away in other parts of town, or in the small town or suburb you head off to. Winding roads in quiet hamlets swirl you by rows of tidy, well-kept, half-timbered houses. And the streets of these towns are as free of trash and litter as you had always imagined German streets would be.

And if your city has an *Altstadt* (old town) section that wasn't totally destroyed by World War II bombs, you will find that storybook Germany you have always wanted to see, perhaps with buildings and streets recalling centuries past, some looking like giant gingerbread-house constructions. In contrast to the 'more like everywhere else than anywhere else' architecture of certain parts of certain cities, you'll find villages (mainly in the new eastern states) that look like they've undergone only minor, incremental changes since the turn of the last century.

So, were your very first impressions so wrong, were your second ones more accurate? No, all of these impressions are correct. But remember what I said in the introduction—you were just rubbing your hands over one small part of the elephant when you first arrived and the more charming Germany belongs to another part of the elephant. Both sets of impressions belong indelibly to Germany. But now you've got to penetrate a little, to seek out the country a little more.

WHY COME TO GERMANY?

In countless conversations with other foreign residents over the years, the question of why people came to this country has prompted a number of answers, but they all fall within a rather narrow range. Mainly it involved a spouse, boyfriend or girlfriend, or a job or some business opportunity—or hopes of one of those. Tellingly, very few people say they came here because of the country itself, that they had always heard of Germany and always wanted to live here, finally seizing the opportunity when it came. For many long- and short-term migrants, Germany is simply the location where they could best do the other things they wanted to do.

Many long-time residents relate how originally they had actually intended to head further west, but Germany, for one reason or another, is as far as they got. Perhaps the most interesting of these cases are the many East European Jews who have sought refuge in Germany over the last 60 years, some of them right after World War II. In many cases, these people had themselves narrowly escaped deportation to the Nazi extermination camps; some of them were even internees in those death camps. And yet, 25 or 30 years later, these same people had gained enough trust in the Germans and the liberal democracy they had built up to brave a rough passage here, through the Iron Curtain, to take advantage of the country's magnanimous political asylum law. Perhaps no greater testimony to the strength of West (now united) Germany's democratic reconstruction exists than this.

THE MALIGNED MECCA

Another curious thing you will discover during your first months of gathering impressions is that very few foreign residents really like Germany that much—or will admit to it. Standard conversation topics of the foreign community here are complaints about this or that aspect of German life, this or that facet of the German personality, their being treated this way or that way. Many go on and on about how much they want to move on to someplace else. But they somehow manage to stay on and on. I have several friends who have been talking about getting out as soon as they can for at least ten years. Yet these folks have been in Germany for 20 years or more, even though they are completely free to leave and go elsewhere.

A view of the Frankfurt skyline: welcome to modern Germany.

More typical than the latter legion of grousers are those who will tell you they originally came for a job or an assignment, expecting to stay only a short time. But then they met a mate, acquired some new friends, got involved in this project or that, found this or that aspect of the country intriguing and then, well, you know. Germany does exercise a strong inertial pull on people. It is fairly well-run and offers a soothing amount of security and peace of mind to those who lock into the fairly open system. Germany-bashing is a favourite light pastime for members of the foreign community here and you'll probably fall into it yourself before long. But for millions of its foreign residents, Germany has provided a comfortable home for quite some time; the country must be doing something right.

I would not need a calculator to tally up all the people I've known who came here and then fell in love with the country or its people (as opposed to some of its people). But most did fall into a sense of satisfaction. What do long- and short-term foreign residents cite as reasons they like living here? "It's a clean, orderly country; Things work very well here; You can generally rely on people; It's fairly safe; I don't feel threatened, even riding public transport late at night; The trains all run on time; yeah, almost everything runs on time; I can make a lot of money here, much more than I could back home; I have a good job here, I get treated well on the job, and I get respect for what I do." You'll most likely nod assent to at least one of these upbeat verdicts after a short time here. And probably add a few of your own.

To supplement your cache of first impressions, those things that jump right out and grab your attention quickly, you might want to learn something about an important aspect of German life that is not so immediately obvious—the country's history. These tragic events in some way affect everyone, including those just arriving in the country as we roll along into the 21st century.

OVERVIEW OF LAND AND HISTORY

CHAPTER 2

'The history of the Germans is a history of extremes.
It contains everything except moderation.'
—AJP Taylor (1944)

'I'm not a German; I'm a Bavarian.'
—Franz Xaver Kroetz,
Germany's most famous present-day playwright.

THE GERMAN LANDSCAPE:
PHYSICAL DIMENSION AND REGIONALISMS
Geography

Up till now, we've been talking of Germany and Germans in ways that might suggest the place is one large homogeneous, if not monolithic, block. But in fact, Germany is a large country defined as much by its regionalisms as by its sense of national identity. These regionalisms are often sources of deep pride, fiercely defended against all wayward attempts to homogenise them.

Once an even more sprawling giant, Germany today occupies an area of some 357,000 sq km (137,744 sq miles), making it the third largest European Union country after France and Spain. Its longest north-south stretch covers 876 km (544 miles), its widest east-west span is 640 km (397 miles). Germany is big enough that it incorporates massively different geographical features and architectural styles within its borders, but small enough that you can travel from just about any point in the country to any other point in less than a day.

The greatly diversified landscapes and geographical areas are impressive and multivariant, running from the low, coastal plains flanking the Baltic and North Seas to the towering Alps of the south; from the thickly forested highlands in the central and southern regions to the sleek plains of the Lüneburg Heide; from the shaded beauties of the Rhine Valley to the misted splendours of Lake Constance, its islands and its surroundings. And we shouldn't forget the imposing beauties of the legendary Black Forest in the south-western state of Baden-Württemberg or its near-match, the Thuringian Forest.

The Call of Nature

Nature lovers will certainly never feel themselves deprived in Germany, with its sharply contrasting beauties and splendours. Even for those residing in the concrete heart of one of the major German cities, it's only a short ride by car or public transport to indulge in some of the beauties of the German countryside.

Germans themselves are quite fond of devoting at least part of their weekends or one of their numerous holidays to a pilgrim's drive in the country. Unfortunately, the sheer volume of these weekend tourists is slowly leading to the asphyxiation of some of the splendorous attractions, as large parts of Germany's famed forests succumb to the toxic emissions of visitors' autos. In addition, the frustrating lines of traffic to certain preferred weekend retreats drain much of the pleasure from the experience.

Germans don't have to leave the country to enjoy the sun, sand and seas: witness this scene from a Baltic seaside resort in the eastern state of Mecklenburg-Vorpommern.

Both winter and summer sports enthusiasts will find much of what they love comfortably within Germany. The German Alps stretch through a wide swath of southern Germany, providing skiing and other winter sports activities to both domestic and foreign tourists. On the other hand—and at the other end of the country—scores of beaches on the North and Baltic Seas oblige bathers and sun worshippers alike with many hours of optimal weather, fun and relaxation. The Federal Republic of Germany gained some of its most wonderful beaches, edged with surrounding landscapes of breathtakingly wild beauty, in 1990 with the addition of Mecklenburg-Vorpommern. This former East German region is becoming one of Germany's more popular tourist areas, as its once pitiful infrastructure has been significantly built up to accommodate all those interested in taking holidays there.

In addition to the splendours of its mainland, Mecklenburg-Vorpommern brought the Federal Republic the third of its most dazzling islands—the Baltic Sea's Rügen, which now joins Sylt and Helgoland in the North Sea as the most sought after island retreats in Germany. Sylt is far and away the most popular, though Helgoland is the more unspoiled and ruggedly beautiful. Probably the main factor keeping Helgoland behind its North Sea neighbour is the fact that it's only accessible by sea, and the boat trips there are notoriously rough and rocky. If you do head off for this lovely island getaway, don't eat a big lunch before boarding ship.

Castles Galore

For those of you who get slightly bored with the beauties of nature neat, Germany also offers a wide palette of architectural glories. It's especially beloved of castle enthusiasts. There were over 200 pre-unification kingdoms, dukedoms and principalities (you will soon read about them in the history section) and the various leaders of these tiny fiefdoms were deliriously fond of building themselves multiple castles, which left the German landscape constellated with the structures. And since modern warfare had stripped castles of their strategic importance, many of them escaped World War II with little or no damage.

It would probably be easier to cite those sections of Germany without castles than those with. Suffice it to say that a drive through many country areas will take you by at least one castle, no matter how minor. Germans and foreign visitors alike favour combining castle-sighting with a trip along the Rhine, Germany's largest and most majestic river. Germany's many petty despots were also impressed with the Rhine's majesty, so they had many of their castles built along its course, affording them a full river view from cosy and snug hillside perches.

Some war damage and the ravages of time have left many castles in a state that allows you to admire them from the outside, but not venture in. But if you would like to know how royalty lived in Germany's not too distant past, there are a number of well-kept castles that have become major tourist attractions. The most famous of these are the four main castles of Bavaria's 'Mad King Ludwig II'—Linderhof, Herrenchiemsee (Neues Schloss), Hohenschwangau and Neuschwanstein. The latter was the real-life model for Disneyland's Magic Kingdom castle, and lies within walking distance of the smaller Hohenschwangau. If you live in Munich, or have the occasion to go there, each of these castles is worth a half-day trip.

Worth at least half a day is Rothenburg ob der Tauber (also in Bavaria). This is the finest preserved medieval city in Europe. Most of the structures within the walls of the old town date from the 13th–16th centuries, and almost nothing was built after 1800. Often called Germany's Disneyland, it is of course a major tourist attraction and, on an average day, you're more likely to catch more Japanese and Americans than Germans strolling through its cobblestoned streets.

Another very popular tourist haunt is Heidelberg, the 'Student Prince' town. Nestled in the lovely Neckar River Valley, it preserves its old glories in the narrow central *Altstadt* area. Today, its famous castle is more ruins than castle, but the town's unique flavour, flowing from the student population at its renowned university, still makes it one of the most appealing small towns in all Germany. In fact, many people who work as far away as Frankfurt, Karlsruhe, Heilbronn or Stuttgart brave the long morning and evening drives to live in the Heidelberg area. So, you see, it's not just a tourist town.

Climate

For those of you who imagine Germany as an extension of Scandinavia weather-wise, it should come as a relief that Germany actually enjoys a fairly moderate climate—rarely does it ever get bone-chillingly cold or stiflingly hot (although several surprisingly torrid summers over the last decade did significantly boost sales of air-conditioning in a country which rarely uses the convenience).

The weather is rawest along the northern coasts, where hearty servings of winter cold join forces with blustery winds to send all but the sturdiest of souls huddling for warm shelter. As a rule, the extreme south-west region of the country enjoys the warmest climate in all of Germany. The tourist-laden island of Mainau on Lake Constance sports lemon, orange and palm trees, along with orchids and other sub-tropical plants and flowers. This area is, not surprisingly, widely sought out by hordes of tourists in the autumn and early spring. The mid-western areas of the country undergo mild winters and tepid summers. Moreover, in these regions, the shoulder seasons of spring and autumn tend to blur into their adjoining seasons.

In general, the northern stretches get colder in the winter and stay cooler in the summer than the rest of the country. Nevertheless, that part of Germany which gets the coldest is the deep south. Why this seeming paradox? Quite simple really—the southern regions boast the highest elevations in the country, ultimately ascending to the Swabian and Bavarian branches of the Alps. Not surprisingly, these regions are also the centre of the German ski industries and other winter sports.

It's often claimed that the Harz Mountain region in the east forms a climate zone all to itself. The raw, unruly winds, cool summers and long, snow-decked winters make the Harz region a favourite for hearty souls who really like to get away from pampered modern life when they take their holidays.

Resources

One of the key facts about Germany is that it is a country rather poor in natural resources. It has almost no oil or iron ore to speak of and while there are significant reserves of natural gas, these can cover only about one quarter of the country's own needs. About the only natural resources the country has in abundance are coal (both lignite and bituminous) and salt.

This scarcity of resources has shaped German economic thinking for centuries. Thus, the German-speaking lands have always been dependent on imports and since the dawn of the industrial age, this import dependence has been critical. As the German soil is not terribly hospitable, agricultural products have also been somewhat limited, in variety as well as quality. But Germany's most important resource has always been its people.

Population

With just over 82 million inhabitants (the most in Europe, except for Russia), Germany is the continent's third most densely populated country. While close to 10 per cent of these inhabitants are officially 'foreigners,' significant differences exist amongst the Germans themselves. Even the Nazis, purveyors of all that 'racial purity' claptrap, conceded that there were many different tribes within the German *Volk*. While career-driven relocations have brought about mixing and meshing in recent years, customs and characteristics can still vary noticeably from area to area and amongst the residents of those areas. But have no doubts that life in one part of the country is sure to be an experience unlike life in another.

In Diversity is Strength

The different regions were able to develop and nurture their unique qualities largely because unification came so late to

Germany. While Prussia, with its stern values, was expanding its influence through the 18th and 19th centuries, other regions and their major cities had already established their own unique features and these continued to evolve—in some ways, even under Prussian domination.

Thus it was that by the start of the 19th century, cities such as Stuttgart, capital of the kingdom of Württemberg; Munich, capital of Bavaria; Hanover, seat of Lower Saxony's rulers; or Dresden and Leipzig, in the wealthy, powerful kingdom of Saxony, had joined towns such as Hamburg, Bremen, Lübeck, Frankfurt and Cologne, which had achieved their status as power centres centuries before, during the so-called Holy Roman Empire (the First Reich).

A Regional Nation

Only when Berlin became the throbbing, bustling capital of a newly unified and industrialised 'Second Reich' did inordinate power begin to accumulate in one German city. Even then, cultural resistance stirred in other regions and continues to this day. Indeed, during the impassioned 1991 debates about moving the seat of government back to Berlin from tiny Bonn, partisans on both sides cited the historical precedents, with the anti-Berlin forces arguing that the major disasters in German history counselled strongly against ever again concentrating such power in one place (Berlin still won). Even so, Bismarck, the grand-daddy of German unification, once wryly observed that beneath the rationality of their togetherness, the Germans nurture a healthy disdain for each other. Today, it would be an exaggeration to speak of intra-German disdain, but it is probably true that Germans do retain a healthy scepticism towards each other.

But the Germans' noted lack of mobility until recent years has allowed persistent regional loyalties to maintain their force in many areas. Many Germans still think of themselves first in terms of their regional or municipal loyalties, then as members of the German nation. Yes, those myriad jokes about Bavarian suspicions of anything vaguely Prussian (which for the comic Bavarian means anything north of the

The 'shoe-slappers' of the Allgäu region in Bavaria in full flight as they practise their speciality.

Main River) have an element of truth in them. It's no joke that one of the major border crossings between Switzerland and Germany sports a sign proclaiming 'FREISTAATBAYERN' (Free State of Bavaria) in huge letters with a small, almost unobtrusive 'Bundesrepublik Deutschland' squeezed in under this.

These regional differences are expressed in variations of food, dialect, religion, mentality, and even, to a certain extent, dress. While the mass media, especially television, and increased mobility amongst the Germans have caused many of these differences to be diluted, the distinctions still persist, especially in smaller towns and villages. I recall watching a television report on a small Bavarian village with my father-in-law, a Frankfurt native. I remarked to him that the villagers' strong dialect limited my comprehension to about one quarter of what they said; he confessed that he himself was able to understand only about half of the chatter.

Regional Kitchens

While one can certainly talk broadly of an identifiable German cuisine, local variations abound. In fact, the border separating the two southernmost states of Bavaria and

Baden-Württemberg is often dubbed the 'Weiss Wurst Equator', a jocular reference to the blanched sausage beloved of Bavarians. Some of these culinary distinctions are dictated by geography, such as the dominant role of seafood in northern coastal regions, or the influences of the French kitchen in the France-bordering states of Baden-Württemberg and the Saarland. Other variations are sidelights—noodles are far more prevalent in the south-west than in the north and east, where potatoes dominate; bread gets darker as one moves through Westphalia; and the northern German diet consists of more fats. Sadly, some of the more interesting regional variations were found in the kitchens of the extreme eastern provinces, sliced away from Germany after World War II. Those Germans who did migrate westward from these areas saw most of the distinct quality of their dishes get blurred in the process of assimilation.

Religious Regionalism

Religious differences between regions have also tended to blur over the last 50 years, though it is still true that Catholics hold sway in the southern and extreme western states up through North Rhine-Westphalia, while Protestants (mainly Lutheran) dominate in the northern and eastern states. In practice though, many Germans wear their religious affiliation more like a style of dress, to be put on or taken off mainly for special occasions.

Regional Dress

Speaking of dress: here too regional differences are sometimes exhibited. For example, if you fancy that classic image of the German male in *lederhose* or with *janker* jacket and jaunty hunter's hat, you are more likely to catch that sight in Bavaria, while the flat, more practical Prince Heinrich (or fisherman's) cap made famous by former chancellor Helmut Schmidt is sported more often in the northern coastal regions. A number of Germans also claim that if suddenly popped down from the heavens in one of Germany's main cities, they could guess the town solely by the fashions being worn there. If these claims are at all true, then well-dressed folks in Dusseldorf and Munich wear more colourful and chic clothing, well-dressed Hamburgers favour the classically conservative styles, while fashion trends in Frankfurt follow more staid and functional lines.

Differences in mentality among the western states are often more those of tone than essentials. Still, as you head southward from about mid-Lower Saxony, you will hear many locals swear that their extreme northern cousins are much more reticent, tight-lipped and likely to keep to themselves than denizens of other German areas. Be that as it may, I myself have been more quickly and warmly accepted by total strangers in Hamburg pubs than anywhere else in Germany.

That untranslatable trait of German *Gemütlichkeit* reportedly flows most freely in Bavaria. The Bavarians are considered (not least by themselves) as the most open, fun-loving, rollicking and beer-guzzling of all Germans (statistics amply support this last claim). Yet Prussians (anyone not a Bavarian native) who have moved south, hoping to immerse themselves totally in this wild and warm spirit, send back reports that this temperament is all lathered on the surface. Supposedly, once an outsider tries to penetrate that surface, he or she bangs into the locked gates of a largely closed society. Still others, both Germans and foreigners, recount unpleasant experiences in small Bavarian villages, where congenital suspicion of any and all strangers is said to run deepest in all of Germany. Even so, Munich tops most polls as the city Germans themselves would most like to live in. This popularity springs not only from the myriad charms of the Bavarian capital itself but also from its close proximity to sports and leisure activity centres such as the Alps and the many large lakes dotting southern Bavaria.

Berliners are also famous for their openness, though it is frequently open expressions of irritation, hostility and discomfort that get sounded. The celebrated *Berliner Schnauze* (big-mouth) is the stuff of song and legend, bumping through the world with its somehow endearing gruffness, as ready to embrace or to offer help as to put someone down for some real or imagined slight. Of course, both modes of behaviour are wrapped in a characteristically rough-hewn humour. In brief, the residents of the Berlin metropolis are the Germans most similar to New Yorkers, Londoners or Parisians.

Because of its thoroughly unique nature from 1948 to 1989, Berlin developed a singular quality brought on by its special status. West Berlin attracted thousands upon thousands of young people through its openness and exciting nightlife. In addition, young men could avoid the military draft by taking up Berlin residence in their teen years. It also became a magnet for immigrants from many different countries because of its general openness, tolerance and opportunities for making a living. Artists were drawn by the heady atmosphere of the town, as well as the generous subsidies to the arts provided by the city's senate.

All of these forces fitted out Berlin with a reputation for wildness and strange behaviour. This reputation is often close to the truth and most Germans in other parts of the country view Berlin either with longing admiration or an indulgent tolerance. Even some staunchly conservative Germans, upon hearing of some strange performance or activity in their recently reappointed capital (such as Christo and Jean-Claude wrapping the *Reichstag* building), will simply shake their heads, laugh and say, "Well, that's Berlin and Berlin will always be Berlin."

The Rhineland area is also seen as having its own unique character that you just have to accept with a laugh and a shake of the head. They are also known for their relative openness and friendliness and, like the Bavarians and Berliners, for their robust enjoyment of life when the time for enjoying life has come.

The East-West Divide

Still, without a doubt, the greatest differences within Germany are to be found between the former East and West Germanys and the denizens thereof. One could hardly expect that 40 years of living under totally different forms of government and economy (and these the 40 years in which some of the most rapid changes in history took place) would not have forged enormous divergences amongst the people living in those two countries.

But the distinctions wrought by four decades of forced separation proved to be more deep-seated (or even indelible) than imagined by those thousands upon thousands who marched through the streets in the last days of the DDR, chanting '*Wir sind ein Volk*' ('We are one people'). Today, more than a decade after the physical walls that separated Germany's two parts were triumphantly torn down, many people still speak of 'the walls within our heads'; sadly, these barriers seem much more difficult to dispose of.

Wessis and Ossis

The key distinctions between the *Wessis* (Easterners' pejorative for Western natives) and the *Ossis* (the Westerners' return volley) reflect the systems they lived under. Easterners argue that Western residents are too materialistic, too superficial, too concerned with themselves and their own narrow circles, too cocky. Westerners answer these reproaches with their own charges that Easterners are too lazy, too unsophisticated, that they want things too quickly, they don't take enough initiative, and they're too insecure.

The massive differences between the two segments exist not only in the psyches of the inhabitants, but also in the industrial landscapes and housing stock. Many of the factories and plants in East Germany were hopelessly antiquated and inefficient. While some of these have been retooled, a great many were simply written off and closed down. Today, new, state-of-the-art factories continue going up, though only the wildest optimists in government or business still predict that over the next five years or so, it will be western Germany's industrial stock that lags behind. Most see this forecast as romantic fantasy. Nonetheless, the industrial and economic upswing of the East is underway, though it has been very much slower than many had once hoped it would be.

The Slow Routes

Two areas where improvements in the East have perhaps been most obvious are the public and private transport sectors and the air and water quality.

For many folks travelling in the new eastern states in those first years after unification, a very practical problem was the significant difference in roads and great inconvenience in just getting around. As many roads, even those considered major thoroughfares or parts of the Autobahn, were in poor repair, inferior, or two-lane affairs, driving in eastern Germany was slower and much more uncomfortable than in the west. And travelling by train was also nowhere near as pleasant as in the western stretches of the country.

However, the German federal government and the Deutsche Bahn (railway) have been spending large amounts of money to improve eastern transport and most of the major differences have now been close to eradicated.

A healthy chunk of the 1.2 trillion euros the federal government has funnelled into the East has been to improve roads and infrastructure. Programmes such as the German Unity Transport Projects have resulted in a situation where today a good many of the highways and railway lines are actually better in the East than in the West. However, be aware than numerous roads in and around villages and small towns are still cobblestoned or in poor condition; bring along some extra time and prepare yourself for a bumpy ride when travelling through some of those quaint parts of old eastern Germany.

Poison for the Masses

Another, even more important, problem the Germans had to face after unification was the often parlous environmental conditions out east. The Communist ideologues of East Germany viewed industrial pollution as an exclusive trait of exploitative capitalist production methods, which gave them license to build and maintain some of the worst polluting plants in this part of the world. As there was no way to quickly cut off this ghastly pollution, short of closing down most of the factories and power plants, excessive air and water pollution plagued many eastern regions for most of the 90s (lingering health problems amongst the population there reflect the long-term abuse of the natural environment by Communist authorities).

This situation has now changed significantly for the better. Admittedly, part of the reason for this dramatic improvement has been that numerous older, poison-spewing factories and power plants have been shut down for economic reasons, so the price paid by many locals for improved air quality is high unemployment. Indeed, the area around Halle, formerly a respiratory tract disaster region, now has the dubious distinction of looking at the highest unemployment rate in the European Union.

While some visitors from the West complain that they still can't always breathe freely in places like Halle, Leuna and Bitterfeld, there's general agreement that even in what were once environmental no-go zones, the improvement has been remarkable.

Berlin—East Meets West

Berlin is, quite understandably, that place where the painful process of full reunification has progressed the fastest and the furthest (though Leipzig's economic progress has been, in some ways, even more impressive). Today, many eastern sections of the formerly divided town have assumed the character of the western parts (much of the city's division was extremely artificial anyway, sometimes cutting right through the middle of a street). True, the wealthiest, glitziest parts of town still lie in the west, but hefty investments are pouring into the East to bring up its level. And as East Berlin had earlier been the government centre of both Imperial and Nazi Germany, as well as the showcase town of Communist East Germany, it already featured a grandeur and glamour that other towns in the East could only marvel at.

But even here, deep psychological divisions persist. Recent TV and radio reports indicate that young Berliners still see themselves as solidly belonging either to the East or to the West—even after 15 years ostensibly together. Many young

East Berliners complain they can no longer flock to their old stomping grounds in the central areas because new glitzy clubs, cafés, galleries and discos have moved in, towing along a wave of new *Wessi* clientele. They feel comfortable neither in the young people's meeting places of West Berlin nor in the newly westernised hangouts in the eastern part of town.

These young East Berliners report that they've had to fan out to places in the more outlying districts of their home grounds (the multiple prize-winning film *Good Bye, Lenin!* caught this sense of dislocation in a humorous if slightly murky light). *Wessis*, on the other hand, report that while they like hitting the new 'in' places in Berlin Mitte (centre city) and funky Prenzlauer Berg, they would never venture out into the peripheral districts as they just don't find the establishments there meet their standards of *gemütlich*. So even in Berlin, the 'walls in the minds' seem to have remained fairly sturdy.

Ostalgie

A remarkable new phenomenon that has developed here in recent years is *Ostalgie* (and apparently it's strongest in Berlin). The word itself is an amalgamation of the German words for 'east' and 'nostalgia', and refers to the desire to recapture as much of the old East German lifestyle as still possible—except, of course, for the dictatorship, secret police, pervasive greyness and mindless propaganda.

To this end, popular consumer products such as Rondo Melange coffee, Spreewaldgürken (jarred pickles) and other old favourites from the days of East Germany (known formally as the Deutsche Demokratische Republik, or DDR) have reappeared after having been swamped off the market in the early 1990s by their Western competitors. (Many of these revived products are manufactured by West German-owned companies, but who cares when you can again bite into a crunchy Spreeewald pickle, then wash it down with Vita Cola instead of Pepsi).

There are now stores, such as the one with a name that means '99 per cent East Products' in Berlin's famous Alexanderplatz, that cater exclusively to those yearning for the planned-economy goodies of yesteryear. A plan has even been floated to open an *Ostalgie* theme park in the Berlin suburb of Koepenick (not a bad idea, as many travel agencies already offer *Ostalgie* tours).

This wave of *Ostalgie* obviously played a role in making *Good Bye, Lenin!* the most commercially successful German film of all time. Tellingly, many of the eager consumers for these once-vanished Ost products and related memorabilia are younger easterners who have themselves taken up residence in the western half of the country.

East Comes West

A good many residents of the 'old' western states came originally from the former East Germany. They arrived in small numbers when the old Communist state looked like it would be around for a long time; streams of them 'came over' in the last days of the regime, or in the early days of unification.

Since 1990, almost one in every seven East Germans has migrated to the western part of the country—or out of the country entirely. The population in the five new eastern states has dropped 10 per cent, to 13.7 million in that time. In certain cities, the decline has been even more dramatic. For instance, the former heavy industrial bastion of Hoyerswerda, saw its population plunge from roughly 75,000 to 45,000 in the 13 years following unification.

The population shift is in some ways even more ominous than the figures suggest, as most of those heading west are young men and women, especially the more highly trained and qualified. This means that the population of the five eastern states is not only significantly smaller, it's also much greyer than in the last days of the DDR.

These former East Germans sense those 'walls in the minds' very vividly. They're content with the higher living standard on the western side, but they rue the loss of a certain human dimension they say they experienced back home. As they see it, the *Wessis* are far too concerned with

themselves and their own affairs. In their account, people in the East were, and still are, more communal, more willing to help each other. And not as judgemental, they say. *Wessis* are so quick to leap to judgement, they aver: about behaviour, clothing, income, manners, many things.

Many westerners are puzzled by some of these charges, while others acknowledge a certain truth in them. But many natives of the 'old federal states' argue that the 'walls in the minds' are carefully guarded by their eastern cousins, which is why they've proven so difficult to get rid of.

The Test of the West

So why do East Germans continue to come west? The huge human transfer had tapered off considerably by 1997, but has picked up again in the last few years. The answer is quite simply the intransigent economic woes in the east. Except for heartening success stories such as East Berlin, Leipzig and Dresden, most of the East remains locked in near-despair, with unemployment rates at Depression-era levels. As talented and enterprising young people in the East cannot find well-paying positions suited to their skills back home, they head west where such jobs exist—leaving behind a population with low incomes and the skills of yesteryear.

Recent internal immigrants share many of the regrets their forerunners from ten years earlier had: they miss the friendliness and camaraderie, the willingness to accept others on their own terms. But they still keep coming to the West. And it's precisely this reluctant intra-German immigration which may eventually help dilute the differences between the two halves of Germany. And finally knock down all those walls in the minds.

HISTORY

It was a German philosopher, Oswald Spengler, who argued in the 1920s that most people viewed history in terms of two basic patterns—either a solid straight line of roughly steady progress, or a dense circle of repeated patterns of occurrences.

If Spengler were around today, he might have added a special, third model for his own compatriots—that of the rollercoaster ride, with breathtaking ups and downs, radical spins and turns, and breakneck swings into uncertain terrain. No other pattern seems to catch the harsh melodrama of German history so fittingly.

Almost no other nation has had its hopes, fears, dreams, allegiances, leanings, fates and passions as deeply stamped with its own recent history as Germany. For this reason, it makes sense to start a book such as this with a quick overview of modern German history.

Early History

But first, an even quicker look at the prelude to the modern era. Early German history is filled not so much with the extremes of Taylor's quote as with a lot of black holes. In the centuries before Christ, the land mass that is today Germany was traversed, settled, fought over and abandoned by assorted tribes of Celts, Slavs, Franks and Teutons. The traditional starting point of German history was set in AD 9 when Hermann, the chieftain of the Cherusker, a Germanic

tribe, defeated three Roman legions. In later centuries Hermann, or Arminius, became a German national hero, athough practically nothing more was known about the fellow than his victory over the Romans.

The first major hero of German history who stood as something more than a very shadowy figure was Charlemagne, whom the Germans claim as their own under the name Karl der Grosse (Karl the Great). Karl brought the Frankish Empire to the height of its power and territorial reach, as well as the greatest blooming of early medieval European culture. But as the French also claim this fellow as one of their national heroes, his position as a German is somewhat shaky.

Karl's empire began to fall apart shortly after his death, with the main split coming between the French-speaking portion in the west and the Germanic section to the east. In AD 911, the eastern empire elected its own ruler, the first truly 'German' emperor. The emperors in what became known as the Holy Roman Empire were then elected by the upper nobility of the area for the next several centuries. That time was largely characterised by repeated conflicts over authority between the emperors and the Church, or the emperors and the various rulers of smaller entities within the empire.

The Reformation

The stew of tensions between the emperor and the lesser rulers, as well as between Church and temporal authority, reached its boiling point in the early 16th century. A German monk, Martin Luther, boldly challenged the theology and authority of the Church and its centre, the Vatican in Rome. Repeated attempts by religious authorities to silence Luther only emboldened him more, until his questioning of Church doctrines, holdings and power reached the point where further debate within the Church became impossible. The result was the Protestant Reformation.

The National Quiltwork

By the turn of the 19th century, this large, important land mass which was to play such a key role in shaping

European and world history was itself just a perplexing quiltwork of kingdoms, grand duchies, electorates and petty principalities—over 200 in all, a simmering stew of mini-states and maxi-powers, loosely bound by insidiously shifting allegiances. Many of these mini-states were led by petty despots, primarily characterised by their zealous self indulgence and incompetence, whose exercise of statescraft involved little more than protecting their own shaky stock of privileges.

The people of this future great power shared a common language, a brilliant literature, music and art tradition, a hefty body of mythology packed with heroes of superhuman virtues and abilities that would have put even Rambo to shame, perhaps even a general view of life—but no common state.

The German Ideal

At this time, 'Germany' existed only in the hopes and dreams of its people. It was fed continuously by books, essays and, especially, songs and poems by Romantic writers. The predominately liberal minded writers and thinkers who propounded the concept of one Germany saw a unified country as the only means of breaking the power of the innumerable petty despots running the various shows, and thus unleashing the enormous creative powers of the German people.

The zeal of these writers and thinkers provided the major intellectual force in the German-speaking world throughout the first half of the 19th century, constituting an ideal they hoped to see eventually transformed into reality. Even the future German national anthem, *Deutschland Über Alles*, was written some 30 years before there was any Deutschland to be over anything.

The First German Unification

A number of political attempts—most notably the democratic revolutions of 1848—were made during this period to realise the dreams of the liberal, democratic idealists. In the event, it was Prussia, with its fabled industriousness, discipline, cultural achievements and devout militarism which forged German unification, following convincing military victories over Austria and its allied southern German states in 1866 and over France in the savage Franco–Prussian War of 1870–71.

Flushed with patriotic fervour, the various German states proclaimed the formation of the German Reich (Empire) in Versailles outside of Paris, where they were otherwise busy dictating peace terms to the soundly defeated French. The kings of Bavaria, Saxony and Württenberg were allowed to keep their titles and certain privileges (mainly printing stamps and pressing coins) but real power was ceded to the Prussian king, now anointed German Kaiser (emperor) and his right-hand man, Otto von Bismarck, who had orchestrated the major events with his cunning policies. Bismarck was named the first German chancellor, the head of government.

The new German Reich did have an elected parliament (the *Reichstag*) and a constitution, but the chancellor was far more than a first among equals and the Kaiser exercised much greater political power than do present day European constitutional monarchs.

The Modern Era

Thanks largely to traditional Prussian virtues such as discipline and hard work, now grafted onto the other parts of the empire, the newly founded state soon assumed its place among the world's great powers.

Germany Up and Running

By 1900, Germany stood as the second largest industrial producer in the world, after the United States. Its accomplishments in the fields of science, technology, the arts and social policies were nothing short of dazzling. They ranged from Wilhelm Röntgen's invention of X-ray technology to Robert Koch's development of modern bacteriology, Paul Ehrlich's 'magic bullet' against a pack of dread diseases and his development of chemotherapy, or Gerhardt Hauptmann's Nobel Prize winning dramas. Not to mention Otto Lilienthal's momentous advances in aviation technology or the separate inventions of automobiles by Carl Benz and Gottfried Daimler (their companies later merged and produced something called the Mercedes Benz).

Military Über Alles

Germany's growth as a military power was also dazzling, and certainly more frightening to its neighbours and potential adversaries. Not everyone in Germany was caught up in militarism; indeed, there were strong anti-militarist sentiments throughout the Reich. But the military in the new Germany followed the old Prussian patterns of enjoying widespread respect and exercising influence which was excessive even by late 19th-century European standards. German military leaders, like their Prussian forebears, did not flinch at getting involved in political affairs whenever they believed their interests may be affected.

Actually, the conservative, imperialistically minded political leaders who dominated Germany over its first 38 years needed little prodding from the generals and admirals to pursue policies of military build-up and expansion of German power. Jumping into the colonial game rather late, the German leaders went at it with typical Prussian zeal, and the new nation had amassed a string of valuable colonies and protectorates in Africa and Asia by the beginning of this century.

World War I

As German imperialism showed no signs of flagging, it was inevitable that the young power would come into conflict with the older, more established colonial empires. An increasing series of frictions with Britain, France and Belgium over clashing interests had raised tensions in Europe to flashpoint by 1914, when Germany started showing renewed interest in once again redrawing the map of Europe itself. The Old Continent had become one large tinderbox, just waiting for a carelessly tossed match to send the whole mess up in flames. And Europe had no shortage of pyromaniacs.

The jumble of events, entangled alliances, tripwire strategic planning and plain bad luck that dragged the major combatants into this conflagration are too complicated to go into here. Enough to say that Germany, allied with the Austrian and Ottoman (Turkish) empires, moved first and

Wilhelm II, the last German *kaiser*.

quickly, though it is patently unfair to pin sole blame for this war on Germany, as some like to do.

Fighting on three fronts, Germany found its not meagre resources severely strained. The United States' entry into the war in early 1917 finally tipped the balance against Germany and its so-called Central Powers allies. Although in early 1918 the situation still looked auspicious for a German victory—or at least a satisfying draw—as the year progressed it became increasingly clear that Germany was heading towards a stinging defeat. The extent and immeasurable human costs of this conflict led it to be called the Great War, though 20 years later it sadly had to be re-christened World War I.

In the final months of 1918, Germany's main allies were not only reeling, they were literally falling, and Germany, which had staked the most in this war, was soon forced to join in. In early November, the progressive forces in the Reichstag declared the first German republic. The Kaiser and the middle-level kings all abdicated, and Germany surrendered unconditionally.

The Weimar Republic

The first German republic, known as the Weimar Republic for the town where its constitution was drafted, had more than its share of birth pains. Not only did the defeat of World War I overshadow its opening months, but so did a failed uprising led by extreme leftists, spearheaded by what would become the Communist Party.

The moderate leftist Social Democratic Party, which had seized the reins of power upon the collapse of the monarchy, found itself in the extremely uncomfortable position of seeking help from right-wing, anti-democratic military forces to put down the attempted revolution. The largely ad hoc military units, known as Freikorps (free corps) were utterly efficient and brutal in putting down the insurrection. In the course of suppressing the coup, the Freikorps viciously murdered two of the radicals' leaders, the popular and respected Rosa Luxemburg and Karl Liebknecht. The Social Democrats' reliance on the military and the subsequent murders of the two coup leaders poisoned relations on the left for the remainder of the Weimar Republic's days.

Within a year, the government found itself faced with another coup, this one from the right, led by virulently anti-democratic military forces. This uprising, known as the Kapp Putsch after its leader, proved more difficult to put down, though the republic survived this crisis as well.

The Great Inflation

The next major crisis to shake Germany's first experiment in full democracy came not from armed groupings but from a monstrously bloated currency. The roots of the almost unbelievable inflationary spiral lay in the old government's financing of the war and the mercilessly unjust financial terms of the Versailles Treaty following the Great War. The vindictive allies had imposed a system of punitive reparations on Germany that many prominent economists, including Britain's celebrated John Maynard Keynes, declared unfair

One of the fascinating scenes from the time of the Great Inflation, 1923: long lines of Germans waiting outside the Reichsbank, many carrying suitcases to be filled with freshly minted bank notes.

and sure to sabotage a speedy German postwar recovery. Indeed, some of the architects of the program had intended just that result.

The government's incompetence when faced with the financial crunch played a major role in fanning the fires of inflation, and to call the inflationary spiral that hit the nation through 1923 dizzying is to engage in excessive understatement. By the end of that year the German mark had fallen to one-trillionth of its prewar value.

At one point, to buy a loaf of bread, a shopper needed a bag filled with paper cash larger than the bag required to carry the bread back home. Before long the government printing presses, working day and night, merely took to stamping extra rows of zeros on the notes already printed. Wives or children of workers stood outside factories and office buildings to catch the twice daily wages tossed out of the windows to them by their relatives and then dashed off to the shops, as waiting until the workers returned home would have depleted the purchasing power of the wages drastically.

Ungovernability

This inflation of mythic proportions was finally brought to an end by the appointment of a new finance minister and a new currency. But it wasn't quite as easy building new confidence in the government.

The 'Great Inflation' merely convinced more Germans that democratic government was incapable of dealing with the problems of a modern society. These sentiments were fuelled by those forces which had been antagonistic to democracy right from the start—some of whom worked in various education ministries and were responsible for the textbooks used in the schools.

Let's Have a Party

The Weimar Republic did have a built-in self-destruct mechanism—its rule for representative voting. According to the constitution, any party receiving the merest scattering of votes earned seats in the parliament. This prescription for representative democracy looked fine in the republic's early days when a few large parties garnered most of the votes and were thus able to establish majority governments or stable coalitions. But as interest groups mushroomed and public opinion splintered, the proliferation of parties reached comical levels. The old joke ran: 'Put three Germans together in a room and they'll start four political parties.' At times the kaleidoscopic make-up of the Reichstag suggested that this joke contained more truth than was comfortable.

By the end of the 1920s and the early 1930s, Germany's governments had devolved into a frustrating series of bickering coalitions cobbled together out of the most unlikely of partners. Predictably, most of these assemblies were able to accomplish little and, after a typically short period of internecine fighting, gave way to an equally ineffective successor.

Frustration and the Führer

The repeated failures of Weimar governments bolstered right-wing intellectuals and other anti-republican forces in their belief—articulated right from the start of the Weimar experiment—that what Germany really needed was a strong leader with an all-encompassing vision—ein Führer, as they designated him. Calls for a Führer to rescue Germany spread as frustrations with the parade of feckless patchwork governments continued unabated.

The worldwide Depression of the early 1930s merely presented the sputtering Weimar government with a mountain of new problems that did not lend themselves to easy solutions. More and more Germans, fed up with the shortcomings of their democracy, turned to extremist parties of the right or the left to seek relief from their misery. And the calls for a Führer resonated with more authority in various parts of society.

The Third Reich

The man who finally assumed the mantle of Führer was a somewhat unlikely candidate—Adolf Hitler, a native Austrian who wasn't even a German citizen until 1932, shortly before he ran for president of Germany. Hitler lost that election, but less than a year later Paul von Hindenburg, the man who had defeated him, tasked Hitler with forming yet another coalition government.

The conventional wisdom in early 1933 was that Hitler and his ragtag group of political amateurs would soon be gobbled up by their more experienced coalition partners from mainstream conservatism.

But Hitler and his cohorts absolutely confounded their political adversaries—not for the last time. The Nazis quickly set out to consolidate their power, used all possible components of the state security apparatus to stifle opposition and silenced or eliminated all their perceived enemies. Within a year, the sometimes cacophonous multitude of parties had been reduced to the dictatorial drone of a single party, and the Weimar Republic was consigned to the yellowed pages of history.

Twilight of the Gods Politics

The next 12 years form that portion of German history with which you are undoubtedly most familiar, unless you have kept yourself pure of movie-going, book-reading and television-watching. The Nazis quickly delivered on two of their key promises—Arbeit und Brot (work and bread) and following this early success with domestic economic problems, they launched their expansionist foreign policy.

At home, the Nazis launched vicious hate campaigns against Jews, Gypsies and homosexuals, as well as political opponents. All of these groups found their civil rights progressively stripped away and would soon fall victim to mass murder when World War II came and the extermination camp system had been set up.

World War II

At first, afraid of confronting a resurgent Germany, the Western democracies watched its aggression with gritted teeth. Britain and France had drawn the line in the sand at the Polish border however, and when German troops stormed over that line on 1 September 1939, the worst war the world has ever known was finally unleashed.

Typically, the Nazis surprised all their enemies early on and scored a series of shockingly quick military victories on every front. But Germany had overextended itself badly and when its main foes regained their bearings, they finally proceeded, in pincer movements, to crush Germany militarily. In 1933, Hitler had claimed, "Give me ten years, and you won't recognise Germany." This was one promise that was certainly kept, though probably not in the way Hitler had intended.

Occupation and Rebirth

Germany had fought to the bitter end, and that end had proved quite bitter indeed. Much of the vanquished 'Thousand Year Reich' lay in rubble, and the entire country was occupied by the four major allies who had combined to defeat the Nazi regime (the United States, Britain, the Soviet Union and France). Now the question was what to do with this conquered giant.

A number of plans were put forward to guarantee that Germany would never again become a military power capable of smashing its neighbours. One of the more radical, proposed by United States treasury secretary Henry Morgenthau, envisioned a collection of bantam agrarian states, too small to threaten anyone and denied the industrial resources to do so anyway.

But any coordinated plan for handling Germany was soon undercut by increasingly acrimonious disputes between the three Western allies on the one side and the Soviet Union on the other. It was clear that the United States—backed principally by Britain—and the Soviet Union each wanted to remake Germany in its own image and likeness. As a result, two very different Germanies started to take shape in the occupied zones.

The Very Hungry Years

For the Germans, the early years of the Occupation were in some ways much worse than the war years, as food production and distribution had almost broken down with the fall of the Third Reich. The occupying powers set levels of daily caloric consumption which fell far short of hearty. The Versorgung (provisions) for a normal consumer in the British zone in May 1946 was roughly that of the inmates in the German concentration camps.

Germans refer to this time as Stunde Null (zero hour) because they were forced, as it were, to begin all over again from scratch. Their very existence as a major nation and significant presence in the world hung in the balance. But the industriousness, ingenuity and discipline that had characterised German societies for so long sprang forth again.

Two Germanies, One People?

There was still a major split between the three western zones and the eastern zone, which only grew as the Occupation proceeded. Under the direction of their respective occupying powers, the two parts of Germany were increasingly developing into two separate and unequal societies. On the eastern side were the Communist controlled committees and councils, while a much more variegated political composition was slowly taking over administration of the western zones. Machinations and posturings on both sides heightened tensions and accentuated differences, but the intransigence of the Communists played the major role in erecting a political and psychological wall that years later would be reified in a physical wall.

In June 1948, Ludwig Erhard, a future West German chancellor, was able to put through his plan to introduce a new currency, the Deutschmark, to replace the nearly worthless Reich Mark. Each German citizen was given 40 of the new marks and, like magic, shortages disappeared almost immediately as shop shelves started filling up.

The Politics of Division

Over the four years of occupation, the Germans on both sides of the cleft assumed more and more administrative tasks and functions, as well as developing strong leadership largely untainted by the Nazi past. The next step was obvious and perhaps inevitable. On 23 May 1949, the areas which had comprised the three western occupation zones constituted themselves as a new independent state—the Federal Republic of Germany. Shortly thereafter, the Communist controlled eastern zone proclaimed its own statehood—the fancifully named German Democratic Republic.

In the first elections for the West German Bundestag, Konrad Adenauer, leader of the Christian Democratic Union (CDU) which he had helped found after the war, was chosen as first federal chancellor by one thin vote over Kurt Schumacher, leader of the Social Democratic Party (SPD). To no one's surprise, the first elections for the Volkskammer, the East German parliament, resulted in an overwhelming victory for the Socialist Unity Party (SED), basically the reassembled Communist Party with a cosmetic sprinkling of some docile Social Democrats.

The Economic Miracle

While both parts of Germany had managed to get off their backs by the early 1950s, they were not quite satisfied with an inferior position. Taking all the energies and resourcefulness that had made them a great power before, they set about regaining their place among the world's major nations, though this time they had to devote far fewer energies and resources to their military build-up.

Guided by the prudent, growth-oriented policies of Adenauer's economics minister, Ludwig Erhard (who had initiated the Deutschmark back in 1948) and stabilised by the mutually beneficial 'social pact' between unions and management, the West German economy took off. What a short time before had been a depressing wasteland of rubble and gutted industries became one of the world's most productive economies. Indeed, by the 1970s, West Germany, with a population of only 60 million, had become the world's third largest economy and a number of times during the 1980s led the entire world in exports.

More importantly, the economic, foreign and strategic policies of the new Federal Republic rooted Germany firmly in the West for the first time in its history. Rather than seeing itself apart from Western Europe, deliberately seeking its own Sonderweg (special way), the larger part of Germany was now developing as a crucial partner in the Western alliance.

While West Germany was playing its leading role among Western nations, East Germany (better known in these parts even today as the DDR) had become the most productive nation in the Communist Eastern Bloc, although subsequent events have shown that much of this productivity was outmoded, second-rate and cosmetic.

So Near and Yet So Far Away

While the two Germanies both excelled in their respective spheres, they did not exactly form a mutual admiration society. One major source of friction was West Germany's refusal to recognise officially its fraternal neighbour. The West German Constitution always held the division of Germany as temporary and considered the eastern regions and its people as ultimately belonging together with them in one, united Germany. All East Germans were regarded as citizens of the Federal Republic and immediately granted passports with full rights of West German citizenship as soon as they resettled in the West, a boon that many East Germans took advantage of over the years.

One event that accelerated this east-west exodus was the 1953 uprising in East Germany. Workers and intellectuals in the DDR demanded free and fair elections, plus an end to Communist domination of most aspects of their lives. Strikes and random acts of vandalism against state institutions underscored these demands.

As this was the first large scale uprising in a Communist bloc country, the rulers in East Berlin and Moscow saw ominous signals in the events and decided to put it down with all due haste. This was done with unapologetic brutality as Soviet tanks and troops joined with East Germany's so-called People's Army to crush all visible signs of resistance to the system.

Now convinced that large numbers of their citizens were deeply dissatisfied, the East German authorities responded by constructing a giant network of fences and walls snaking all along their common border with West Germany. Heavily armed soldiers, and later, hidden machine guns that fired automatically when tripped off, were added to discourage any Germans intent on fleeing to West Germany, or presumably any fugitives going to the East, though the fugitive traffic was pretty much one-way during the decades of German division.

The Berlin Wall

While the fortified borders were somewhat effective at keeping East Germans in at any of these points, there was one giant, gaping hole in the shield—the city of Berlin. For a dozen years after Germany had been officially split into two states, it was still possible for disenchanted East Germans to simply walk into one of the three Western Allies' zones—or ride an underground train there, if they wished to bring along a few bags of their worldly possessions—and become instant West German citizens.

This was happening more and more as the Cold War headed into deep freeze, especially amongst well-trained professionals who realised their skills could earn them many times more in the West than what they were drawing in East Germany. The DDR continued to haemorrhage its best and its brightest, reaching a level of over 8,000 a day, when East German leaders decided they could no longer tolerate this opening to the West. Shortly after midnight on 13 August 1961, they announced a cancellation of all local transport moving through the two parts of the city and then set to work stringing barbed wire fencing all around the western sections.

The Great Wall

East German officials always maintained the Berlin Wall was merely a protective barricade to prevent an impending invasion by the small contingents of Allied troops stationed in West Berlin, thus shooting down two stereotypes with one pop—that neither Communists nor Germans have a sense of humour.

It was a well planned, lightning fast operation, so much so that West Berliners woke up that morning shocked to find their city totally surrounded by a fence, reinforced by armed East German soldiers. As soon as architecturally possible, the fences were replaced by a thick concrete wall with an imposing height of 4.10 m (13.5 ft).

The Normality of the Abnormal

Both Germanies continued to develop along divergent paths, earning prestige and envy for their many achievements. A matter of special pride for the East Germans was finishing second in medals won at the 1988 Summer Olympics, ahead of the United States (though many cynics point out that this triumph was a matter of pride for East German chemistry as much as its sports).

Early in 1989, Erich Honecker, leader of the DDR and ideological architect of the Berlin Wall, gave a speech in front of his concrete pride and joy in which he confidently declared that the structure would stand for another hundred years.

At that point, there were few on either side of the Wall who would argue with him. But events proved Honecker and his believers to be roughly 99 years off.

Voting With Their Cars and Feet

Later that same year, Hungary ripped down its part of the Iron Curtain, and hundreds of unhappy East Germans stormed across the Austrian border, from there travelling on to West Germany. When the liberal Communist regime of Hungary refused to act as border guards for the DDR, the East Germans took a startling, unprecedented step—they forbade their citizens to travel to another Communist nation.

But once the flow had started, it was impossible for the East Germans to staunch it. Denied a Hungarian opening, East Germans sought an exit through Czechoslovakia, with thousands scaling fences to get into the West German embassy in Prague. Televised images of East Germans desperately seeking access, handing frightened children over to those who had already made it onto the embassy grounds, stunned many people around the

East Germans were welcomed by their West German cousins as they poured through the breach in the Berlin Wall.

world and touched a raw, easily exposed nerve in the West German consciousness.

A hastily constructed tent city continued to grow day by day in the mud of the embassy compound until a beaming West German foreign minister, Hans-Dietrich Genscher, came out onto the embassy balcony to announce to the jubilant crowd that the two Germanies had struck a deal and all those present had been granted exit visas to the Federal Republic.

Almost as soon as these lucky ones had arrived in the West, others took their place in the Prague embassy. The sardonic joke of the day recalled that West German officials had always spoken of the eventual unification of the two Germanies, never realising that they would both be united on West German soil. Another joke, painted at various sites along the western face of the Berlin Wall, reminded Communist leader Erich Honecker to turn out all the lights in the DDR, as he would soon be the last one to leave.

Wir Sind Das Volk!—We Are The People!

In spite of the jokes, many East Germans elected to stay home and push for substantive changes in their government and society. Numerous marches and demonstrations showed an unanticipated resolve for change and they grew in number and size as summer moved into autumn.

The biggest and most famous of these marches were the so-called Monday night demonstrations in Leipzig. As these mushroomed in size and intensified in their demands, the top figures in the DDR government decided they had gone far enough. According to some in the inner circle (who admittedly had much to gain personally from circulating this account), shortly before one of the October Monday marches, Honecker gave orders to send troops to Leipzig to stop the protest. If the demonstrators persisted, the troops were to fire on them, taking down as many as necessary to force a halt to the protests.

Erich, Adé!

At this point, other key DDR officials decided that Honecker had lost all touch with Perestroika-era reality and shoved the 'Old Warrior' into early retirement. He was replaced by Egon Krenz, until then primarily known as a party apparachnik, who proved that he knew how to take the pulse of the times. Krenz let the demonstrations go on and spent a couple of weeks mainly walking around smiling and talking about openness and change.

On the evening of 9 November 1989, Krenz made a startling gesture of openness and change—he instructed guards at the Berlin Wall to open gates and allow East Berliners to visit the western half of their city. Within hours, tens of thousands had availed themselves of this opportunity and for the next few days Germany celebrated an impromptu national holiday, centred in Berlin.

The gates stayed open, and more and more of them opened as the year drew to a close. Hundreds of thousands of East Germans visited various parts of the Federal Republic, with quite a few of them deciding to stay indefinitely. Egon Krenz was himself supplanted by Hans Modrow, the mayor of Dresden long regarded as one of the leading reformers in the party.

Under Modrow, arrangements were made for the first free and fair elections in the history of the German Democratic Republic. These took place in March 1990, with the Eastern branch of the CDU (whose Western wing had led West Germany since 1982) surprising many and coming out as the largest single party. The CDU-led coalition government of the DDR then set out to close shop on the DDR. The two Germanies moved towards unification with what some observers considered breakneck speed and on 3 October 1990, the 41-year division of Germany came to an end. The Federal Republic of Germany had five new states on its eastern flank—and a mountain of new problems.

Post-Unification Headaches

In the lead-up to reunification and the first all-German elections two months later, German chancellor Helmut Kohl had promised people on both sides a 'blooming landscape' in the East within five years, and a united country in which, 'Things won't be worse for anybody, and will be much better for many.'

The reality proved to be much more prickly. Many overstaffed and/or antiquated factories in the East were compelled to make wrenching changes or even forced out of business. The reunification occurred just as West Germany itself was heading into a major recession, which only intensified the dislocations in the East. The five new states today suffer persistently high rates of unemployment and underemployment, and this in areas where for 40 years, unemployment didn't even officially exist.

Blessed with a weak opposition chancellor candidate, Kohl's party and its coalition partners managed to squeak by as victors again in the national elections four years later. But in 1998, the main opposition party, the SPD, came up with a strong candidate for chancellor, Gerhard Schröder. Many Germans, including many within Helmut Kohl's own party, felt that the Grand Old Man had been on stage too long and that it was time he step aside for a younger candidate. But Kohl, still wielding enormous power, insisted that he lead the party and its designated coalition partners into the fray once more.

But this time, Kohl had piled up too many negatives. The intransigence of the dire economic situation in the new eastern states along with relentlessly stubborn unemployment in the country as a whole, plus reduced quality of life factors, turned many people against the 'Eternal Chancellor' and his government. The ruling coalition was handed a resounding defeat, and the SPD returned to power, promising to get the German economy humming smoothly again, as well as introducing more effective environmental policies. Plus, for the first time, *die Grünen* (the Greens) entered the German national government, taking over as junior partners in the two-party ruling coalition.

But even as the new government started its work, with the media-savvy Schröder at the helm, many sympathetic observers in all parts of the country wondered whether it would be any more successful at solving the nation's economic problems and the woes of the eastern states. For all too many Germans, many of these were beginning to look like intractable problems.

For a long time, most Germans thought that they would never live to see the fall of the Berlin Wall; today, most Germans believe they will never live to see the end of the solidarity tax surcharge used to finance the reconstruction and relief of eastern Germany.

Despite widespread dissatisfaction, the SPD-led coalition managed to squeak by to a repeat victory in the 2002 national elections. Another one is slated for September 2005, and most observers predict that the still sluggish economy and significant changes made in entitlement programmes (necessitated by demographics and globalisation), some of them jettisoning core principles the SPD had paid fealty to since the beginning of the Federal Republic, signalled another tectonic shift in the political landscape and the end of this government. A few, however, felt that the ever resourceful Schröder might still turn back the challenge from the opposition, whose Chancellor candidate was not as strong a personality.

This then is the Germany of the 21st century, a country that bears the burden of its recent history in a way few other nations do. Anyone wishing to live and succeed in Germany needs some understanding and appreciation of this star-crossed, rollercoaster-ride history in order to understand and appreciate the Germans themselves.

GERMAN CHARACTERISTICS

CHAPTER 3

'We are like children lost in the woods,
Afraid of the dark,
Who have never been happy or good.'
—WH Auden

AUDEN'S BLEAK LINES WERE WRITTEN as an indictment of all the major nations that had allowed the world to slide into the morass of World War II. But they could easily be recycled as a pointed description of the typical German of the postwar period. Many sympathetic observers have been baffled by this central German paradox: these people have built the fourth or fifth largest economy in the world; they have erected a model social system; their infrastructure is exemplary; they have acquired a sterling reputation for competence and achievement—so why do they still suffer from a sense of insecurity?

THE LEGACY OF HISTORY

A large part of the answer seems to lie clearly in German history, with its repeated ups, downs, spins, turnarounds and collapses. History plays a role in the development of all nations, but in Germany, it casts a particularly long and heavy shadow. In areas ranging from German political institutions to its industrial relations up through the many spheres of daily life, one senses the indelible legacy of this treacherous history—in ways both positive and negative. And it provides a key to what we might, for want of a better phrase, call the German character.

Why is History so Important?

Germans themselves often speak ruefully of the burden of their own history, which they correctly take as a many faceted burden. Obviously, much of this burden is connected to the central trauma of modern German history, the Nazi experience and its lingering effects.

The Nazi experience has exercised a massive influence on the present day German character. Today's Germans tend to be more distrustful of authority and to have much less respect for uniforms than their forebears had. Indeed, a strong scepticism of the military runs through all levels of German society, with large sections of the German public embracing a largely pacifist viewpoint.

A Permanent Debt?

Almost all Germans realise that their whole country is still frequently judged by the Nazi experience. Shortly after moving here, I myself was asked a number of times, in both America and Britain, why I wanted to live 'over there with all the Nazis'. My response, back then in the early 1980s, that there were at least as many neo-Nazis in the United States and Britain as in Deutschland hardly made my decision more palatable to these sceptics. The crimes of the Third Reich remains, for many, a stigma that can never fade nor be washed away and which will always be immediately associated with Germans, no matter what their age or background.

A similar irritation echoes in the lament of some of my German friends and acquaintances when they relate why they always try to speak English when visiting the Netherlands or Belgium. Many Dutch and Belgian citizens, they aver, still harbour strong negative feelings towards the Germans, and the treatment given German speakers is undeniably shabbier than that afforded English speakers. James Joyce's Stephen Dedalus said, 'History is a nightmare from which I'm trying to awaken.' For most Germans, history is a mega-nightmare that they can't simply awaken from; they must battle fervently to overcome it.

VALUES

Until quite recently, those attributes which served to insulate the nation in some way from the vagaries of its own history and its negative consequences dominated the German value system. While some of these once-sturdy core values have been shaken considerably within the last decade or so, many still retain their force. Even those which have been weakened cling on tenaciously with quite a few groups in society. These values inform the way the Germans view themselves and others, the way they act in business or social situations, as well as the way they skew their dreams and hopes. Any inventory of the most important ones would have to include the following.

The Lust for Security

This, I believe, is the major key to understanding the German character. After all the shattering uncertainties and radical reversals of fortune that were a standard feature of German history up through the 1950s, today's Germans crave security. Germans are not risk-takers and they insist on having things reasonably under control—and what the Germans see as reasonable, others might well consider irrational.

This may be why Germans like things placed just so, why they often seem resistant to change, or why they often come off as arrogant in new, uncomfortable situations. That harsh veneer of arrogance is in many instances an overreaction to the insecurity created by the situation; a strong-willed attempt to get the situation under control.

An uncertain future of any shade is anathema to most Germans, and their lives are structured around avoiding such a calamity. One of the first questions many Germans asked after I told them about my medley of self-employed bread-winning activities was, "Oh! But what do you do for your old-age pension?" (still some way off in my case, I hope). And in how many other countries will you find 20-year-olds absorbed in discussing their own retirement plans? Or full-page ads in popular magazines urging young people to supplement their government pension plans with private plans?

You will encounter some of these efforts to keep things under control very quickly and in their most rigid form: all German residents are required to register with some authority or other scores of times, from the moment they first take up residence, through every subsequent change of residence, through opening bank accounts or getting a library card, through taking up many occupations. Moreover, for just about any well-paying, skilled occupation, you're further required to go through some certification exam, often at the end of a set course of study.

Expertise, Please!

This latter requirement results in a society of highly qualified people and here in Germany, you can be reasonably sure that craftspeople will know their jobs pretty darn well. (A ready source of jokes amongst Germans is the alleged incompetence of British or French craftsmen.) Even engaging in low-risk activities such as buying bread, pretzels or cakes, you'll know your goods have been baked by some certified master, or at least someone apprenticing carefully under that master.

But even the greatest backers of the system must occasionally shake their heads at how far it can be taken. Case in point: some years back, we bought a bathroom cabinet with a lighted mirror. The mounting instructions were written for countries throughout Europe. For ten of the countries, they told you where to place the mirror and electrical equipment and how to mount it—for Austria and Germany, they informed you that this work could only be

In Germany, great importance is place on qualifications. Here, restaurant cooks are going through an officially recognised training programme.

done by a certified specialist following a specifically cited electrician's regulation procedure.

The Future is Always Very Near

Perhaps the more striking element here is the way Germans plan their lives and try to manage the future. I remember discussing with a 19-year-old her apprenticeship program with a big company. She informed me in a chipper manner that she would work at this one activity for about a month, then switch to another, then learn another, then yet another—at that point, her apprenticeship would be over and she would settle into the one specific job she would do for the rest of her life. And as far as she was concerned, that was that.

This is no isolated case either, as the example of young people actively planning for their pensions indicates. Of course, major changes wrought by economic factors beyond German borders have made many here aware of the growing need to prepare for multiple occupations during one's lifetime—even for Germans. Still, for both young and old, security is that the ballast that keeps German society on its even keel.

Neither Borrowers nor Lenders

Because of this deep attachment to things, borrowing and lending are not the casual matters in Germany that they are in many other places. With friends and relatives, you can always feel relaxed about asking to borrow something or offering to lend something out. But it gets much stickier with neighbours, mere acquaintances or fellow workers: Germans are loath to lend out anything of any value whatsoever to people they aren't close to, nor will they ask to borrow such items from these people. And it is essential that no matter from whom or what you do manage to borrow, you always return that object in at least as good a condition as you received it.

Home and Hearth

Primary among those assets to be savoured and protected like one's own skin are the home and the beloved automobile.

Of course, the home represents a special, almost sacred ground for people all around the world, an abode where one can find that momentary stay from the cold, ominous world outside. But it takes on a special meaning in a country which has seen dark periods when people or their neighbours were dragged out of their homes by security police in the middle of the night, and where many homes were severely damaged or destroyed by bombs in a devastating war.

A major part of the German population therefore views the home and all those possessions that go into making a home fully one's own in a very special light. That is one reason that people who come to the door unannounced—be they strangers hawking products, magazine subscriptions or religious beliefs, or lost travellers requesting directions—are treated suspiciously, sometimes even harshly (admittedly, the sharp rise in house-call crimes has contributed significantly to this already inbred hesitancy). Even visiting a friend or acquaintance unannounced can be taken as discourteous or at least thoughtless. Remember that the German's home is more like a vault than a castle. You may notice the preponderance of gates, walls, fences and hedges around German houses. They are there primarily to indicate that here is where the public sphere ends and the private begins.

You should always respect this special character when visiting someone's home and you will be judged as somewhat aberrant if you don't pay as much attention to your own home. In fact, one charge levelled indiscriminately at many foreigners is that our lack of obsession with the home and its care proves the intended transience of our German residence.

Concern for the Environment

Over the last few decades, this love of the home has expanded for large segments of the German population into a pronounced concern for the environment. The heightened environmental awareness that one frequently encounters here is one of the more positive manifestations of the sense of insecurity. Germans like the environment they have grown up with and don't care to see it radically altered by human recklessness.

Fears of the destruction of nature and the many dangers associated with environmental pollution have effected a raft of changes in lifestyle quite unexpected in a society so fundamentally resistant to rapid change. Indeed, the country's third largest political party and now the junior partner in the ruling national coalition is *die Grünen* (the Greens), originally formed in the late 1970s as an environmental protest group, retains staunchly pro-environmental policies as a centrepiece of its platform.

Automobilius Glorious

The private car gets a closer look later in the book, but we can't close this topic without noting that 'your own four wheels' is one particularly prized possession in Germany. Despite the excellence of public transportation and the large numbers of bikes, the ownership of a car bestows a certain prestige upon the German burgher, a sign that he or she has achieved a requisite level of respectability.

If you think you sense a contradiction here, you're right. In fact, the plethora of private cars in the face of both strong environmental concerns and Germany's excellent public transportation system suggests that the automobile represents something above and beyond just a means of getting from one place to another.

Of course, different cars reflect different expressions of success or self-image. Accordingly, even when Germans get their car, they often strive to move up to another which will better express (or even increase) their sense of self-worth. The ultimate expression of achievement is generally the BMW or Mercedes, with the Porsche being the vehicle of choice for the more raffish. Remember that all three are German-made and therefore considerably less expensive here than in most other countries.

Please Step Away from the Car

The psychological importance of the auto to Germans explains why most cars are so meticulously kept up. Cars in Germany generally shine and gleam as if they had just rolled out of the showroom. And woe betide you should you not treat that car with its due reverence. Nothing casual about cars here—you might just as well sit on a German's child, spouse or dog as sit or lean on his car.

Compartmentalisation

As Germans reckon it, one good way to breed insecurity is to allow various areas of life to start spilling into one another. Such mixing can, of course, produce messiness, which translates rapidly into insecurity.

To thwart this as much as possible, Germans strive to keep the most important areas of their lives scrupulously compartmentalised and as far from each other as possible. Work activities belong exclusively to the work sphere, while family life has its own unique sphere. Activities with certain friends belong here, with other friends somewhere else, while club activities enjoy their own special nook. Even when these activities do somehow merge, Germans still twist to preserve the compartmentalisation in some way. For example, there are cases aplenty where colleagues who have built up a friendly relationship outside the office maintain the formal *Sie* form of address in the workplace, reverting to the familiar *Du* form only when work is finished.

Keep it Where it Belongs

The German home is a wonderful laboratory for observing this phenomenon at closer range. Most rooms have their own assigned function, and should be used for no other purpose, except under extreme duress. The structure of many homes underscores this attitude. For example, most German kitchens are small and barely suitable for anything other than cooking meals. Certainly they would not serve well as family conference centres, as they often do in North American or Mediterranean cultures.

Objects, too, usually have their assigned place in a home. Consequently, most things stand where they do because the residents have resolved that this is exactly where they belong—and nowhere else, thank you. Certain objects have multiple functions, of course, and these things will be moved about as they are needed and then quickly returned to their originally assigned places. If you are visiting German friends, or if you happen to move in with Germans, don't move things around, unless you want to seriously disturb the peace.

A Time for Everything Under the Heavens

To assure that this careful compartmentalisation works effectively, Germans commonly assign a proper time for most activities and they can be quite disconcerted if something is inserted into an erroneous time slot. After living here for a while, you will understand why all the major Western philosophy on the subject of time comes from Germans; these folks are truly obsessed with time.

Germans are devout clock-watchers, especially in factories, stores and offices. Should you turn up at an office or store shortly before closing time (or the holy lunchtime break) so that it appears that your business might drag on past that magic hour, you will either receive chilly service or be turned away altogether.

This rigid attitude also extends to the home or leisure activities. There are times to do just about everything, especially sitting down to meals. It's useless to protest that you aren't really hungry yet—if it's lunchtime, dinnertime or *Kaffee*-time, you're going to eat, period. But let's not get too wrapped up in our stereotypes: most Germans do exercise some flexibility in this regard, but that flexibility is measured in minutes, not hours. The practice of 'grazing' that has replaced regular meal times in some other cultures is something that most Germans would just never swallow.

There are also times to take long walks, to open the windows in a room and let in fresh air (a compulsory ritual, independent of time of year or any but the most inclement weather conditions) and to watch television. Violating any of these time slots can knock people off greatly and, worse still, it may then take them some unplanned time to recover. To take one example, you should be very careful about phoning someone between 8:00 pm and 8:15 pm when the main evening news is broadcast. (Especially, don't ever call me during this time!)

Germans even have a long-established measure of how late is too late—*das academische Viertel* (the academic quarter hour, after which students could give up on a tardy professor). Should you arrive more than 15 minutes late for an appointment, you had better have an extremely good excuse ready.

The Importance of Planning

Closely allied to this obsession with time is an unshakable commitment to careful planning. As planning forms one of the best bulwarks against uncertainty, most Germans frame their lives with a great deal of the stuff. You'll soon discover that it is not advisable to extend a last-minute invitation to Germans as they have almost certainly made plans for that day, even if said plans entail nothing more than spending a quiet evening at home.

As this suggests, spontaneity is no major virtue for most Germans. One important radical political movement of the 1970s and 1980s called itself the *Spontis,* a diminutive of spontaneous. Indeed, few things could be taken as more subversive of the German social system than programmatic spontaneity. (And, of course, a lot of this group's activities did involve carefully programmed spontaneity.)

Start Planning Now

You won't need to be here too long before you, too, are drawn into the undertow of planning, as much of the German way of life doesn't merely support this insistence on planning, it positively forces it. Most club memberships, subscriptions to theatre or concert seasons, magazine or newspaper subscriptions renew themselves automatically. It is your obligation as the client to cancel these commitments, and cancellations must often occur three to six months before the expiration date. If you don't cancel by that date, you will be renewed for another year, and then just have to remember to cancel by the following year's notification date. I know one short-sighted lady who had to pay her dues to Germany's largest automobile club for two or three years after she had junked her car because she routinely neglected to cancel her membership. And no courts or consumer advocacy groups will step forth to help you out of these unwanted commitments. The rules and the sentiments all stand on the side of careful planning.

Thoroughness

Another good way to fight back against insecurity is to be thorough in just about everything you do. Which is why the Germans have secured their well-deserved reputation for thoroughness. There is a pervasive commitment to doing things thoroughly, a quality that you are sure to find, by turns, both reassuring and irritating. Foreigners here frequently discover that Germans will come in and put the finishing touches on what they thought they had already completed in a fairly decent manner. Or the Germans will tell them that the job has been done well so far—now complete it.

A good example of German thoroughness came up several years ago when our landlord had some windows in our flat replaced with more energy saving units. A trio of workmen came in and worked a few days installing the new windows. A week or two later, our landlord informed us that their boss, the master carpenter, would be coming in to inspect their work. He did, and reappeared a week later, to give it one more inspection. That's the sort of thoroughness you can expect with the Germans. It goes without saying that we had no problems at all with our windows following that process.

Frankness to a Fault

Many people relocating here are quite taken aback by the brutal frankness Germans sometimes display. Whereas many other peoples will weigh their words most carefully, will be extremely tactful, will take care to shield the feelings of others, Germans like to give it to them straight. The German credo seems to be, 'The truth hurts—but it is good for you nevertheless'.

So when you come to Germany, be prepared to hear criticisms or unkind judgments of a kind you're probably unfamiliar with. Casual acquaintances or fellow workers may tell you things that even your best friends back home would hold back. They may even criticise you on things which happen to be personality flaws that are hard to remedy and thus pretty much taboo subjects in most other societies.

A number of German acquaintances, colleagues and students have told me that they don't really feel comfortable dealing with Americans or Asians. Why? Because they just can't trust them, they say. What they mean with this put-down is that Americans and Asians tend to be altogether more circumspect in their criticisms, that they will pad the truth to protect the other person's feelings. If this is also your way of doing things, be aware that Germans don't see it as any kind of virtue. You are better advised to become a little more blunt in your pronouncements, to drop all the rhetorical airbrushing and adornments and serve up a more point-blank account of what you think and feel—even if it starts to enter the tender zone.

The Credibility Factor

Perhaps one reason that Germans are so painfully frank is a difference in the way they wish to be perceived by others. While people from cultures like North America's often have a need to be liked, Germans have a need to be credible, to be believed (*wahrgenommen werden*). This need surfaces in any number of situations, but mainly in the fact that Germans hate to make mistakes and hate even more admitting they have made a mistake.

Crossed Lines

In no other country have I ever received a wrong number phone call, informed the caller that he had dialled incorrectly, only to be hit with the sharp retort, "No, I haven't, now let me speak to Herr X." Does such a thing really happen in Germany? Yes indeed—for instance, while I was in the middle of first writing this chapter!

Arrogance

Does all this mean that Germans are arrogant? Well, arrogance is to some extent in the eyes of the person being sneered at, but yes, Germans do display a streak of arrogance more often than many other peoples (though many will argue that they still trail the French badly in this regard). When you can't bend very far, you have to stiffen yourself in ways that demand a tough, arrogant stance. This is one of the less endearing qualities discernible throughout large parts of German society. Even if the root of their inability to bend comes from their deep insecurity, the bitter fruit of this is an exasperating arrogance.

Aggression

A South African living here for decades has often reported how, after a few hours back in Germany from trips abroad, he starts feeling a tightness, a knotted tension in his neck and shoulders. He offers this diagnosis of his syndrome: "This society is so aggressive. It starts to get to you right away."

Allied to their perceived arrogance, this pervasive aggression is an even less endearing Teutonic trait. Sadly, many Germans do come on much too strong when they want something. At such times, they can indeed be pushy, overbearing, palpably impatient, if not truculent.

Rationalism

The vast majority of Germans are strong rationalists—or at least they cling to the irrational belief that they are strong rationalists. They like to judge things empirically, to assemble all the hard facts they can before reaching a decision. Ergo, they believe that any decision they do make was based on unassailably rational grounds. This is why it is not very profitable to argue with Germans about decisions they have arrived at after long consideration, or question long established practices in German society. Most of the Germans you meet will be convinced there couldn't possibly be any viable arguments on the other side of the issue.

An adjunct to this rationalist commitment is the stock German attitude towards sentimentality. Most Germans claim to hate the stuff, and their standard response to songs, films, stories, or poems lathered with sentimentality is either a contemptuous snort or a nervous, sneering laugh. So don't try to push any products of sentimentality on Germans or you are bound to get an unpleasant response. Nonetheless, catch them in the right mood, under the influence of the right beverages, in the right situation and you will find that a good many Germans are just chock-full of sentimentality. Why this apparent contradiction? Read on.

The Dynamic Split

Goethe, Germany's greatest poet, had his most famous creation, Dr Faust, proclaim that, 'Two souls beat within my breast.' The good old Doc could have been sounding the lament of a large number of his compatriots. Germans do often find themselves split by competing passions, and they tenaciously hold seemingly contradictory views. For example, repeated polls through the 1980s and 1990s indicated that the overwhelming majority of Germans considered themselves optimistic about their country and their own future, but you are apt to encounter some of the most pessimistic sorts you've ever run into over here. And while an even larger majority believes human nature is basically good, distrust of others is rampant and can get rather annoying.

Some baffled foreigners consider the Germans hypocritical. A deeper analysis might indicate they are torn, with the tear line running somewhere between the head and the guts. All too typical of Germans is this split between 'head feelings' and 'gut feelings.' That's why they can often be deeply committed to mutually exclusive views or passions—

the one view is lodged firmly in the guts, the other planted in the head.

This split nature actually gives a dynamic tension to the national personality; these people can't decide which feelings to be guided by. For example, contrary to popular stereotype, Germans can be very emotional, indeed extremely passionate, even though they tend to keep these capacities under rein much of the time. This is why they are more often perceived as cold, mechanical, overrational. Furthermore, as the floods of emotion frequently come out in negative situations (you've probably seen this in the behaviour of football hooligans or right-wing extremists), the rare outbursts merely underscore some of the world's other negative images of Germans. But if you happen to develop close relations with Germans, you will discover these emotions, these passions can also be released in very positive contexts.

There's Always Room for Gloom

Back to that point about pessimism. A deep capacity for gloom is one of the qualities their dark history has bequeathed to these people. They know all too well that things can go horribly wrong. Hence, Germans do worry a lot. And if they are not busy worrying about some problem, they are probably worrying about why they are not worrying.

Short-term visitors and new residents, unaware of the German capacity for fun and joy, often take this as proof of one enduring German stereotype—that they are a gloomy people. The fact is, gloom is a staple of German life, informing the way most people here perceive things. Sorry, but Germans are just not a naturally sunny, upbeat people. You have to prove to them there's a reason to be joyous, to celebrate, or it has to be publicly declared with some holiday. However, when you do, you will be surprised at just how boisterous they can get in their celebrating.

Wertewandel

When I first arrived in this country, I found myself praising the exquisite punctuality of German public transport to a somewhat disaffected young German lady. "At least the trains run on time!" I noted as one rolled in true to schedule. "Yes," she responded morosely, "The trouble is, in Germany, everything runs on time."

Little did she or I know back then at the start of the 1980s, but we were just sliding into the full swing of what many Germans often refer to as the *Wertewandel,* or transformation of values. Starting in the late 1960s with the fabled student rebellion and other radical movements, then spreading to most other parts of German society over the next two decades, the *Wertewandel* has significantly altered many German ways of doing things. Today, there are quite a few things that no longer 'run on time'.

Much of this shift in values was perhaps predictable, considering the development of German society. After all, the virtues necessary to rebuild a devastated nation after World War II were not as indispensable once the country had achieved a level of affluence the war generation could hardly have dreamed of. Younger Germans with no first-hand experience of the lean years began to ask, "If we're so rich, why aren't we happy?"

The result was a determined rejection of many of those very values that had helped Germany reach levels of prosperity making such a rejection possible. German society today is clearly different from what it was 40 or 30 years ago, even from what it was some 20 years ago when I first arrived. Many of these changes will continue into the foreseeable future. Others have themselves fallen victim to campaigns to re-evaluate the re-evaluations. But it's undeniable that Germany today still finds itself in a period of considerable flux, slipping more and more away from that image portrayed in the old stereotypes. (This trend is, of course, even more pronounced with the dislocations brought on by the unification of the two Germanys.)

The Body Public

In sharp contrast to the prudery that prevailed for the first decades of the post-war period, German society is today more characterised by open displays of the body—in newspapers and magazines, in public saunas, beaches and promenades, and in certain protected prostitution 'tolerance zones'. Prostitution is legal in most German cities, though it is controlled and limited to certain areas, such as Hamburg's famous Reeperbahn. Unfortunately, in towns like Frankfurt, the red light district lies right outside the main train station, making the sex zones the first view of Frankfurt that many visitors are treated to.

Countless news-stands and shops prominently display magazines with nude bodies on the cover, often a whole array of them. And it's not just the sex mags that flash those nude (mainly female) bodies on their covers; even quasi-serious publications such as *Stern* seem to find the occasional nude on the cover a sure sales booster. The point here is, it is virtually impossible to avoid such explicit images completely if you ever venture near a news-stand or magazine rack, so those coming from more modest societies had better brace themselves for some shocks here.

That goes doubly so for public beaches, baths, parks or river bank stretches where full nudity in its live presentation is not at all unusual. Whereas just a few decades ago, this would have been considered scandalous in Germany, today it's routine. What is not routine, and is in fact judged rather harshly, is staring at those nude bodies. And be strongly advised—just because some sunbathers are fully stripped down, this does not mean that they are advertising their availability, or even looking for some companionship. Approaching someone engaged in solitary sunbathing is considered highly offensive, and can earn sharp reproach from everyone around.

In winter, the scene of mixed public nudity shifts to the sauna, where stripping down to the essentials is not only optional, but required. Should you feel squeamish about sitting around in the nude sweating with members of the opposite sex, stay out of public saunas. The modest practice of wearing swimming briefs into the sauna, something that many Asians and Americans seem to favour, is more than frowned upon. I have seen instances where the swim-suited miscreant was asked to remove the offending piece or else leave the room. This is not entirely reverse prudery either, as wearing clothing in a sauna is considered unhealthy (on the other hand, you should always bring a large towel to sit on and catch the flows of sweat).

As there are unfortunately a good many louts anxious to display their crude senses of humour in public saunas, many of these institutions have introduced ladies' nights, where entry is barred to men. Sadly for shy males, no sauna has inaugurated a men's night as far as I know.

DRUGS

Another bigger shock in store for many newcomers is the fairly open use of drugs in Germany. The personal use of so-called soft drugs was effectively decriminalised by an April 1994 decision of the German Supreme Court, and the authorities in several jurisdictions have slipped into a policy of malign tolerance towards even the use of hard drugs. These latter are, however, mostly confined to certain 'tolerance zones' and then only in certain cities. Berlin, Hamburg and Frankfurt are notorious as drug centres whereas states such as Bavaria and Lower Saxony take a rather hard line on all drugs, while the attorney general of North Rhine-Westphalia in the mid-1990s interpreted the court's decision to permit even small amounts of heroin and cocaine.

From time to time, especially before an important municipal election, cities initiate a tough crackdown on the public use of drugs, and the junkies suddenly become scarce. Despite such cosmetic treatment, the problem has reached epidemic levels in some cities, often forcing the police to just shrug their shoulders and turn to other problems. Thus, in cities like Berlin, Frankfurt or Hamburg, you may be subjected to the spectacle of junkies shooting up more or less in the open as you walk through the major train stations and surrounding areas.

RELIGION

Considering that two of the largest and most powerful political parties in this country both bear the title 'Christian' in their names, you might be tempted to think that Germany is halfway to a theocracy. The truth is quite the opposite in that religion today plays a rather negligible role in German public life. While religious beliefs can be a most important part of an individual's private life, most Germans choose to keep it stashed away there. The vast majority appear very uncomfortable with religious discussions, and make it rather clear that they are.

Sure, the major churches often speak out on social and economic matters, but their less popular admonitions are usually ignored by the elected representatives of the people. (Some of those politicians who most strongly supported liberalisation of the country's abortion laws in the 1990s were ostensibly devout Roman Catholics.)

Perhaps paradoxically, Germany maintains no strict separation of church and state such as one finds in many other democracies. In fact, 12 of Germany's 15 legal holidays are Christian feast days (*Refer to* 'Public Holidays' *in* Chapter 7: Enjoying Germany *on pages 198–204*). Moreover, the major churches are supported by taxes paid by the official members of those churches, with a majority of Germans still ranked as official, tax-supporting members of the two largest faiths (Lutheran and Roman Catholic). But then, even amongst

German Catholics, required under the pain of mortal sin to attend weekly mass, only about 16 per cent are actually regular churchgoers. And that percentage dips even lower for Protestants here.

Even more striking, a number of baffling polls throughout the 1990s indicated that more burghers belonged to a church than actually believe in God. This apparent discrepancy is probably explained by the fact that church membership plays a major social function for many Germans. Many minimally religious or even, evidently, atheistic citizens value this social aspect. Also, once you've become an officially registered member of a religion, withdrawing your membership can be a troublesome process that requires going to different government offices and drawing a lot of bureaucratic attention to what might be essentially a private matter.

Despite such roadblocks, more and more people have officially found their way out of the Church, with the two largest reporting total losses of around 115,000 annually—which follows an unwavering trend of the past decade. Much of this decline seems related to a general rise in taxes and drop in disposable income which has led many residents to seek unloading the one tax they bear that is optional.

The only religious groups that make any large public displays of their faith are sects like the Jehovah's Witnesses and the Unification Church. The former also engage in a serious proselytising program, often going door-to-door to seek new recruits (and we know what impression invading the privacy of the home creates). Even the staid, stolid Mormons are considered a weird sect in this country because they go around actively proselytising, trying to market their faith, and this is simply not done in Germany. So be aware that if you go around speaking too openly of your own religious beliefs, you could also be considered somewhat weird, perhaps even someone to be avoided.

LAW AND ORDER

Perhaps as a consequence of all these major shifts in values, weakening of authority, and the marginalisation of religion, Germany has experienced a dismaying rise in criminality over the last few 20 years. The shredding of the social safety net over the last decade also undoubtedly plays its part, as does the mind-boggling leniency of many court verdicts. While German crime rates are still comfortably low compared to some other Western societies, they seriously disturb many Germans and long-time foreign residents who remember their country as a bastion of law-abiding burghers.

Actually, the vast majority of German residents do remain admirably law-abiding. But by the early 1990s, the total number of reported crimes had more than doubled in less than 20 years (since then, it has plateaued, remaining with more or less steady crime rates). As usual in this area, however, the problem looks worse on paper (and in the pages of the boulevard press) than it does in the streets. In fact, that type of crime which sparks the most fear, violent crime, has stabilised and even dipped in some categories (such as murder). The biggest, ugly chunk of Germany's crime is still against property, not body.

One type of crime that doesn't wait for you, but comes right to your door and beyond, is burglary, which has seen the most dramatic jump in rates, increasing threefold in less than ten years. Through the early 1990s, our own building, situated in the middle of a safe, middle-class section of Frankfurt, had at least three break-ins within a two-year span. Our flat was one of those so honoured, though our ham-handed culprit made such a ruckus forcing his way in that a neighbour heard him, called the police, and he was forced to flee before grabbing any booty. (He himself was nabbed a few streets away.) We were lucky, but not completely so: we had to cover the costs of that broken door ourselves.

Following this rash of incidents, everyone in the building became more diligent about taking basic precautions against burglary, such as double-locking the front door so visitors can't simply be buzzed in, and there hasn't been a single break-in since. On this matter, as well as others, police departments offer a series of pamphlets with helpful hints in various languages. In short—always look out for that ounce of prevention that makes the pound of cure unnecessary.

Crime and Punishment

While surges in crime rarely have a single cause, many people here blame the leniency of the criminal courts for the upswing. While it is undeniable that many high-profile verdicts, such as the appallingly light sentences meted out to neo-Nazis who have attacked and in some cases murdered foreigners or German Jews, or the two-year suspended sentence handed down to the Steffi Graf fan who stabbed Monica Seles in the back and effectively ended her high-flying career, or the short sentence for manslaughter given out to the infamous 'Internet cannibal' have been at the very least questionable, their high profile probably lends them more weight than is justified. Many other sentences are fittingly tough. (And note that in April 2005, prosecutors successfully appealed the sentence meted out to cannibal-killer Armin Miewes, securing a new trial to make their case that Miewes deserves a much longer stay behind bars. On the other hand, Miewes and his agents have made a lot of money selling the rights to his story and one public-funded institute doled out 20,000 euros to make a cheesy film based on the grisly affair.)

The tenor of many sentences is itself another example of the legacy of German history. Obviously chastised by the viciousness and arbitrary nature of the Nazi-era courts, German judges of more recent vintage have bent over backwards (and beyond, according to some critics) to protect the rights of the accused and understand the motives of the convicted, assuring that no sentence should be seen as unfair or too harsh. To this end, the death penalty was abolished in the West German Basic Law of 1949.

Some of these ultra-acrobatic judicial acts of bending over backwards have also aroused outrage abroad. Germans themselves just shake their heads sadly, recalling a time when everyone knew what was right and what was wrong, when you were rewarded for doing right and punished for doing wrong, and everything contributed nicely to the common pursuit of security. Now there is this major transformation of values, or whatever it is, and again we are like children lost in the woods, afraid of the dark brought on by all these uncertainties. Thank God we're Germans, and know how to really worry about these things the right way. Right?

FITTING INTO GERMANY

CHAPTER 4

'Everybody is a foreigner. Almost everywhere.'
—Slogan of the German
anti-xenophobia campaign

'Whatever is not forbidden is permitted.'
—Friedrich Schiller, *Wallenstein's Camp*

THE AUSLÄNDER PROBLEM

Let's cast our glance back to late 1945 for a moment: Germany lay devastated, its industrial capacity smashed, its agricultural base ravaged, large sections of its most important cities and towns little more than sprawling piles of rubble. This people who for 12 years had been exhorted to fancy themselves as the 'master race' destined to rule much of the world suddenly found themselves occupied by the people of other nations—some with different skin colour, others from ethnic groups Germans had been taught for over a decade to despise.

Then, four years after the collapse of Nazi Germany, when the three western zones of occupied Germany united in a democratically elected republic, one of the laws enshrined in this republic's new constitution was an absolute right to political asylum in Germany. This statute, at once a conscious act of atonement for the crimes of the Nazi period and a recognition that many German Jews and political dissidents had died because other nations had refused to accept them as refugees in the late 1930s, was considered more symbolic than applicable when passed in 1949. After all, how many victims of persecution would really seek refuge in a shattered country which wasn't even fully able to feed, clothe or shelter its own people?

Now zip ahead a few years: The Germans, possessed by an extraordinary determination to rebuild their country, surpassed all but the wildest of optimists' forecasts with their rapid pace of reconstruction—the *Wirtschafstwunder* (economic miracle). By the mid 1950s, German economic recovery had been so fantastic that the country actually ran up against a labour shortage. Unskilled and semi-skilled workers were actively recruited abroad, first from southern Europe, then from Asia Minor or North Africa. By the early 1970s, when German economic ascendancy was recognised and envied the world over, the number of these so-called *Gastarbeiter* (guest workers) and their families or associates had reached 4.1 million. As a Turkish friend in London once remarked, "Those Germans have been damn clever at colonialism—they just went out and imported themselves some colonies.".

Flash back to the present: The number of foreign residents has swelled to around 7.5 million (in a population of 82.4 million). Within a short span of three or four decades, a people who had been conspicuously homogeneous

This Turkish grocery store is just one of thousands of *Aüslander*-owned and -operated shops and businesses in Germany.

found themselves living in a richly multicultural society with people from cultures sometimes radically different from the mainstream.

Nor are all of these foreigners 'guest workers' any more. As Germany grew rich, it became a most tempting lure for political refugees wishing to take advantage of the country's ultra-liberal asylum laws, including not a few with rather dubious claims to political asylum. The number of asylum seekers more than quadrupled between 1980 and 1992, when it hit a record 438,191. Stiffening of laws and greater stringency in guidelines have cut that figure significantly every year since.

Moreover, as European integration continued to advance, the Germans were suddenly being told they had to start thinking of themselves in terms of their new European identity, within the context of a united Europe 'without borders'. Throw all these factors together in one pot, stir them roughly, and you've got the brew which many Germans of all ages, classes and faiths today characterise as *das Ausländer Problem* (the foreigner problem).

While this phrase may sound a bit ominous, perhaps even echoing some of the darker chapters of recent German history, you have to keep in mind that many Germans tend to look for the problems in a situation as, for them, problem-solving is a kind of national sport. In this case, the solutions offered differ radically and have ranged from dual citizenship for all who have lived in Germany for a certain number of years, to beginning repatriation of large numbers of foreigners, including many of those born and bred here.

The more common reaction is a state of bewilderment. A commonly heard remark amongst some Germans today is, "I really have nothing at all against foreigners, but they should stay out of Germany." This, you should note, is said without a hint of conscious irony. Upon further inquiry, you find out that they don't mean all foreigners, just a vaguely defined lot who should be kept out of Germany. But in this era of shrinking incomes, high-pitched terrorism and raised tensions, when even traditionally hospitable lands such as the United States, Britain and Australia have produced some frothing anti-immigrant sentiments, even some restrictive legislation, how many countries can claim to throw out the welcome mat to all new arrivals?

Unfortunately, large numbers of people have indeed tried to abuse Germany's humane and liberal asylum laws, which has soured many German citizens on the whole concept of asylum for persecuted refugees. And it is undeniable that shortly after the fall of the Iron Curtain, a stream of illegal workers, mainly from Eastern Europe, found their way into Germany and took many jobs at wages below the legal base, usually in the construction industries. This stream may have become a trickle in the last few years, but it still irks many here.

WHAT IS A GERMAN?

Possibly the best place to break out of this dilemma is with the question 'What is a German?'. This actually has two answers, a legal one and a common-sense one. As this concerns Germany, which loves legalisms, we'll start with the legal one.

Germany is one of the few countries in the world that still largely bases its citizenship on 'blood'. Yes, blood. This legal definition of a German as someone filled with 'German blood' harks back to a law passed in 1913, during the Imperial period. While most enactments of the Federal Republic were scrupulous in trying to amend the abuses of the Nazi period, this law with its distinctly 'race-conscious' bearings has somehow managed to stand—though not as straight or as proud as before.

The application of this law spawns a number of anomalies. For example, immigrants coming from, say Rumania, Poland, or an area of the former Soviet Union who have never seen Germany, who can't speak a word of German, and who are totally unfamiliar with the German way of life can arrive here and automatically lay claim to German citizenship because their forebears emigrated from some German area centuries ago. On the other hand a Turk, Italian, Croat, Spaniard or

Moroccan born and bred in Germany, who has never seen his or her parents' homeland, who speaks fluent, flawless German and would be like a fish out of water living in any other society doesn't quite qualify as a full-fledged German citizen. Those in the latter group assume a limited-term dual citizenship that requires them to choose one allegiance and renounce the other sometime between their eighteenth and twenty-third birthdays.

Common sense would argue that those in the latter group are actually Germans and the former not, and that's the approach we largely take in this book. Although these limited-term dual citizens may have dark hair and eyes and swarthy complexions, their behaviour marks them as being every bit as German as anyone conforming to the old Aryan ideal. This is especially true of those 'immigrant children' who have largely broken away from the bonds of their homes. Indeed, everyday in any of

A group of foreign school children posing next to a wall which shows some of the countries the school's students come from.

Germany's big cities, one runs into countless 'foreigners' who seem to be trying to 'out-German the Germans'—for better or worse.

Further, in the last few years, the government has made it easier for foreigners to become Germans, almost halving the time of their 'habitual residence' to just eight years. However, they also have to prove adequate knowledge of Germany, show a clean criminal record and commitment to the tenets of Germany's Basic Law (constitution), and be 'in a position to pay for his/her own maintenance'.

Immigrants? What Immigrants?

Fogging up this whole matter considerably is the fact that, officially, Germany has almost no immigration policy; German law simply does not recognise the fact of immigration to this land. Most of the foreigners who arrive without the benefit of 'German blood' get classified under that rubric of *Gastarbeiter*. Perhaps inevitably, this causes any number of confusions, embarrassments and bruised feelings.

In recent years, debates have been heating up throughout German society, as well as in its state and national parliaments, as to whether Germany is, in fact, a country of immigration. One piece of legislation intended to spur an influx of foreign talent was blocked by the German supreme court in late 2002 after the conservative opposition parties filed an appeal against it. The federal government then set about redrafting the bill to bring its immigration intent more in line with German constitutional principles. Only in June 2004 was Germany's first-ever immigration bill passed, after the federal government made major concessions to the conservative opposition parties which control the lower house of the parliament.

Having moved nowhere near resolve, these debates look set to continue at least through the end of this decade. And one reason for this is that many Germans simply refuse to recognise even those life-long residents as Germans—in any but the most superficial way.

The Gastarbeiter Syndrome

The fact that many foreign residents, even after having lived here ten, 20 years (their whole lives in some cases) are still referred to by their neighbours as 'guest workers' shows an unsavoury tendency to permanently view them in a temporary light (despite the fact that one-third of the officially-registered foreign population of Germany in 2002 had already lived here for 30 years or more, while at least 50 per cent of this group had resided here for at least 20 years). All of which stirs inevitable resentment within the rejected foreign population.

And even though, as we saw above, there are many cases of abuse and illegal residence, the overwhelming majority of foreign residents pay their taxes and obey the laws like most Germans. They also contribute to the government-sponsored health and pension programs, though it's possible they'll never be able to fully participate in those programs. But still, they don't qualify as full-fledged members of German society. And more and more, they want to know why.

All these elements together seem to be a recipe for serious trouble, and that's exactly what they produce sometimes. You may be familiar with some of these 'sometimeses' from TV or newspaper reports: foreign youths fighting pitched street battles with German rowdies or police; random acts of mindless vandalism; attacks upon foreign residents or their businesses. These extreme eruptions are can't-miss headline-makers; much more often though, the situation results only in minor irritations, misunderstandings, and frictions. And then, at other times, the product of these elements is just the opposite—something really warm and humane.

The Importance of the Foreign Community

Look, the simple, incontrovertible fact is that if Germany's entire foreign population left the country tomorrow, the vaunted German economy would totter on the brink of collapse. Major operations would lose scores of their key people, banks would be bereft of essential foreign experts,

German companies and government agencies would lose important conduits to partners abroad. Meanwhile, factories and mines would soon stumble to a virtual standstill, thousands of shops or restaurants would disappear while the remaining ones would find themselves desperate for sales personnel or waiting staff as the streets of most towns piled up with trash and garbage. Not to mention the loss of those thousands of foreigners in the German entertainment industry who keep the country entertained when the workday comes to an end.

Any honest, informed German has to admit this central fact of contemporary German life, and probably the majority of them do. Unfortunately, not every German citizen is as appreciative of the countless foreign contributions to contemporary German society. Which forms the perfect breeding ground for a low but unsettling level of xenophobia (or, as the Germans call it, *Ausländerfeindlichkeit*). Fortunately, most of these feelings today remain at the stage of pedestrian xenophobia. But it's probably not this pedestrian brand that has you a little worried about living in Germany; it's the most virulent form—the skinhead or neo-Nazi phenomenon.

The Skinhead Phenomenon

Chances are that when you started telling friends and acquaintances back home that you were planning a move to Germany, they heaped fervid warnings upon you about attacks upon foreigners there, about the hordes of neo-Nazis marching throughout the country, about fire-bombings of foreigners' homes, businesses and places of worship. Without wishing to minimise either the threat or the viciousness of these elements, let me assure you that the problem is absolutely nowhere near as widespread as television reports around the world might make it seem.

One would have thought, certainly one would have hoped, that the unspeakable horrors of the Nazi period would have scoured vicious xenophobic sentiments from the German soul for all time. Unfortunately, that painful lesson just didn't take on each and every German. One poll not too long ago found that 15 per cent of the German population had strong anti-foreigner leanings, while 15 per cent were described as 'manifestly anti-Semitic'.

Many Germans still harbour fears, suspicions and misconceptions about the non-natives living in their midst, many of them for decades. For example, one highly educated German I know (he actually studied law) once assured me that 80 per cent of the crime here is committed by foreigners, even though there are no statistics at all to remotely support such a claim.

The most vicious outgrowth of this is all too familiar to many people—those images or reports which have been beamed around the world of skinheads and other neo-Nazis whose hatred of anyone and anything foreign has more to do with social and psychological pathology than any ideology.

Sadly, in addition to the minuscule percentage of Germans belonging to these groups, there is a sizable number who generally agree to a large extent with the neo-Nazis' view of foreigners, even while rejecting the Nazis' final conclusions, their methods, or possibly just their fashion tastes. It's hard to say what portion of the German population belongs to this latter group, but it is larger than anyone, especially we foreigners, can be comfortable with.

The Bright Side

There is a much brighter side, and this demands to be presented, especially in a book written for non-Germans contemplating a move to Germany.

There are literally millions upon millions of Germans who welcome the presence of foreigners, who sincerely believe their country has become a richer, more interesting place because of the abundant contributions of *ausländische Mitbürger* (foreign fellow citizens). Many people in other countries look at me sceptically when I tell them that I have not seen all that many real live skinheads in Frankfurt, the town where I lived for over 15 years and the town which has the highest percentage of foreigners of any large German city. But it's true. I've also seen a few dozen Skins in my frequent visits to Berlin, and a scattering on trips to other major cities. Like you, the largest number of German neo-Nazis I've ever seen has been on my television screen. Yes, they are out there alright, and they do come together in critical masses for their theoretically illegal marches and demonstrations. (Any dissemination of Nazi philosophy or views is strictly contravened by German law.) But they are no daily threat to most foreigners living here.

Many Germans today, all too aware of the negative image conveyed by the neo-Nazis and other, less virulent manifestations of racism, now actually go out of their way to make foreigners feel more at home here, doing whatever they can to smooth their way to cultural acclimation.

The Ausländer Hierarchy

A further complicating factor here is the clear hierarchy which exists amongst the *Ausländer,* a ranking devised and recognised by many Germans. For instance, I myself am of northern European stock, and my physical appearance immediately betrays the western Irish birthplace of my grandparents. This accords me a higher level of respect amongst many Germans than if my skin were darker.

This prejudice was vividly brought home to me shortly after my arrival in Germany when I went to a *Makler* (real estate agent) looking for a flat. When I told him what price range I was interested in, he showed me a long list of available properties in that category. But almost every one was tagged with the ominous *Keine Ausländer* (No Foreigners) warning. When I moaned to the agent that I seemed to be effectively barred from doing business with any of his clients, he rushed to reassure me: "Oh, don't worry, when they say *Ausländer*, they don't really mean your kind of *Ausländer*."

I was then informed that in this particular exercise in bigotry, *Ausländer* referred almost exclusively to non-Northern European foreigners. This was my own backdoor introduction to that pernicious hierarchy that all too many biased Germans bear allegiance to.

Anti-Americanism

A peculiar strain of German xenophobia is anti-Americanism. This strain, not as virulent as the other forms of xenophobia, is strongest amongst those on the political left.

This cluster of anti-Yank sentiments stems largely from America's world stature and policies, and it has grown considerably, in both numbers and intensity, during the years of the George W. Bush presidency. (Pew Research Center polls indicate that favourable attitudes toward America among Germans plummeted from 61 per cent in the summer of 2002 to just 38 per cent in March 2004. It had inched back up to 41 per cent by May 2005, but the trend holds.) It's not just American military actions such as the war in Iraq that upset many, but also America's abrogation of weapons and land mine treaties, its stance towards the World Court, and especially the US rejection of the Kyoto Protocols on global warming. (Remember that pronounced German concern for the environment?) Contemptuous statements by the U.S. Defense Secretary on the relevance of the 'old Europe' (mainly France and Germany) did not serve as balm on any festering wounds either.

For many Germans, in particular those of a more traditional or conservative bent, the anti-US sentiments are born more out of disappointment or a sense of betrayal that the nation they once looked up to as their redeemers and protectors has now taken on the appearance of an arrogant bully.

The good news for Americans living or travelling in Germany is that most of this anti-Americanism is directed at the current administration and its policies. Only a small minority of those far over on the left or right practice knee-jerk anti-Americanism. However, if you defend current US policies and postures too vocally, you do risk ruffling the feathers of a much wider portion of the German population. (Conversely, there is still a small coterie of Germans who are almost blindly pro-American.)

As this little tale reveals, Germany is a little short on anti-discrimination laws. However, statutes combating such unfair treatment have spread throughout the country, partially promoted by European Union initiatives. Owners of flats or houses can still refuse to rent to and eating and drinking establishments can refuse to serve people simply because they belong to the wrong ethnic or racial group. The latter rarely happens, however, except at discotheques, where admission is sometimes barred to certain types of foreigners. The more common treatment at offensive eating and drinking establishments is cold, curt service. But as you'll discover in Chapter 7: Enjoying Germany (*Refer to pages 196–222*), this could be applied to all outsiders, foreign or domestic.

There are, of course, other factors fixing you on higher or lower rungs of this hierarchy. For example, as English remains very 'in,' native English speakers enjoy a huge advantage over those who speak a language that the Germans look down upon or just can't fathom. As Italian and French are also 'in,' though nowhere near as economically valuable as English, speakers of these tongues snuggle in just under English speakers in the hierarchy. Christians are regarded more highly than non-Christians, or at least Muslims, who are sometimes perceived as a cultural threat. And since late 2001, sometimes even as a real security threat, (Remember that the core of the September 11th suicide brigade plotted out their strategies in Hamburg.)

The type of job you hold can also accord you more respect, especially if it sounds like a position which advances German economic interests abroad. You drop like a stone in German estimation if you perform unskilled or semi-skilled work. Germans actually confide some of these prejudices in private discussions with those foreigners who score high on all or most of these points.

But it's also important to steel yourself against paranoia in this regard. Always keep in mind that many Germans are just not overly friendly to strangers in general, so a harsh glance, a cold stare, a chilly rejoinder, or ignoring your presence may actually have little to do with your skin hue, your accent or your place of national origin.

THE GERMAN WAY OF MULTICULTURALISM

The image of Germany as a land packed with blue-eyed, blond-haired giants never even approximated the reality, but it deviates even further from reality today, when the bountiful waves of unofficial immigration have lent a rich, kaleidoscopic look to contemporary German society. It's true, you'll get your fair share of blond, blue-eyed giants here, but in most of Germany's big cities, you are at least as likely to run into representatives of the Mediterranean rim, South-east Asia, Africa or just the darker types of southern

Germany. Much more importantly, the cultural contributions of these groups to German society have grown exponentially over the last few decades, thoroughly enriching the overall cultural life in the process.

Ironically enough, the stilted resistance of German society to full assimilation may have actually aided this process in many ways. Rather than pushing its foreign communities to assimilate into the German mainstream culture, Germany has in some ways widened that mainstream, allowing diverse parallel tributaries to flow productively alongside the main culture. In fact, it is possible, if residing in one of the big cities, to carry on a full life in Germany without coming into contact with traditional German culture at all.

Promoting Multiculturalism

For some time now, German authorities and non-governmental organisations have recognised the importance of allowing and encouraging the various outside cultures transplanted here to flourish. This feeling has intensified and spread as a reaction to the series of vicious attacks against foreigners that began erupting in the early 1990s. As a result, government moneys and funding from non-governmental organisations have flowed into the promotion of other cultures, along with the promotion of understanding for the foreign communities living here. Today, many German cities, large and small, have followed the lead of Frankfurt am Main, which boasts Germany's highest concentration of foreigners, in opening an official Department for Multicultural Affairs that promotes, coordinates and sometimes funds activities by various non-German cultural groups living here. Activities include lectures, social events, music and theatre companies, and cultural festivals featuring music, dance and other arts from various countries, often ringed with food stands serving ethnic dishes.

In addition, government bodies have in recent years contributed to and coordinated various marches, educational courses and programs arranged to combat resurgent *Ausländerfeindlichkeit*. German and foreign residents' groups have worked closely in almost all of these marches and programs, which try to promote mutual understanding between the various cultures living here.

The Department for Multicultural Affairs also offers a wide range of advisory services of which many foreign residents avail themselves, especially in the early stages of their residence. They're especially helpful in guiding people whose German is limited through the *Behörde* jungle (*Refer to 'The Behörde Jungle' in this chapter on pages 89–91*). These services can be especially beneficial either in seeking some advice before going to a particularly difficult agency or after having encountered problems there. Should you find yourself in either one of these situations, you might want to call on your local foreigners' assistance office.

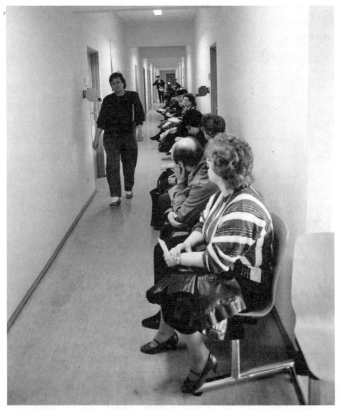

The wait at a German *Behörde's* office can often be long and frustrating.

FINDING YOUR PLACE AMONGST GERMANS

As the above paragraphs show, you are not obliged or expected to fully assimilate into the German way of life. It is actually much better to bring your unique qualities and perspectives and offer them as an enhancement to German society. The later parts of this chapter will show how you can use those qualities and perspectives to your best advantage. But now let's look at how you can better adapt to the German system.

Becoming Another Number

Believe me, Germany is no loosey-goosey land; its reputation as a well-run society is well-earned. But such reputations only get earned by herding citizens and other residents into certain structures. Ergo, you are required by law to register with a number of government agencies when you establish residence in Germany. This process can be fairly painless if done properly and promptly. If not, there can be plenty of pain and no gain.

The Behörde Jungle

Behörde and *Amt* are the German words for the various government agencies that play such a crucial role in keeping Germany running as Germany. Like all who went before you, you will soon learn that in Germany there are three things that are inevitable—death, taxes and *Behörde*. You will have to deal with some *Behörde* or *Amt* throughout your stay in Germany, though perhaps your worst dealings will come soon after your arrival.

In fact, many newcomers never survive the ordeal. I have known quite a few souls who decided to leave the country after their initial string of negative run-ins with German authorities. That's unfortunate, as those who do make it past the early stages generally agree the whole process becomes much easier after the initial unpleasantness. The officials at these *Behörde* are not famed for being friendly or helpful. They have a job to do, and being friendly or helpful to you is not a part of their job description, so they tend to skip over such niceties. A scowl often seems to be part of the regulation dress code of the people tasked with meeting the public, especially foreigners. Grin and bear it if you can.

You can still claim tourist status for the first three months of German residence, but then you must begin the trek through the registration maze. So why wait? So many other things depend on or are contingent upon your first steps that it is foolish to delay them.

Your first stop will be at the forbidding *Ordnungsamt* (Department of Order), where you will be directed to the *Ausländerbehörde* (broadly translated, Immigration Office, even though Germany doesn't have any official immigration). This is where you apply for an *Aufenthaltserlaubnis* (Residence Permit). If you're a European Union national, this is more or less a formality. If you come from a non-EU land, there are a number of hoops you have to jump through to get this magic stamp. What you should know is that these hoops are held rather high when you first apply, but are eventually lowered to accommodate most foreign applicants.

For example, you will probably be warned that you can't get your *Aufenthaltserlaubnis* until you have an *Arbeitserlaubnis* (work permit) firmly in hand. But when you trot over to the *Arbeitsamt* (Employment Office) where the trusty bureaucrat at the *Ordnungsamt* sends you, the good people there will tell you that one can't acquire an *Arbeitserlaubnis* until one is the proud possessor of an *Aufenthaltserlaubnis*. Slam! Sounds like a vicious Catch 22 intended to make your stay in Germany rather short, doesn't it?

Don't worry; it's intended to look much worse than it is. What you need is a job or the promise of one. A prospective employer will write a letter for the *Arbeitsamt* declaring that they need your unique expertise for this job, that you're taking a position which no German or EU national could possibly fill. The proximity of this claim to the truth is of no great importance as you return to the *Arbeitsamt* with this note, which will usually secure you a tentative *Arbeitserlaubnis*. With this you return to the *Ordnungsamt* and register.

After a background check and the other rigmarole, you'll be granted your *Aufenthaltserlaubnis,* which gets stamped into your passport. With this, you return to the *Arbeitsamt,* where they will award you a work permit if all the other forms have been properly seen to. And you thought I was kidding about jumping through hoops. If you came here following up on a job offer, your employers, knowing the system, will probably have taken care of the first stages of this process, squeezing visits one and two to the *Arbeitsamt* into one quick stop.

After you have successfully taken this first series of hoops, there are others you have to face. One of the first is registering with the *Einwohnermeldeamt* or *Ordnungsamt* to let them know where you live. This is much easier than your first encounter with the *Ordnungsamt* and merely entails going there with passport and filling out the long form you are given. You then receive a slip asserting that you have registered, which you are supposed to keep on your person at all times.

This last form of registration is required of all residents, German or foreigner. You must repeat the process every time you change your place of residence, unless that change merely involves moving from one flat within a building to another. Failure to do so within a 'reasonable time' of moving will earn you a fine of between 10–38 euros when the authorities finally catch up with you—and they have quite a few opportunities to do that. Again, do yourself and the bureaucrats a favour and quickly re-register whenever you move.

Let's Do It All Again

Now just because you got through all the hoops doesn't mean you are finished with the process for good. For the first few years, you will probably have to renew your residence permit annually. After the first time, it's mainly a formality, so you can skip the work permit and health certificate. Just go to the *Ordnungsamt* with your passport and apply for your extension, or *Verlängerung.* On about the fourth run, you will get a two-year permit. By your sixth year here, when you've grown to like many things about Germany and have gotten used to going through the permit mill, they will give you an unlimited residence permit and tell you that you need not come back any more!

Never on Sunday, Tuesday, Thursday or Holidays

Now if you are one of those super stout-hearts who feels all this is beginning to sound a little too easy, add this little hoop to the act: most *Behörde* only open their doors to the public three days a week (Monday, Wednesday and Friday) and then only in the mornings. Mornings means roughly 7:00 am or 8:00 am till noon. Some *Behörde*—but mainly in the larger cities and towns—have extended their opening times to Thursday afternoons, until 6:00 pm or even 6:30 pm Be sure to call and check the times of *Sprechstunden* (hours open to the public) before you collect all your papers and trek way across town only to be greeted by locked and guarded doors.

Banking on Foreigners

Banks are required to check your major documents every time you make a deposit of 10,000 euros or more (we should all be so lucky). Nevertheless, there are banks, and I myself have had this unexpected pleasure, that require all these documents anytime a foreigner opens any account. This is something you've also got to get used to quickly, namely that foreigners often get different treatment than German citizens, with additional regulations and then stricter enforcement of the standard regulations. This may be seen as discrimination, but let's not be too quick to vilify the Germans on this one—more than a handful of foreigners have left the country suddenly, leaving rental leases, tax bills, even bank overdrafts dangling. Banks and other businesses know the system is arranged so that they will usually be able to find German customers who sting them, but with foreigners, unfortunately, they have to be a little more careful.

Der Führerschein (Driver's Licence)

For many foreigners, a major step towards fitting into German society is when they can get behind the wheel of their own car and join the legions of racing maniacs on the Autobahn. The

Autobahn gets a longer treatment in the Chapter 5: Settling In (*refer to pages 164–166*), but before we get that far, we have got to make sure you've got a valid driver's licence.

For EU nationals, this is no problem at all: if you have a driver's licence from another EU country, you don't need to have a German driver's licence. You can use your licence from home as long as you live here. That is, unless you are a bus driver or the like, in which case you have to acquire a special German licence for your job.

For all others, your own licence from your home country is valid in Germany for one year from the date of your arrival in the Federal Republic. After that, you have two choices: give up driving or get a German driver's licence. This you do by taking a driving test (*Prüfung*). But it's not quite that simple, as the test is both practical and written and you need to know German road laws for both.

The way you learn these laws is to take a special course just for this test at a driving school (*Fahrschule*). But be wary. Many *Fahrschulen* will tell you they don't offer the simple *Prüfung* brush-up course and you have to take their full course, which is very arduous and costs a lot of money (1,500 euros minimum). But you don't have to take this course. What you must do is find a *Fahrschule* that offers the special course for your situation. But if you wait beyond your first year of German residence, you will need that full course—so don't wait!

Excuse me, I made something sound too simple. Even during your first year here, your home licence alone is not enough, you have to affix it to a translation of that licence. This doesn't mean a translation that you, a friend or a spouse whips off, but rather a translation by an officially certified translator. If you don't know where to find one, just go to your local ADAC office. (ADAC is Germany's largest automobile club, with offices all over the country.) There you can get the official translation done for between 36–42 euros, depending on the language (English would be cheapest). By the way, ADAC offers a wide range of services, including extensive information, emergency road assistance, and special insurance packages. If you are going to drive here, you should inquire about membership.

Don't try to get by with an international licence here. If you read the quasi-small print on that licence, you'll find there are two countries where the permit isn't valid—the country that issued the licence and any foreign country you are residing in. As Germany will qualify under the second rule, your international licence is useless here.

The Generous German Social System

Before you get the impression that living in Germany is just a maze of regulations and registrations, let me assure you that these elements generally support a system that will provide you with many clear advantages. Germany has developed a generous system of social programs and benefits that every foreigner who is actively involved in productive work can participate in.

The *Arbeitsamt,* for instance, can offer various job-finding or job-training programs that enhance your skills or earning abilities. And the government-sponsored health insurance plans contain a wide array of benefits that go beyond mere coverage of medical and dental treatment. Shortly after settling in, you should inform yourself of most of these benefits. After all, you will be helping to support many of them with your taxes—why shouldn't you partake of those benefits when they apply to you?

EXPERIENCING GERMAN SOCIETY
Your Place Amongst The Germans

As the first part of this chapter strongly suggests, no matter how long you live here, you will probably never be fully assimilated into German society, so don't even try. One can never really become a German, the way you can become an American, a Canadian, an Australian, an Argentine, and maybe a few other nationalities. But as our discussion of multiculturalism shows, you don't have to, as it's often much better to bring your own unique qualities and perspectives and offer them as an enhancement to German society. Unfortunately, in addition to the legal hurdles you have to clear, which we have already discussed,

there are also quite a few psychological hurdles you need to master to make the most out of your German stay.

Before we start examining some of these hurdles, I want to warn you that the next few pages are apt to be the most discouraging part of this book. So brace for it, it's much better that you hear it from me before you get overwhelmed by the real thing in your daily doings.

If you're looking for a place where the vast majority of people are friendly, helpful, warm, open and considerate, you've probably chosen the wrong country. These qualities are unfortunately not the oils that keep the engines of German society humming. We've already touched on many of the plus points about living in Germany and many more will come up in later chapters. But now let's look closely at some negative factors you may not care to experience but will undoubtedly have to.

Courtesy and Friendliness Optional

If you hail from a society where established norms of courtesy are expected, where affability with strangers is routinely exhibited, where civility is the very air the society breathes, then you're in for a rude awakening in Germany. Here, such pleasantries are more the exception than the rule. The sad fact is, common courtesy can be a most uncommon thing in these parts.

The entrenched German attitude towards strangers is more that of coldness, suspicion or, more usually, determined ignorance. Strolling along most German streets, even those in your own neighbourhood, you could easily get the impression that smiles are a rationed commodity hereabouts. Striding along public thoroughfares with their eyes fixed straight ahead, most Germans seem rigidly oblivious to everything around them. The common alternative, to fix others with an uncomfortable, inquisitory stare, doesn't help one feel any more accepted.

Service? What's That?

Of course, city streets are more and more the scene of dogged anonymity in many societies. But a greater shock probably awaits you in those places where friendliness and courtesy abound in most countries, if for no other than commercial reasons—in shops and other places of business. Glares greet the new customer as often as smiles in many German stores, banks or service desks. More common than both, however, is the bored look of compulsory compliance. Regardless of which of these you're served up, all too often you get the feeling that your service provider is doing you an enormous favour just by waiting on you.

How pervasive is the problem? Hilmar Kopper, who headed Deutsche Bank—Germany's largest private bank—through much of the 1990s, once remarked that if only his personnel would greet every customer in a friendly manner, the bank's business could increase by at least 25 per cent. But a quick visit to other competing banks will show Kopper needn't have lost sleep over the competition snatching customers on this count.

But let's pull back for a moment. Had I written the above 15 years ago, it would hardly need this qualifying note, but the last decade-and-a-half witnessed a very positive *Wertewandel* in this area. Many businesses have come to realise, none too soon, that hostility and rudeness might not be the best ways to draw and hold customers, so they have initiated new training procedures where their sales staff learn ways to make customers feel welcome once they have wandered in. Such a receptive atmosphere has given many, including me, a pleasant shock at various times in the last several years. Even today, they remain rare enough to provide that little jolt of surprise. Interestingly, a number of refitted salespeople and even some customers express a distaste for this new style, declaring that it's a little too much like 'superficial American friendliness'. Well, you can't please everyone—especially when they're customers.

Arrogance on Demand

The chafing caused by this lack of courtesy and affability is all too often exacerbated by an arrogance or know-it-all attitude that can be thoroughly irritating until one learns how to defend against it. Such offensive behaviour is usually exhibited in a business context, especially in offices. The arrogance frequently makes the client feel not only that he or she is receiving a favour but that said client is exhibiting unmitigated gall in just soliciting the almighty's help or advice. "I'm giving these (expletive deleted) people business," exclaimed one seasoned émigré, "They should be treating me with gratitude, not like I was some panhandler!"

Let's turn amateur psychologist on this one. Such arrogance possibly springs from that German lack of security. In fact, it is almost the mirror image of that security deficit, a way of dealing with their insecurity, or at least shielding it from public view.

Watch Their Step, Please

A former New Yorker, exasperated after a few months of bruising strolls through German streets, finally barked out, "These people should all be sent to New York City for a month of survival training just walking down crowded streets. Then they'd return to Germany much better off for the experience. Make it a lot more pleasant for the rest of us too!"

His frustrations are understandable to anyone who has sauntered along the busy streets of any big German city. German pedestrians do tend to have a lot of side-swiping accidents with other pedestrians. While there are no statistics on this sort of thing, I would imagine that the Germans lead every other Western nation in the area of public bumping. You'd have to travel to places like Hong Kong to find streets more prone to such sidewalk collisions.

The main culprit here? That straight-ahead, non-registering stare of most Germans. As this is the accepted German stance for pedestrian travel, its practitioners are apt to misjudge the distance between themselves and other people. Most Germans seem to feel that making simple eye contact, which many other nations do just to sense where the oncoming pedestrian is going to step, is too personal a relationship to establish with all those strangers. Presumably, making precautionary eye contact could be interpreted as indiscriminate flirting, something the Germans abhor (The problem there is the 'indiscriminate', not the 'flirting').

So how does one adjust to this sort of behaviour? Get set for the contact, don shoulder and elbow pads every time you hit the streets, and give as well as you take? Hardly. Remember that this bumping is mostly unintentional, so any premeditated collisions would be judged and treated very harshly. No, in German cities you've just got to keep an eye out for the other pedestrians and do the best you can to avoid such collisions.

And please don't expect that absolute rarity, someone actually apologising for having bumped into you. The more typical response in Germany is simply to ignore it, to pretend it never happened. Of course, it happens so often that people have probably become inured to it. I've even heard quite a few Germans joking sympathetically about how those poor, polite British are always apologising for brushing people on the street. Here, such a thing, far from being a dictate of etiquette, is seen as more of a comic mannerism.

No Queues Please, We're German

Those who still believe Germans are addicted to order in all things have clearly never tried to line up for anything in Germany. Germans just don't take to queues and when files of bodies become absolutely necessary, they are commonly made so unpleasant that anyone can readily understand the Germans' distaste for them.

Many daily situations where queues form elsewhere have no German variant. For example, bus stop queues are unheard of. At crowded bus stops, waiting passengers just move themselves in a pack to the door, clambering on the bus in whatever way they can.

Just as there is no natural tendency to fall into line amongst the Germans, there's is also no sense of duty to continue forming that line in many situations. For instance, even when queues have formed, as at long information counters, it is not unknown for a new arrival in a hurry to quite simply start a new line of his or her own.

The Lines of Sorrow

This certainly doesn't, however, mean that queues don't exist in Germany; being one of those indispensable parts of modern life, the queue has snaked its way into German society. But when it does, it is generally one of the more annoying variants of the queue.

In standard queue country, such as supermarket check-out counters, post offices or banks, only now is any effort being given to making the process more pleasant for the poor customer.

Germany is one of the few countries I know of that abjures the single line system; you know, where the next customer is simply called to the next available counter. Sorry, but in Germany, most of the time, you still have to choose a line, hop in and hope that the people in front of you don't have some extraordinarily complex business that will make your line the slowest one possible. (Though the famous von Mürphy's law postulates that it always will be.)

Another thing that may puzzle shoppers from other lands is the almost complete absence of special lines for shoppers with fewer items. Most supermarkets or other large stores maintain a set policy of one line fits all shoppers. Thus, the poor schmoes toting two or three articles can find themselves camped behind a string of shoppers with full carts, with little hope of getting through quickly. (Though some sympathetic, well-packed shoppers do let the two or three item person slip in ahead of them.) I've even asked a few times why the 'X Items or Less' lines haven't caught on here and was told by supermarket personnel that they had tried it, but quickly abandoned it when too many customers with big orders complained that they were being discriminated against. Yeah.

Rules For Daily Intercourse

Of course, cultural norms are a two-edged sword. Just as people from other cultures will at first find the Germans unconscionably rude in certain situations, Germans can find outsiders ill-mannered when they don't observe certain well established rules for daily intercourse in German society.

We've just spoken above of the chilliness one encounters in many shops and stores. On the other hand, Germans do expect a certain mechanical politeness in these situations. For example, upon entering a small shop, one should always intone a robust *Guten Morgen, Guten Tag* or *Guten Abend* (Good morning, afternoon, evening). And thank-yous (*Danke*) are in order following any type of service.

Phone Felicities

Germans customarily answer a phone by giving their family names, but much more important is that the caller identify him or herself fully in the first sentence or two. This is essential for both business and private calls, and it will do you well to learn this rule quickly.

Who's that Calling?

One American friend of ours recounts an incident from some years ago when he rang up a young German lady he was interested in. The woman's mother answered the phone, and our friend merely asked for the daughter without identifying himself. The offended mother immediately issued him a stern tongue-lashing, reacting as if he had been caught making an obscene phone call. She almost refused to turn the phone over to her daughter; well, with such a reprobate on the other end, who could blame her?

Speaking of telephone calls, remember our discussion in the 'German Character' section, about a right and a wrong time for everything? Well, the egregiously wrong time to call most Germans is after 10:00 pm. Shortly after I arrived here, I made that mistake a few times, and was read the riot act for my misdeed. This used to be a major commandment, but there has been a little bit of a *Wertewandel* here. A good many Germans under 40 now go to bed later and they will permit you to call later, up till 11:00 pm or maybe even midnight. But don't ever do so without first asking friends, acquaintances or business associates how late you can call them. (As you'll see, Germans often rise early to get to the office early.)

You will find another handy collection of *faux pas*, ones mainly dealing with the home, in the 'Public Selves, Private Selves' section later in this chapter (*pages 105–107*).

The German Sense of Humour

You've probably heard that old gag about Hell being the place where the French direct the traffic, the British do the cooking and the Germans tell the jokes. Well, just as British cuisine has made some remarkable advances over the last two decades, the German sense of humour has developed in a positive direction. (In fact, it's arguably improved even more than British cooking has.)

In sharp contrast to the stereotyped dour German who, when forced to, will mechanically recite some pointless joke and then bark out a wooden laugh, you will often find Germans producing rapid-fire jokes or engulfed in

Those Funny English

As an English-speaker, you will enjoy a great respect from the Germans in the region of humour. But be warned: a superb sense of humour is almost assumed to be a genetic trait amongst English-speakers, so you will also be expected to keep friends and colleagues well entertained when the time calls for lightness. Do come packed with lots of jokes and a deftness at telling them as you will very possibly be called upon to uphold the honour of the English-speaking world in this domain.

streams of hearty laughter—at the right time and place, of course. The German principle of compartmentalisation can strengthen the force of the dour stereotype, as German business partners or customers generally go at the task at hand with a brusque seriousness. But afterwards, relaxed jolliness will redeem all that seriousness of the workday.

German domestic production in the area of humour tends to fall into either broad slapstick or satirical humour, the latter full of piquant wordplays and stirred with thick flows of irony. The former type is encountered most often on German television, or at parties and festivals, while the latter is the staple fare of the celebrated German Kabarett clubs. (Sadly, the language barrier may keep you from joining in on the appreciation of this for a long time.) During Fasching (*Refer to* Chapter 7: Enjoying Germany *on pages 201–204*), you are apt to get both varieties in pure, unfiltered form.

That Spot of Bother from 1933–1945

Let's face it, you're living in Germany. You've gotten to know many Germans on a personal level. There is one question that has just been gnawing at you for the longest time and it comes in two uncomfortable sizes. For those over 70: "What did you do during the Nazi era?" For those under 70: "What did your parents or grandparents do during this time?" Unless you get to know some Germans extremely well, or they broach the subject themselves, it's probably best to keep that question gnawing away inside you.

For all but the frightening fringe, the Nazi period remains a source of bruising shame for Germans. You may arrive here with the film and television-fed notion that every German was a true-brown Nazi who had command of but one phrase in English—"Ve haff vays of making you talk." When you've settled in here a little, you might be tendered the impression that except for a small circle around Hitler, every German was a secret resistance fighter.

Neither picture is correct, though, sadly, the first comes a little closer to the truth. Yes, many Germans had their irritations with the Nazis, maybe even strong doubts about them, but anyone who was an active dissident went to jail or a concentration camp. Quite a few of these people did survive—unless they also happened to be Jews or Communists. Otherwise, the general population pretty much went along with the program—either grudgingly, enthusiastically, or somewhere in between.

To be fair to the Germans of that period, their government kept them malignantly misinformed about many things: they were constantly fed distorted propaganda, if not outright vicious lies. Those who knew never revealed, for instance, that most concentration camps were large-scale extermination centres. There was also an element of threat and fear involved, which made speaking out against the Nazis a dangerous pastime.

Keeping Quiet

The prevailing mentality of those days is poignantly suggested in a story my father-in-law told about a summer evening late in the war when he was visiting relatives in Berlin. The family was clandestinely listening to the BBC broadcast on radio when the 'Beeb' reported that their section of Berlin was to be the target of that evening's bombing raid. They quickly decided it might be healthier to sleep out in the nearby woods that night.

Before packing up their sleeping gear, they thought of telling some neighbours in the building, old and dear friends of theirs, about the impending raid. But they finally decided to keep these good friends in the dark about such an important matter—because to inform them meant revealing that they listened to prohibited BBC broadcasts. And though these neighbours were old and close friends, the family still couldn't trust them not to report this 'crime' to the authorities. Such was the mentality that gripped the whole nation at that time.

SURVIVING THE INITIAL SHOCKS

I realise much of the foregoing may sound rather bleak, but
there are many rays of light which, unfortunately, are usually
tucked away at the far edges of the shadows. But be of stout
heart: the Germans can become more accommodating, even
open to strangers in a variety of situations. But you have to
learn the fine art of drawing this out. When you do, life in
Germany becomes distinctly more pleasant.

Where Do You Fit In?

The prime question is how can you fit yourself into German
society without changing yourself in ways you don't
necessarily want to change. One curious phenomenon
reported by many foreign residents of Germany involves
unconscious change. These people still consider themselves
quite different from the Germans, but upon returning home
for a visit, the homefolks start asking why they are now so
aggressive, impatient or aloof. They find they need a few days
to a week to become fully themselves again. This is normal;
don't let it worry you, it comes off quickly. The important
thing is that you take something valuable from your German
experience, while still retaining the most positive parts of
your own personality and cultural identity.

Just remember that this is a society in which channelled
aggressiveness is frequently rewarded and where courtesy
or conflict avoidance is sometimes regarded as weakness
or retreat. One of the more obvious ways to react in such a
situation is to do as the Romans do—to bark back, to assert
yourself. I've often found that when faced with German
arrogance, a sharp return volley of arrogance can get me
what I want. I may not win the affection of the salesperson
or business partner, but if I can quickly determine that such
treasure is just not there to be won, I find it more realistic to
bark back, get what I came for, then leave.

The Softer Way

At other times, the display of arrogance is too obviously just
a shield to cover feelings of insecurity, lack of expertise or
bending under pressure. In such situations, the best way to

proceed is to reassure the other person and offer patience, sympathy or even help in solving the problem at hand when you can. This approach has proven to be very profitable for myself and others, often inducing a Jeckyll-and-Hyde transformation in salespeople or civil servants.

Showing Confidence

Perhaps a greater key to success here is to keep in mind that German society respects and rewards those who exhibit confidence, control and expertise. This can also be done, or neatly feigned, with demeanour. Casting your eyes down in a sign of deference, as is common in some Asian cultures, gets judged very negatively over here. Indeed, if you do that, your partner is liable to sense real weakness and try to stomp all over you (figuratively, of course, but the German version of figurative can be very painful nonetheless). To get along well in Germany, always look the other person right in the eye. When you meet people, offer them a firm handshake—limp handshakes are also taken as signs of inner weakness, the limper the weaker.

Another method that frequently works in warming up Germans is to disarm them with a bit of charm and friendliness. I have often found that ending some commercial exchange with a robust, sincere "*Schönen Tag noch*" (Have a nice day) elicits a surprised smile and warm return wish. Germans aren't really much different from other people under the skin, and it is almost as if sometimes they are just waiting for someone to give them the opportunity to be nice in a social situation. You could just be the one who provides them with that opportunity. But don't come on too strong with the charm, or Germans will think you are out to get something from them and just ratchet up their mistrust level.

PUBLIC SELVES, PRIVATE SELVES

Hopefully, those last few paragraphs provided you with a soft landing from the rough stuff earlier. Now you should know that it gets even better—even that batch of negatives is only half the truth. There are, in fact, two clearly discernible types of behaviour one finds in most Germans. This is where the German personality splits most dynamically, where the solemn principle of compartmentalisation reaches into the very deepest regions of the self—of the selves actually.

The type of behaviour, not always terribly endearing, described at the beginning of this chapter belongs to the German public self. This is a self to be displayed on the street, in business or work situations, or in most situations involving strangers. The other self, the private, is reserved for times when one is with family, friends or particularly close colleagues. Only then, from this self, does a rather different personality emerge, one that is more open, friendly, helpful—in short, more engaging in almost all ways.

Of course, a similar split between public and private spheres can be found in almost all modern, complex societies. But it is more pronounced in Germany, where the lock of social norms and rules renders the role of the private self that much more important. Here, the fluctuation between the two selves actually functions as a kind of psychological safety valve, allowing people to be true to both social restrictions and themselves.

Sie and Du

This split in the German personality is underscored and probably even bolstered by a division in the German language itself, which has three forms for the word 'you': the formal *Sie,* the single familiar *Du,* and the plural familiar *Ihr.* The rules governing the use of one form or the other tend to be rather rigid, and they essentially force German speakers to divide the whole world into people they must be formal with and those they can be more casual and relaxed with.

While Germans may come off as somewhat cold and arrogant in many daily situations, they can be disarmingly kind, helpful and warm to those who have been admitted into their guarded *Du* circle. With some friends or family members (through marriage) I have discovered that the merest hint of a problem elicits inquiries of the source and quick offers to find remedies for it, even when that demands taking considerable personal pains.

An interesting phenomenon that one discovers in Germany is what we might call 'the charm-debt syndrome.' As German society most certainly does not insist on false displays of charm and warmth, when these qualities are spun out, they are often much richer and positive for being genuine, and not rehearsed. The other side of this phenomenon is that when Germans try to fake charm, friendliness and kindness, they are so inept that the whole exercise becomes comically transparent.

Friends and Acquaintances

Actually, the *Du* circle itself has a deeper, tighter inner core, and this further division is also reflected in the language. For Germans, the word 'friend' (*Freund*) denotes a special status conferred only on deep, special relationships. When women use it, it most often means that they are involved in a romantic relationship with its bearer, and for men it translates into the English 'close friend'.

Germans are sometimes puzzled by how promiscuously English speakers hand out the appellation 'friend'. Most of the people I refer to as friends, Germans would designate as merely *gute Bekannter* (good acquaintances). Yet, I know that if I ever called these people acquaintances in English, they would be roundly insulted.

Sound a little complicated? Well, I did warn you that the Germans were a complicated people. The key point here is that to be a *Freund* is to achieve a very special status that takes time and emotional investment. That's where you begin to see the real person within. And the only way you get there is by first going through the *Du* circle.

THE HOME—THE GREAT SANCTUARY

Being wedged into such a thorough compartmentalisation of their lives, Germans place a special value on their homes and all the activities centred there. This is where the private selves are allowed to bloom, where you can put aside that hard face you prepared to meet the faces you meet. For many Germans, this is where the real person slips out to do all the things they somehow wish they could do out in the wider world.

As the house plays such a special role for so many Germans, they have clear rules as to how one should behave there, assembled together under the rubric *Hausordnung*. Foreigners ignore these rules at their own peril.

Greetings

Though Germans frequently ignore most everyone in the neighbourhood (including all the people living right next door), protocol insists that you always greet everyone living in your own building as often as you see them—virtually from the day you move in. This necessitates learning everyone's family name quickly, as the greetings are best served up in the following manner: "*Guten Tag, Frau Schmidt; Guten Abend, Herr Müller*". And once you've got that, you'll probably never have to learn the first names, as last-name greetings tend to last a long, long time here. One couple in our building has been here at least 30 years, another over 20 years and a third 15 years and they all continue to exchange their cheerful greetings in last-name terms. And they all still employ the *Sie* form in all conversations too!

Oh, very important—leave all decisions to switch to the *Du* form, or to address people by their first names, to the others in your house. Germans still feel quite uncomfortable with forced familiarity, and your flying into informality will squeeze them into a tight social corner. Using *Du* in inappropriate places, such as with people in shops, even if you see them everyday and know their surnames, can even be taken as an insult, since it is the standard form for addressing children. Some thoughtless Germans even use *Du* with most foreigners, indicating that they put them on a level with children.

Cleanliness is Next to the Law

Hausordnung literally means 'house order' and order is a key element of maintaining smooth harmony with your housemates and/or neighbours. For instance, keeping common areas clean is important and your lease will probably stipulate that you wash your steps once a week. Even if it doesn't, that's an unbreakable unwritten rule of German society, and you should strongly adhere to it. Every week doesn't necessarily mean every week—even Germans aren't fanatics—and if the steps look pretty clean, you can probably skip a week here and there without scandalising the neighbours. But blatant dirtiness is something of a mortal sin within a shared residence.

There are also clear rules about noise. You are never supposed to produce enough noise that you disturb the neighbours. Everyone has his or her own level of noise tolerance, but even loud television sets or stereo systems can be protested according to German rules, if one has an inclination to do so. Parties, notorious noise producers, are allowed, as long as they don't become too frequent, or too boisterous (one or two parties a year are allowed by common consent). Any time you do plan a party, you should inform your neighbours a few days in advance, so that they can prepare their nerves. This, too, is one of those unwritten rules of German *Hausordnung*. This doesn't mean you have to invite them; that's generally neither expected nor desired.

Quiet, Please

While we are on the subject of quiet, Germany traditionally has its own official quiet time (*Ruhezeit*), usually between one and three o'clock in the afternoon. Although this practice has fallen victim to the hectic pace of modern life, you are still expected to tone things down a bit during this time. For example, children shouldn't play too energetically at this time, and even dogs have been ordered by a German court to hold off their barking during this period!

Sunday doesn't have a *Ruhezeit;* it is a total *Ruhetag* (day of rest) on which one should observe all the rituals of quiet. So don't plan to get all that noisy handy-work done on your one totally free day; drilling, hammering and related activities are officially prohibited on Sundays. Indeed, in small towns and country regions, you are not even supposed to wash windows or hang out wet laundry on Sundays; doing so is a fail-safe way to ostracise yourself from your neighbours.

Which raises another point: in Germany, hanging out laundry is never done from a front window, a matter often set down in the rental contract. People in your neighbourhood will take offence if you violate the appearance of the area. The head of the theatre where I worked when I first arrived here some 20 years ago swore that the police once came to their door ordering them to take their laundry from the window because neighbours had called in a complaint (on a Sunday of all things!). A backyard or an inconspicuous balcony are fair territory for drying or airing laundry. But if your dwelling has neither, you'll just have to appropriate a nook in your bathroom for this purpose.

Flexibility is German Too

This may be a good time to introduce you to the German saying '*Es wird nicht so heiss gegessen, wie es gekocht wird*' ('It doesn't get eaten as hot as it gets cooked'). Some of these regulations regarding house order are not taken all that literally, especially in urban areas and amongst younger people in these areas. Parties can certainly be thrown more often than once or twice a year if they are not too raucous; you can occasionally take off on cleaning the steps; you can take a bath after 10:00 pm; from time to time, you can even do some drilling on Sunday. But bending the rules on these matters depends on maintaining generally good relations with your neighbours, which in turn depends on fulfilling the core elements of *Hausordnung*.

No matter how far you go in adapting to German customs on the outside, remember that the home is where you live, so try to keep the general atmosphere there as pleasant as possible. Two American friends of ours moved into a splendid building in a choice section of Frankfurt some years ago, and after an initial period of grace, violated a few of the unwritten rules with regard to the long-time occupant of their building. Following these infractions, this lady became rather finicky on the minutiae of *Hausordnung*, reading them the riot act whenever they made some little slip in this regard. Life was not too pleasant for them for the rest of their German stay, despite their elegant dwelling. Also keep in mind that certain elements of *Hausordnung* are actually set down in the law and can be grounds for terminating your lease upon repeated violations.

HOSTING

As a rule, Germans make a special effort to be pleasant to those living right around them, so by and large it is easier to get along with than to offend people. The same holds true for inviting people to your home. There are, of course, established rules for playing the good host and hostess and you'll note these when you are invited to somebody's home. More importantly, you should learn the most important of these rules quickly and apply them whenever it is your turn to play host.

We've already mentioned in Chapter 3 ('Home and Hearth', *on pages 55–56*), the special significance bestowed on one's home by the Germans. Being invited to someone's home is therefore something of an honour in this country, so the visit itself is fraught with all kinds of duties and rituals that should be carefully adhered to.

Hosting others is an opportunity for Germans to really show the true selves that must be partially suppressed in offices, factories, shops and on the street, so they typically go at it with a good burst of Teutonic fervour. With the advantage of being on their home ground, they will probably be much more relaxed than they were at that business meeting or conference.

The first rule of being a good host or hostess is, of course, to make your guests feel comfortable. This is true almost everywhere in the world, but Germans have well-formed ideas of what makes guests comfortable. One thing to always remember is that German obsession with time and there being a proper time for everything. Inviting people at specific times conveys very specific ideas of what awaits them when they arrive.

Any invitation for Saturday or Sunday afternoon around 3:00 pm or 4:00 pm always entails a duty to serve coffee (with the option of tea for non-coffee drinkers, and soft drinks for children) and cake, or at least a plate of cookies. An invitation for 7:00 pm or 8:00 pm automatically includes the idea of serving some dinner—and the food should be served shortly after that time, as there are entrenched times for dining in Germany. If you wish to spend some time just chatting first, then pitch the invitation for 5:00 pm or 6:00 pm and lay on some pre-dinner drinks and finger food snacks.

Food and Drink

As is typical of most of the well-fed world, Germans usually prepare and offer more food than the assembled group could possibly eat—and Germans can be awfully good eaters. It is considered extremely embarrassing to run short on food, so most Germans over-prepare.

Alcoholic drinks (wine and/or beer, depending on what food is being served) are generally offered with any serious meal, with mineral water standing backup for abstemious guests. You can always refuse alcohol, though your hosts will generally repeat the offer more than once, just to be sure. On the other hand, if religious practice makes it difficult or impossible for you to offer wine and beer, you should make this clear with the invitation. Otherwise, your guests may feel somewhat short-changed.

Smoking is another matter entirely, and there are no longer any society-wide standards on this point. There has been some minor concern in Germany about the dangers of second-hand smoke (though nowhere near comparable to the concern evidenced in places like the United States, Canada or Britain). While German authorities still show a pronounced reluctance to restrict smoking in restaurants or other public places, one's home is a different matter, and it is generally accepted that the final decision there belongs to the hosts.

We ourselves did not permit smoking in our home, and none of our guests ever objected to this prohibition or made more than a few pointed jokes when escorted to the balcony to indulge in their addiction. On the other hand, some folks have reported that certain guests insisted on their right to enjoy a cigarette right at the table or in the living room, and our friends conceded rather than cause a scene. (Those people were not invited back, as we've been told, so one can probably take a lesson from that.)

Being a Good Guest

The reverse side of this coin features the rules for being a good guest. And considering the importance of the home to most Germans, these rules are at least as meaningful as those for the good host/hostess.

The first thing you'll probably do is arrive. The host and/or hostess will presumably be there to greet you at the door, so the first order of business is to return their greeting, then inspect the children, if there are any. Now is also the time to present your gift, if you've brought one. But be aware that German etiquette, unlike that of some other cultures, does not necessarily require guests to bring gifts. If you feel nevertheless that you should, appropriate gifts include flowers, a bottle of wine or a small book on a subject you know your host or hostess is interested in.

The toilet, or WC, is frequently a separate closet-sized room in Germany and you should ask for it by one of those names. Requesting the bathroom may get you escorted to a larger room housing only a large sink and a bathtub. It is also considered extremely rude and coarse to leave the toilet door open after you've used it; almost as crude as leaving it open while you are using it.

While keeping these few warnings in mind, perhaps the most important rule for being a good guest is to enjoy yourself. Unless you've offended them by committing one of the above infractions, German hosts are highly edified by knowing their guests have enjoyed themselves and they have succeeded as hosts. And if you have anything at all in common with your hosts and the other guests, you'll find Germans can be quite engaging, open, entertaining and informative, with a wide range of interests and experience to delve into. Those private selves are much richer and more fascinating than the stone-faced public selves you meet so often on the streets. Try to take full advantage of every opportunity to meet those selves within.

LEARNING THE CUSTOMS

Later in this book we'll see how important to success in Germany learning the language is. Learning some of the key customs is just as important. In fact, mistakes here are usually less readily forgiven than slips in language.

Doing just the right thing in the right situation can make you a *persona very grata* with your German friends and colleagues and as these social grace notes are neither too numerous nor too complicated, doing the right thing at the right time can be somewhat easy.

For a people so bound to ritual in their daily lives, the Germans are curiously short on celebratory rituals. But a tidy number of such rituals do still play a significant role in smoothing and sweetening a German's passage through life, and you yourself may be asked to participate in one, or more, of the following.

Birth and Baptism

Not surprisingly for a society with a threateningly low birthrate, the addition of a new family member is a cause for great joy and mild celebration. And you can often be invited to share in that celebration.

If a colleague or acquaintance does have a birth in the family, you might express your good wishes by sending a card. A small gift might also be appropriate, according to how close you are to the new parents. A fitting gift would be any small but useful item for the baby. In the office, a collection is usually taken up by either the secretary or the colleague closest to the proud parent, and a joint gift from the entire office is then presented.

You can also expect a little bit of cheer from the jubilant parent, especially in an office setting. Non-smokers will be delighted to hear that proud fathers in Germany almost never hand out cigars to honour the arrival of a new tax deduction—the general offering is a glass or two of *Sekt* (the German champagne).

Baptisms aren't as big a deal in Germany as they are in many other Western cultures, and in fact the family often waits until the children are a few years old—in other words, just old enough to get really scared about what is happening to them up there. Attendance at the baptismal ceremony itself, and the small party that follows, is usually limited to the family and the closest of family friends.

The First Day of School

In today's largely secular Germany, the first day of school has replaced baptism as the approved rite of childhood passage for many people. At the start of their school careers, children are presented with a *Schultüte*, an oversized and brightly decorated cardboard cone stuffed with candy (allegedly to sweeten the start of that new career). Photos are taken and the adults in attendance, usually the parents and possibly the grandparents, make a proper fuss about the whole matter.

Birthdays

We are all born just once, but many of us commemorate that day for the rest of our lives. In Germany, everyone expects you to commemorate it in an extremely public manner. People from the Anglo-American world are in for something of a jolt here. In Germany, it is the birthday boy or

Youngsters on the first school day with their proud parents and the distinctive *Schultüten*.

girl who treats everyone else. Now you know why so many people here keep asking you when your birthday is.

You are expected—very expected—to lay on a little spread of birthday goodies for all the people at your place of work. This usually means cake, or rolls with cheese and sliced meats, with coffee, juice or *Sekt* to wash it all down (though some managers, noticing a drop in productivity in connection with these celebrations, advise their people to go easy on the *Sekt*). In addition, it is common practice to invite your closest friends to a restaurant or pub that evening—with you footing the bill, of course. For all this goodwill you've spread, you can expect some small presents from your friends, and a fervent handshake or slap on the back from your colleagues.

If you are one of the lucky ones invited to the evening meal, you don't want to forget that little present. The best gift is, of course, something personal that your friend will appreciate. If you don't know him or her well enough to make that judgement, a good wine, cognac or liqueur can fill the bill nicely. Birthday presents are never given before the big day, as this is considered a gratuitous tempting of fate. If you can't be there for the event, present the gift later.

Weddings

A most important rite of passage for many people is when they bind themselves permanently—or, considering the lamentably high German divorce rate (around 40 per cent), temporarily permanently—to that one special other person. This is one rite where you'll see very clearly that compartmentalisation in German society we have spoken of several times before.

All weddings in Germany must be performed at a *Standesamt,* or registry office. For the religiously inclined, there is the option of a church wedding after the civil ceremony. German churches won't join you in the eyes of God unless you've already been joined in the eyes of the state. The church ceremony ordinarily takes place the weekend after the *Standesamt* ritual, though that depends entirely on the wishes of the couple.

Who gets invited to what ceremony is a question of closeness. As *Standesamt* offices tend to be smaller than your average church, attendance at the civil ceremony is generally limited to the happy couple, their two witnesses (required by law), the immediate family, and a very tight circle of friends. Often the friends don't even attend the actual ceremony, but gather outside the town hall to greet the couple as they emerge as newlyweds. A quick trip to a nearby café to partake of the goodies there often tops off the civil ceremony.

In some German towns, weddings are still carried out in the traditional local garb.

Attendance is usually higher at the church service, with a larger group of friends and acquaintances, as well as more distant relatives getting invited. The service itself can be simple or elaborate, depending on the religion, the wishes of the couple and the individual parish. A wedding meal in a restaurant, hotel or merely the church hall may be provided for all the invited guests, courtesy of the bride's father. Presents are usually given to the couple at this event if it is held; if not, they may be presented right after the church ceremony.

There's a third German ceremony in connection with weddings—the *Polterabend* (noisy evening). This affair takes place on the evening or two before the *Standesamt* ceremony. This is where the soon-to-be-wed couple invite a wide circle of friends and acquaintances, relatives one hardly remembers any more, and many co-workers. The *Polter* of the *Polterabend* is provided by the guests, who are expected to come armed with old plates, cups, any kind of porcelain (one of our more inventive friends turned up with an old toilet bowl), which then get smashed against the ground, in a huge pile assembled for this ritual. At the end of the evening, the married-couple-to-be has the honour of sweeping up all the broken dishware and disposing of it. The practice harks back to pagan days and was supposed to ward off evil spirits and assure life-long happiness to the union. Today, it mainly assures good turnover rates for the German crockery industry.

After making their contribution to the clutter, *Polterabend* guests bestow their presents upon the couple and then join the party, traditionally held within a tent, though this arrangement is fading away as the size of the festivities grow. Standard German fare is served and the mood is one of presumed ebullience.

Getting Married

Should you yourself decide to get married while living in Germany, there are a number of steps you are required to take. First of all, you have to present yourself at the *Standesamt* office. They are usually in the *Rathaus,* or city hall, but check in the phone book for the one in your locality. It is best if both parties come, and be sure to bring some time with you.

You should also be aware that Germany has what many claim to be the most complicated marriage laws in the world. There are no set requirements of what you have to present to the *Standesamt,* as they require different documents for every nationality, to ensure that the marriage will be recognised in your own country as well as in Deutschland. The civil servant at the *Standesamt* will inform you exactly what documents are needed in your case (a short sampling: passport, of course; birth certificate; parents' marriage certificate; records of any previous marriages with divorce decrees or death certificates; and court decisions about children from previous marriages). All or most of these documents will then have to be officially translated into German.

In addition to discovering what documents you need, you will be informed about the required waiting period. Finally, before the big event, there must be an eight-day 'posting of the banns'. This public posting of all wedding applications is to foil under-aged or polygamous partners.

Many foreigners, as well as some Germans, decide to escape all this red tape and waiting by taking off to Denmark, known as the Las Vegas of Europe for its speedy and simple procedures. Armed with nothing more than your passports and birth certificates, you can get married there within a few days. There are even German travel agents who offer special three-day Danish wedding and honeymoon packages.

Standesamt ceremonies used to be flat and perfunctory, and a married couple not planning on a church edition often felt a little empty or let down right afterwards. To correct this, the registry offices have begun putting flowers around the room, and the public servant officiating often tries to spiff up the proceedings with a little more ceremony. Even so, many still find the civil wedding a tad too cold and colourless for one of the most important rites of passage in one's life.

Funerals

No one likes to plan for these rites, but if someone you know, or the loved one of someone you know, dies, there is a pattern of decorum you should observe.

If your relationship to the deceased or the survivors is tangential, all that's expected is a sympathy card. On the other hand, if you did know the deceased or survivors somewhat better, your attendance at the funeral service is quite appropriate.

Wakes have become extremely rare in Germany since World War II, and today take place only in small, devoutly Catholic towns. Normally, services are held at the church, mosque or synagogue, with the mourners then accompanying the coffin to the graveside. Frequently, all in attendance file past the lowered coffin to pay one last moment of respect, then pour a small scoop of dirt onto the coffin. Close family members are provided by the funeral parlour with flowers to drop onto the coffin. Following the funeral, mourners are often invited by the family to a café or restaurant for coffee and cake, though attendance at this event is not necessary.

By the way, if you are not an official, tax-paying member of a recognised religion here, no German church will marry you, bury you or baptise your children. These are considered some of the services members pay their taxes for. But the churches are not at all mean-spirited about this and they usually let you join just before you marry or before the birth of a child, thus permitting you to partake in all church ceremonies. Of course, these churches then expect you to start paying your church taxes regularly. That, too, is a well-established part of German custom.

WHY IT'S ALL WORTH IT

Hopefully, the main lesson of this chapter has come through clearly. To wit: the Germans are not the easiest people on the planet to get along with, but when you do learn how to interact with them, the whole experience can be quite fruitful.

The entire process of experiencing German society may get easier in coming years. Remember, we are in a period of heavy *Wertewandel*. Both natives and foreigners who have lived here for decades report they have discerned some major modifications in German attitudes and behaviour. Some are positive changes, while in other areas, the changes are more negative, apparently brought about by the stubborn economic doldrums of recent years. You just have to learn to deal with it all. Many people who have built up successful careers and lives here thought at the beginning they wouldn't stick it out. The fact that they did strongly suggests that you can too.

SETTLING IN

'... common sense is frequently in short
supply here, particularly when it comes
to bureaucracy and a chance to make money.'
—Barbara Burris van Voorst,
in the *International Herald Tribune's* 'Meanwhile' column

THERE'S NOT A LOT YOU CAN ACCOMPLISH in the way of pre-arrival preparation, as the Germans have an inordinate trust in the wisdom and efficiency of their own bureaucracy. Most of your serious bureaucratic slogging will just have to be done here. The most you can do beforehand is make sure that all your documents are in order and that you have all the papers you need: passport, university records or recommendations from former employers if you'll be looking for a job, certification papers for your handcraft trade, marriage certificate, driver's license. In addition, if you find the opportunity back home, you might attend a prep class in the German language.

In point of fact, if you're coming here to a job, your future employer can do more for you than you can yourself. Clearly the most important of these tasks is taking care of the spadework on your work permit with the *Arbeitsamt*. As we already took you on a quick aerial safari of the *Behörde* jungle, we'll now skip that part of your journey and leap right into the search for living quarters.

HOUSING—THE RENTAL MARKET

As we've already seen (*Refer to* Chapter 2: Overview of Land and History *on pages 8–49*), Germany is one of the most densely populated countries in Europe. Taken down into practical terms, that means that the task of finding appropriate housing can be somewhat daunting. Let's see what we can do here to make it a little less so.

If your company or an associated firm has transferred you here, they will often take care of providing your initial housing. That will save a lot of emotional wear and tear in the early going. But the more common experience of those moving to Germany is that they must fend for themselves in the housing market. There are three options available to you, each with its own advantages and degrees of success.

The option that comes closest to having your firm providing your housing is knowing someone who has a flat or house available, who is leaving, or who knows someone with available accommodation to offer. This is, in fact, how we found our flat, a relatively spacious, pleasant sprawl of rooms in a favourable location at a stunningly reasonable rent.

Such an occurrence still happens often enough to list it as an option, but if you're arriving in Germany without any contacts or relations, it is an option you can't even hope for. So let's turn to contingency number two.

Going the Newspaper Route

This is by far the cheaper of the two remaining possibilities and, perhaps not surprisingly, it also holds less promise of success. Every week, on a specific day, at least one of the major newspapers in towns across Germany runs a special section featuring all available rentals in a wide range of price and comfort categories. All you have to do is pick up the paper, find some property that appeals to you, call up, make an appointment, then go over to see the place and meet the owners.

That, of course, is 'all you have to do' in the sense of all you have to do to climb the Matterhorn is put one hand and foot over the other one until you reach the top. Admittedly, finding housing through a newspaper is easier than scaling the Matterhorn, but only relatively.

Actually, your success along this route will depend on how high you are willing to go in terms of rent. There is much less competition for properties in the upper reaches of the rent scale, so your searching there will mean less scrambling. It's in the middle and lower rent regions that the real adventure comes in.

A typical scene around big newspaper offices on the day the rental sections are printed is of people arriving in pairs, then splitting off. One half of this search team heads to a nearby telephone and waits while the other half of the team goes to the front of the newspaper building, purchases the coveted edition hot off the press, then returns with all due haste to the partner waiting in the phone booth. The next sequence is worthy of high film comedy, though it is all deadly serious to those involved. One part of the team scans the notices frantically for suitable offerings while the other taps out any promising phone numbers just as frantically. Mobile telephones have stripped some of the more athletic elements from this competition, even reducing the number of people needed to look for a flat to one. But the rush at the seller's end remains every bit as frenetic.

Even if you are an Olympic sprinter, or the fastest finger on a mobile phone the world has ever seen, you still might have a lot of trouble getting your dream flat simply because you are not German. Many of the real estate listings say point blank, *Keine Ausländer* (No Foreigners), a nasty roadblock which is legal in Germany. Even if this detail is not provided in the listing, when you do get through, some polite landlords or landladies will inform you that they refuse on principle to rent to foreigners and the impolite ones will simply hang up the moment they hear a foreign accent.

The Secrets of Agents

You can spare yourself all of this aggravation by simply availing yourself of our third option—but it will you cost you money. Still, many choose to take this path of least resistance, which involves going to a *Makler*, or real estate agent. Actually, the newspaper route will often flow right into this route, as many of the ads are placed not by property owners themselves but by these *Makler*. (The plural form of this noun is the same as the singular in German)

The *Makler* handle a wide range of properties, though most of them shun the lower end of the rental scale as they don't find them profitable enough to make them worth their bother. Your *Makler* can also save you some unnecessary trips, as they often have a good idea of what kind of tenants the owner is willing to accept, having conferred with that owner or even rented for him/her before. A seasoned *Makler* can even get you past the *Keine Ausländer* barrier by putting in a good word with the owner before sending you over there.

While some *Makler* will merely supply you with phone numbers and addresses and then scoot you off on your way, others will meet you at the prospective property to smooth the way or even drive you there themselves.

A helpful note about the *Makler* route: Experiences of a number of friends indicate that even after you've registered as a client with a *Makler*, they are often too busy to call you. You must call them every week to see if they have any new properties that fit your needs. And two friends recount how they once rang up their *Makler* regarding a flat he had listed in the newspaper. He told them that the particular property was already gone, but he had another which hadn't yet gone into the paper. It turned out to be a wonderful flat and they snapped it right up. The moral? Even when dealing with a *Makler*, a good strategy is to phone a day or two before real estate listings run in the paper, as many prime properties have already gone by the time they appear in print.

Makler Sharks

Makler have a bad reputation in many parts of Germany, and quite a few of them go out of their way to earn this notoriety. For example, what seems to have become a widespread practice amongst the less scrupulous agents is charging desperate seekers an additional 'service' fee or demanding more than the three months' rent, both of which are illegal in most German cities. They will then insist that you sign a paper declaring that they didn't impose such a fee. If you refuse to sign, or rebuff any of the *Makler's* demands, you can just forget about ever seeing or getting the longed-for property.

While all of these services are much more pleasant than fighting with 20 other people to get into a phone booth, don't think that *Makler* perform any of these deeds out of their love for humanity. They make good money on these deals and most of that money will come from you. If you do take a *Makler* negotiated flat or house, you must pay the agent's fee, which usually runs to the equivalent of three months' rent. This is all on top of the standard *Kaution* (security deposit) which goes to the landlord and generally amounts to three months' rent. This security deposit must be held in escrow by the landlord and paid back to you, with interest, within that notoriously nebulous 'reasonable time' following your vacating the property and after any expenses for damages or necessary repairs. So, for the more expensive properties, you are looking at paying a lot of money before you even cross the threshold of your own home.

In any event, don't pay a cent until you've signed the lease. Charging an agent's commission before you've actually landed a property is highly illegal and any scoundrel engaging in this activity should be reported.

Home, Bittersweet Home

So, let's say you've cleared all the hurdles and managed to find an apartment or house that suits your needs. What can you expect with regard to the lease, its obligations and your rights?

We have already mentioned the security deposit. If you are renting a place on your own and not simply moving into a company property for a short time, you can often work out a lease with a length mutually satisfying to both parties. If you have to leave before the expiration of the lease, you are required to give the landlord ample notice, which can mean from a minimum of three months up to a year, depending on the length of the lease, or provide the landlord with a few prospective *Nachmieter* (sub-tenants). The number depends on your agreement with the landlord, who has no legal obligation to accept any of them. If he rejects all of your *Nachmieter* and fails to find one of his own, you might be required to cover the rent for the next three months (which will, of course, simply be subtracted from your security deposit).

If there is disagreement as to whether you fulfilled your obligations as a tenant, you always have legal recourse to recover all or part of your *Kaution*. Except in flagrant cases, it's hard to predict which way a verdict might go, though some German states are known to lean more towards the tenants, others more towards the landlords.

Furnished or Unfurnished?

Flats and houses can come in furnished and unfurnished varieties; the furnished, of course, command a considerably higher rent. And in Germany, when they say unfurnished, they mean unfurnished—all you should expect are four walls, a ceiling and a floor. All lighting fixtures, all external wiring, almost all amenities are your responsibility (toilets, bathtubs and showers are generally thrown in by the landlord, as are sinks, though even the latter are in some rare cases left up to the tenant).

You then have the freedom to make the property a home of your own. You can install any electrical wiring, hang any paintings or posters that you want and so on and so forth. BUT—when you leave, you are required to turn the property back over in the condition in which you received it. That means filling any and all holes you may have drilled or nailed during your occupancy, removing any new wiring, repairing any damage to doors and windows, including small chips caused by bumps. And then paint the whole place anew before you clear out. Failure to do any of this entitles the landlord to have it done himself, and then deduct the costs for this work from your security deposit—and it will always be more than you expect.

Help for Tenants

There are a number of books and computer programs on the market that inform you of your rights and duties as a tenant in a much more detailed way than this space allows us to do. Unfortunately, for those whose German is not up to snuff at this time, none of the material seems to be in English, though that may change. Just go to one of the large bookshops in your town and check what is available.

There is also an organisation, *Der Mieterschutzverein* (Tenant's Protection Association), which offers legal advice, in English as well as German, and other valuable services to all of its members. You become a member simply by paying a yearly fee of anywhere from 6–50 euros, depending on the locality and the extent of assistance (those groups charging lower annual fees will often ask payment for additional services). Many foreigners have found these organisations to be highly beneficial in helping them find their feet upon moving here.

UTILITIES

Having taken that first major hurdle, you've still got a few more to clear before you've made your new abode liveable. Aside from furnishings and any wall decorations, this basically means getting those basic utilities flowing. And this is how you go about it.

Electricity and Gas

Utilities were deregulated in Germany within the last few years, which means you can now shop around for gas and electricity providers. The easiest course (and you're going to have so many other things to take care of when settling in) is to keep the same provider as the previous tenant. But if you do want to change providers, you can call up a power company serving your area and ask about rates and offers. (Ecologically-friendly and water-generated electricity are just two of the options. Some companies even let you mix the types of electricity used.)

To get electricity and gas turned on, you have to fill out forms wherein you provide minimal information such as your name, address and bank GIRO account (*Refer to* 'GIRO Accounts' *on page 134–135*). The power and gas will then be turned on automatically. If you take over immediately upon the departure of the previous tenant, you can make an agreement with the public utility company to assume all responsibility from such and such a date. But if you do so, be sure to check the reading on your meter the day you move in and make sure it jibes with the last reading from the former tenant. Otherwise, you could find yourself picking up the tab on their energy use.

Telephones

After decades of functioning as a government-run monopoly and another half-decade of maintaining near monopolistic power, telephone services were deregulated at the beginning of 1999 with private companies being given full access to the network. Nevertheless, Deutsche Telekom, the former government monopoly, still holds absolute control of phone installation. A battery of smaller companies offering cheaper, often more flexible local, regional and international services have sprung up, and you can subscribe to these companies—referred to as resellers—for those services. But you still need to deal with Telekom for the basic service. Several of the private companies will bill you separately for regional or international calls made through them; others use Deutsche Telekom to bill their customers.

To get a telephone, you have to make your way over to the nearest Deutsche Telekom 'T-Punkt' service centre or simply call 01-114. Deutsche Telekom leases and sells telephones, and you can also purchase telephones at most electronics shops. (But *caveat emptor:* all outside equipment must be Telekom-approved, so look for a sticker confirming this fact.)

You fill out a series of forms, and your telephone service will be installed soon thereafter. Actually, you can cut the wait by simply taking over the phone from the former tenant if that's still possible. (In many cases, the former occupant may have moved out by the time you see the flat.) Even if you do have this good fortune, there are still forms to be filled out at the Telekom office. Currently basic installation charges run to 52 euros, while a charge of 26 euros is levied when you take over an existing phone line from a former tenant.

The essential thing for you to know is that switching to smaller companies for some services does not require you to change either your telephone number or your basic equipment. These Telekom competitors offer the same basic services as the Big Guy, but at somewhat better rates. However, as it's much easier to go the full Telekom route, many customers elect to swallow the small price difference and go that route.

In Germany, telephone billing is calculated on both a monthly basic fee and calling units, which are themselves based on a preset number of seconds based on the distance of the call. You also have to pay for most extra services, such as call waiting or caller ID. One factor to be weighed in working out the best deal for your phone service is the number of seconds per unit. The fewer the better actually, as this way you only pay for the actual time employed in making the call.

The basic fee for fixed-line service can run from around 13 euros for a plain vanilla analogue line up to over 30 euros for a DSL or ISDN digital line. With the latter, you're given different numbers which you can use for separate units, such as a home phone, a second phone, a business phone or a fax. The DSL is roughly 12 times faster than the ISDN and is thus generally preferred for Internet service. (Though to take advantage of the DSL, you also need a DSL modem, which runs about 150 euros.)

One other important point about billing procedures in Germany: standard telephone bills here are not itemised, supposedly because of Germany's strong personal privacy laws. You can, however, get itemised bills listing each call and the cost thereof, but only if you specifically request this service from Telekom. To get this service, you must ask for a *Einzelverbindungsnachweis*—if you can ever get that out of your mouth at one go.

Water

Water supply is arranged by the landlord, but you usually have to pay for your water use yourself, after the overall bill has been presented to the landlord. Landlords determine how the bill will be divided between the various occupants of a building. Some simply work out a calculation dividing costs according to the size of your flat. A much fairer way is for the landlord to engage a company to come in and read individual water meters and then bill each residence for the water it actually used.

This service is called an *Ablesedienst,* and the company performing the service will, a few days before coming, put notices with the date and time of the readings on the front door of a building. You are then required to be present in your flat at that time. If you can't be (the readings occur almost exclusively during workdays), you have to give your key to a neighbour to facilitate the reading. If you don't provide for either of these possibilities, the *Ablesedienst* firm will arrange a second visit to your residence. This sounds very kind, except you will then have to pay the firm for this extra trip and it can be expensive.

Even dearer can be having your electrical power shut off. This is usually done after failure to pay one month's bill. In the second month, you will receive a number of warnings from the electric company ordering you to pay or face the loss of your electricity.

To avoid such unpleasantness, you can simply have your utility bills paid by registering through an *Einziehungsermächtingung.* While this German mouthful might suggest a complicated surgical procedure, the only thing that gets removed is your money. You sign a form allowing the utility company to withdraw the amount of your monthly bill automatically from your bank GIRO account, and this relieves you of all responsibility and saves you from paying the wages of the sins of omission.

Einziehungsermächtigung or *Abbuchungsverfahren* can also be tapped for any regular payment schedule, such as health, auto and other insurance, subscriptions, monthly rent or even monthly or quarterly payments to the tax authorities.

Electric Shock

About 12 years ago, a friend of ours who had gone off on vacation forgot to provide for his utility bill payments. Shortly after his return, he came back one evening to find himself powerless. He then had to go to the *Stadtwerke* office the next day and pay his back bill—plus DM 400 (200 for shutting the electricity off, 200 to get it back on)!

DEALING WITH BANKS

Now that everyone's second favourite topic—money—has reared its head, it might be a good time to talk about where to put your money. At first, you might get the impression that the main purpose of German banks is to protect you from your own money, but the German banking system is actually a well-ordered and regulated arrangement that provides stability and order to the economy. Still, regulations seem to be tight for both large and small customers, with penalties and other disincentives applied for getting at your money too frequently or too heftily.

German history again casts its dark shadow here. As British economist JM Keynes once noted, every nation has its own form of economic nightmare, and Germany's is inflation. (Remember the frantic spiral of 1923?) As a result, the government and the central bank, Deutsche Bundesbank, continuously pursued a fairly rigid policy of securing currency stability at close to all costs. (Such a task was even set down in the Bundesbank's charter.) The policy filtered down to the individual banks tending to customers' needs, which means keeping the flow of money not all that fluid.

In practical terms, that means you are somewhat restricted on how much money you can draw from your savings account. The prevailing bank policies stipulate that you're

allowed to withdraw up to around 1,500 euros within any calendar month. (This amount was set by law until the mid 1990s, and the vast majority of banks still continue the practice—something very much in their interest.) Any amount withdrawn over that results in a penalty charge, which entails a loss of interest determined by a percentage of the amount exceeding the legal limit. For a standard account, you can only withdraw the entire amount after giving a three-month notice of your intention to do so. (This period is commonly listed on bank signs as *vereinbarte Kündigungsfrist,* or agreed notification period.)

GIRO Accounts

If you are going to exist as a financial entity in Germany, you will need a GIRO, or current account, as well as a savings account. The total amount in a GIRO account is at your disposal at any time and, although at present very few of these accounts offer any interest, there is a trend in that direction. Actually it's more of a trickle than a trend, but it is still an improvement.

Beyond the disappointment of not getting interest, you have to pay fees just to maintain most GIRO accounts, and they can amount to over 10 euros a month with all the trimmings. Despite that, you are going to need your GIRO as the overwhelming majority of bills, salaries, fees, reimbursements, etc. are paid through GIRO transfers.

Cheque? What's a Cheque?
Payment by cheque is quite rare in Germany; so rare, in fact, that when my wife received a reimbursement cheque some years back, she thought it was a notification of transfer and didn't even cash it until the payee asked her why she hadn't. But the main point here remains that if you don't have a GIRO account, you are going to make things quite inconvenient for yourself and anyone who wants to pay you or get payments from you.

As standard costs for maintaining a GIRO account differ substantially from bank to bank, it would be a good idea to shop around a bit until you get the best deal. One good rule of thumb that applies to both GIRO and savings accounts is that the giant German banks with international branches aren't all that excited by private clients, so you are most likely to get the best deals, not to mention the best treatment, at smaller institutions.

DOMESTIC HELP

Finding good domestic help in Germany is not unlike the process in most Western countries; in short, it can be quite difficult. There are a limited number of Germans who take this work, and they demand a fair amount of money for doing it. In addition, you are required to pay for the worker's social programs (i.e. health and unemployment insurance, pension, etc.) calculated on a percentage of the income they receive from you.

The low-budget method of acquiring domestic help involves engaging foreigners who are not yet totally integrated into the German social network. These men and, principally, women charge significantly less per hour than their German counterparts and the people they work for are not required to pay for the package of social benefits. But as these workers are not yet fully integrated into the German system, you won't be able to acquire their services through either the *Arbeitsamt* or the standard agencies. That means you're dependent on word of mouth, asking friends, acquaintances and colleagues if they can recommend a reliable person in this field.

All of your problems in securing reliable domestic help will increase manifold if you don't speak German. Adding a working knowledge of English to the job description cuts the number of qualified workers drastically. Most foreign cleaning ladies speak some German, and they occasionally have picked up a smattering of English in their travels. But any complex communication or instructions will usually work only in German.

SHOPPING

One of the biggest shocks awaiting many foreigners settling in Germany is the restrictive shopping hours. Those coming from countries where one enjoys flexible shopping times are apt to find the rigid German laws regarding trade frustrating, aggravating, irrational, even mean-spirited. Gradually, things seem to be changing, although it will be some time before Germany has unrestricted shopping hours.

Until recently, almost all stores engaged in retail trade were required by law to close on weekdays by 6:30 pm, on Saturdays by 2:00 pm (a little later on the first Saturday of each month), and all day Sunday and legal holidays. After wrangling and haranguing, law-makers loosened things up a bit in the late 1990s. Now shops are allowed to remain open until 8:00 pm, Monday through Saturday. Sunday trading is still banned, except for bakeries, which are allowed to open their doors for three hours on that hallowed day of rest.

Beating the Restrictions

Most of Germany's main railway stations and several of its airports have supermarkets or larger grocery shops, fruit stands and bakeries that do stay open later, often seven days a week. Theoretically, you should be a *bona fide* traveller with a valid train or plane ticket to use these facilities, but that requirement was dropped long ago (if, indeed, it was ever enforced).

Unfortunately for those ensconced in smaller towns, where neither airports nor main railway stations are at hand, this is not an option. Even for folks living in major cities, it is not always that convenient to hop over to the airport or main station. But there is still one possibility for late shoppers in this group. Recently, a number of service stations have opened travellers' shops that stock the bare necessities. Some of these outlets even operate 24 hours a day!

But as is often the case, you have to pay extra for this convenience, especially at the service station shops. And those in very small towns are bereft of even these few options. The moral: take a tip from your German neighbours and learn how to plan.

The Sales Season

In Germany, storewide sales can only take place at two specified periods, the *Winterschlussverkauf* (winter close-out sale), confined to the last week of January and the first week of February, and the *Sommerschlussverkauf,* which covers the two-week July–August cusp.

As small operations could never compete with the large stores in snatching up huge consignments and selling them at reduced prices, this practice is limited to those two periods. Stores of any size can, however, mark down prices on specific items at any time—as long as the sales are limited to what can reasonably be judged to be 'individual pieces'. Further, though the official periods cover the above dates, the very best buys on the best items are usually shortly before the start of the sanctioned sales periods.

Good Buys, Bad Buys

While sheer practicality dictates that you buy many things in Germany, the country is hardly a shoppers' paradise, and you may want to hold off on certain purchases until you are back home. This is especially true for those who frequently travel home, as do many foreigners who can afford to.

For example, I used to try to buy good wool clothing in Britain when I was there. Not only were British prices for these goods noticeably lower than German tabs, but the range of styles, colours and sizes was considerably more extensive.

On the other hand, there are some products that a shrewd shopper will pick up in Germany and maybe even take home. Some household appliances or other consumer electronics items, if produced by a German company, can often be had cheaper here. Plus, it is altogether more convenient buying such things here, although be aware that many electrical appliances bought here won't work back home.

Other good buys include things like the highly praised Solingen steelware or the immensely popular Hummel figurines. These items can be found in any big urban area. The Hummels are readily available at most department stores, as are Solingen products, though the latter are often offered in a wider range at small shops specialising in Solingen wares.

Large crowds flock to the major shopping areas, such as Cologne's Hohestrasse.

And, of course, how could we forget the world famous Black Forest cuckoo clocks. These can be found at speciality shops (not only in the Black Forest region) and a few department stores. Here, the clocks will run you far less than they would in much of the world but do be careful here—there are enormous differences in quality amongst these tick-tockers. As many shops believe the buyers are predominantly tourists from abroad who won't try to set the thing working until they get back home, they carry a lot of shoddy products which they flog at unjustified prices. If you don't exercise a lot of caution here, you might discover you have simply purchased an expensive wall decoration. (This, sadly, happened to us once with a gift for relatives back in the States.)

Where to Buy

Although the system does its part to make your shopping inconvenient, there are many places for you to shop when you can catch them open. Large-scale shopping malls such as those in North America, Asia and Australia haven't caught on to the same extent here, though they are sprouting up more and more, especially in cities like Hamburg, Munich and Berlin.

More typical of the German mode is a main shopping district in the centre of town, or in one part of an urban quarter, with department stores and a string of small shops set along a main avenue and the tributary streets serving that main thoroughfare. Examples of these main shopping strips are Berlin's famous Kurfürstendamm, Munich's Maximilianstrasse, Dusseldorf's Königsallee and Frankfurt's Zeil. As they are both popular and accessible, these areas tend to get packed on Saturdays, so you should be forewarned and maybe get there very early on that day.

Verbraucherzentrale

If you are at all confused about the purchase of electrical appliances, big-ticket items for the home, bank accounts, private or public-funded health insurance, or even the proper toothpaste or deodorant, there are agencies in most German towns that offer free advice on an amazingly broad range of consumer topics. These *Verbraucherzentralen* (consumer advice centres) will allow you to access their copious files and usually feature photocopiers where, for 10–20 cents a page, you can copy any material available. Most of these centres also now charge 1.00–1.50 euros to trawl through their files. They usually have a trained, helpful staff who can answer many of your questions or at least direct you to the file or other agency that might have the answer you need. Their addresses and phone numbers are listed in phone books under *Verbraucherzentrale*, but their phone lines are relentlessly busy and they can't give that much information over the phone anyway, so it's often best to go there in person.

Shopping for Sustenance

One aspect of shopping in Germany that has changed radically in the last 25 years is food shopping, thanks largely to the abundant influx of foreigners. Today, you will find a surprisingly wide offering of all your food needs, as well as various outlets.

Up until the late 1970s, fruit and vegetable offerings were limited by season and to what was available in Germany or

Weekly outdoor markets, such as this one in Bonn, are a fixture in many German towns and cities.

other western European nations in that particular season. My wife remembers a time not too long ago when a humble coconut represented a special present for her grandmother and fresh pineapple was a bit of culinary exotica, prohibitively expensive for the average consumer. Now, produce from southern Africa, Asia, the Middle East, Australia and New Zealand, as well as the Americas regularly fills the stalls of German markets. Although these items will be found most easily at stands run by foreign residents, they now even occasionally pop up at businesses run by the third and fourth generation of German stall-keepers and can be found in ample supply in the supermarkets of most big cities.

Supermarkets, many of them pocket-sized by North American or British standards, are spread widely throughout the country and almost every significant shopping district in today's Germany is dotted with fruit and vegetable stands or produce shops. The offerings and quality are usually best at the big central markets, such as Frankfurt's Kleinmarkthalle, Hamburg's Fischermarkt or Gänsemarkt, and Munich's Viktualienmarkt, but it is possible these days to scoot around to the corner market and pick up a mango, papaya, cape gooseberry or lychee at almost any time of year. Such is the power of a country with a huge export surplus and a keen curiosity about the rest of the world, fed by massive vacationing in foreign lands.

Shop-O-Metric

Those of you who haven't yet been schooled in the metric system will need a bit of adjusting in Germany, where all groceries are sold according to that measure. It is quite a simple system really. Things sold by weight are calculated in grammes, which run from one gramme to a kilogramme (or kilo), which is a thousand grammes, before starting all over again. For those of you better versed in the English system, a kilo is a little over two pounds. By the way, Germany has its own variant of the pound, called *das Pfund* but this *Pfund* weighs in at exactly half a kilo, or 500 grammes, while the classic English pound only hits 474 grammes. This is something to keep in mind in both comparison shopping and handling any recipe calling for pounds.

The same principle operates with regard to lengths and widths, though here the basic measure is the centimetre, which becomes a metre when you have put together a hundred of them. The metre is a little bit longer than the English yard.

Flea Markets

Some of the best buys anywhere in Germany are to be found at the local *Flohmarkt* (flea market). These markets, which usually operate only on weekends and in specific parts of a town, allow freelance hucksters and salespeople to bring whatever they care to sell from small stands, or even sometimes just from a dowdy blanket laid down on the ground.

It would take a small book of its own to describe the miscellaneous objects proffered at flea markets. Suffice it to say that at any of these open air sales-fests you are sure to find lots of clothing, appliances, cassettes, CDs and old vinyl records, as well as accessories and parts for cars and bicycles (many whole bikes, too, though I haven't yet seen any entire automobiles being sold). Many sellers seem to have dragged all their family heirlooms along. The range of quality is also enormous, running from pure junk to amazingly high-quality items. Even if you are not buying, the show itself is well worth a Saturday or Sunday stroll through the flea market.

KNOW YOUR EURO

German currency is every bit as easy to learn as German measurements. The euro is, like the revered mark it replaced in 2002, of the decimal system persuasion: 100 cents equal 1 euro, with euros then proceeding in orderly decimal variations. Euro coins come in supplies of 1, 2, 5, 10, 20 and 50 cents and 1 and 2 euros. Bank notes or bills are offered in denominations of 5, 10, 20, 50, 100, 200 and 500 euros. You needn't worry about mistaking any of this even on your first arrival, as every coin and bill has its value prominently printed in Arabic numerals with nary a word of German. In addition, bills or bank notes are of different sizes with raised, tangible symbols for the blind.

HEALTH

It has often been claimed that if a German is feeling too healthy, he thinks there is something seriously wrong with him. The broader truth behind this crack is that Germans are quite concerned with their own physical well-being. Germans also understand that asking someone, "How are you doing?" is just a rhetorical question, but despite that, when you ask it here, you are quite likely to get a quick synopsis of some health problem in response.

The health problem you will become familiar with very quickly is *Kreislaufprobleme* (circulation problems). Minor malfunctions of the *Kreislauf* system seem to be pandemic in Deutschland. Symptoms of this scourge mainly involve dizziness, weakness, minor sight problems, a general lassitude. Other widely reported symptoms include headaches, inability to concentrate, job dissatisfaction and the intense craving for a day off from work.

Visiting the Doctor

The general concern for one's health means that you will have a lot of company when you visit a doctor. The vast majority of doctors maintain posted *Sprechstunden* (visiting hours) as well as special times set aside for appointments. Waiting rooms are packed during the *Sprechstunden*, and if you venture in during the last hour, you can expect to be there until even after the end of the posted time before the doctor sees you.

But making an appointment doesn't necessarily relieve you of a wait. It is not unheard of for people who have scheduled an appointment—even during those special times—to have to wait an hour or longer before getting in to see the doctor. Because of this, you should always budget a lot of time when you have a medical appointment. Also be aware that many people book appointments during the regular *Sprechstunden*; so don't feel abused if someone who entered the waiting room some time after you gets called in for attention first.

Many specialists have abandoned the practice of *Sprechstunden* altogether, even though the signs outside their offices still list these times. But dropping in unannounced on dermatologists, neurologists or orthopedic specialists will often get you nothing but a future appointment.

Health Insurance

Other than overwrought concern for one's health, the main reason for congestion at doctor's offices is the splendid health insurance system Germany enjoys. The system involves an interlocking matrix of private and public health care plans. Everyone who is officially employed with a monthly gross income of under 3,825 euros (as of this writing, but sure to go up before too long) must be enrolled in one of the government-run health care plans. Usually the employer decides which plan, and all workers in the company are shuffled into that plan. Employees with incomes above that level or the self-employed have the option of becoming voluntary members of the government plan, locking into private health care plans, or taking their chances with no insurance. Most insurance plans cover non-working spouses and children of registered members.

The costs for insurance can be stiff. Regular members of the state-sponsored plans have a percentage of their monthly incomes automatically deducted from their pay; half of the costs for officially employed people are borne by the workers themselves, the other half by their employers. Voluntary members, lacking the employers' contribution, pay a smaller percentage of their incomes, although government officials have set minimum and maximum payment amounts. Long-term unemployed, some retired persons, college students and young people serving in the military or alternative service generally get their contributions to the system covered either fully or partially by the government. Most of these folks are put into AOK, the largest of the state-supported systems.

Paying for health care in Germany can be almost as painful as the ailment that drove you to the doctor in the first place. Ordinary visits can ring up to between 40–60 euros, and that's before the doctor even does anything to you. Each element of the treatment adds to the overall cost and, worldwide, Germany ranks near the very top when it comes to health care costs. Unless you happen to be rolling in money, going without any health insurance in Germany is not recommended.

Hospital Admission Procedures

If what ails you cannot be handled at your local doctor's office, or if it starts ailing you on a weekend or holiday, you may have no recourse but to go to a hospital. If so, there are two main methods of admission.

When doctors diagnose your ailment as one requiring hospital treatment, they will contact a hospital and arrange admission for you. Depending on how urgent your case is, you could be admitted that same day or be given an appointment for admission at a later date.

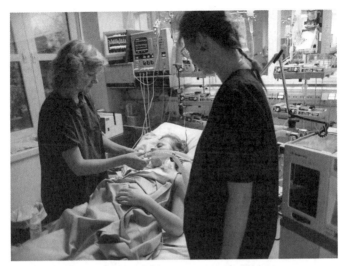

The sick and the disabled receive extensive medical treatment in most German hospitals, irrespective of income level or social status.

Emergencies

Unfortunately, there are certain health problems that we can't plan for. We've mentioned that Germans generally abhor accidents and the unexpected (*Refer to* Chapter 3: People on *pages 50–73*), but even in Germany such nasties do sometimes happen—so they do have ways of dealing with them.

If your particular emergency is something that can be handled by a general doctor or dentist, these are available even during strange times when your regular doctor or dentist isn't. Lists of these *Notärzte* (emergency doctors) are provided by *Ärztliche Notfalldienst-Zentrale* (the Medical Emergency Service Central Office), whose telephone numbers are generally listed at the beginning of the *Yellow Pages* phone books. People working the phones here will listen to your complaint, then tell you which is the nearest *Notarzt*.

If, on the other hand, you have a serious accident or some other serious and sudden health problem, you can always be admitted to the nearest hospital as an emergency patient. In such a case, you'll be taken or—if you can still move under your own power—you'll go to the *Notaufnahme* division of the hospital. If your problem is deemed an emergency, you will be taken in for treatment.

As many German hospitals today are strained past capacity, the first hospital you are brought to may be able to provide only first aid or emergency treatment. They will then arrange for you to be transferred to the nearest available hospital.

If your problem is of a more minor nature, which you think lends itself to mere apothecary treatment, there is a similar service with pharmacies. Pharmacies (*Apotheke* in the German parlance), being commercial operations, are subject to the same restrictive business hours all other shops suffer from. Indeed, as a rule, pharmacies hold to the old 6:30 pm shop closure time.

The emergency pharmacies are permitted to dispense all prescription and non-prescription drugs, as well as their other products (should you ever have a desperate need for sun tan lotion in the middle of the night). But you do have to pay a little penalty for not planning to get ill at a proper time—the emergency pharmacies get to charge a supplement of 2.50 euros for all products sold outside normal business hours (this sum is prescribed by the law).

FAMILY MATTERS
Children's Needs

Many politicians, writers and sociologists have spilt a lot of classical German anguish over the perception that Germany is a *kinderfeindliches Land* (a country hostile to children). A great many others deny this charge, though the very tenor of their denials underscores the fact that some problem in this area does exist. Happily, Germany has certainly shown progress in making the place more hospitable to children over the last 25 years—probably because fears of 'the Germans dying out' convinced movers and shakers in many fields that they had better start giving people encouragement to have and raise offspring.

Actually, on paper, Germany appears to be a country that does a lot for its children. The government operates a Federal Youth Plan, which it further supports with a yearly expenditure of around 100 million euros. While this figure does represent a slight drop from that of a few years earlier, the money helps to support a broad range of political, social and cultural youth activities, including youth exchanges, as well as an increasing number of programs of an extra-curricular nature.

By law, since 1996, every child has the right to a kindergarten slot from the age of three, and there are a raft of other programmes aimed at meeting younger children's needs. Attendance at a kindergarten is voluntary rather than obligatory, and comes in two sizes, suiting the needs of the families. Children can attend just the morning sessions or spend the entire day there. The fly in this sweet ointment is that there aren't enough kindergarten slots to fulfil the promise for all children, so every semester sees parents scrambling for the available slots, especially at the more sought-after locations.

Of course, government and private programs are fine things in and of themselves, but there is also the matter of the larger social environment. And this is where Germany often comes up short in meeting children's needs, which perhaps reflects yet another German trait: a belief that if the government or some responsible agency has set up a programme to tackle

Daycare centres are still rather rare in Germany, as are summer programmes such as day or overnight camps where kids can go away without their parents and interact primarily with their peers.

some problem, the rest of us have little more to contribute to its solution.

In this case, sadly, that's not true. A number of parents from other societies note that the German environment is not the best one in which to raise children, because of the widespread shortage of warmth, friendliness and openness that pervades the society.

Education

An equally celebrated feature of German life is its educational system. All children living in Germany are required to attend some school between the ages of six and 18. Those who attend a Gymnasium usually add a 13th year to this spell and finish their school days at age 19 (although some influential pedagogues and politicos have been talking seriously about cutting this to a standard 12 years). If your children fall between these ages, you must see to it that they are registered in an officially recognised school. Failure to see that a child attends school will draw you repeated warnings and eventually a fine.

One of the first questions foreign parents living here have to address is whether to send their children to a German state school or one of the alternatives. Most foreign children take the former track (in fact, 40 per cent of the schoolchildren in Frankfurt are officially 'foreigners', and other towns show comparable high percentages), though many international business people elect to send their kids to private institutions. While the German educational system is still widely praised and stands as a model for many other countries, standards have slipped a notch or two during the *Wertewandel* and some features of the German system may take more than a little getting used to. To help you in your decision, here's a quick overview of this system.

State Schools

First, the plus points. Attendance at state schools is free, as are some (though not all) teaching materials and resources, such as books. Compared to many other present-day state systems, German education offers quality instruction and commendable results. At least as important when considering your child's education is that sending your children to a German state school is also one of the best ways to integrate them into German society.

The first four years of school, called *die Grundschule,* mix all students together in basic classes. The next two years may, depending on the city and state you live in, involve what is called an orientation or promotion stage allowing students and their parents to decide what kind of school the kids should continue onto. There are four such choices: *Hauptschule*—the lowest form, which basically prepares its charges for jobs in trades and industry; *Realschule*—a slightly higher form providing a broader education, thus preparing its students for middle level positions in business or jobs in public service; Gymnasium—the academically select form, emphasising traditional academics and preparing *Gymnasiasten* for university and better positions in industry and commerce. A *Gymnasium's* seven to nine years culminate in the *Abitur*, a battery of tests which help determine what college or university students get into, or what kind of job they will be offered; and *die Gesamtschule*—comprehensive schools, which combine the three other forms. There is some general mixing of students in the *Gesamtschulen,* but even here students are tracked according to abilities and inclinations.

Other than deciding on the type of German school for your child, there are a number of sticky logistical problems linked to the school system. For one, after the *Grundschule,* you may discover that the appropriate school for your children is not the one closest to you. This may then entail packing your kids off to travel by public transport all the way across town.

A more distressing factor for many parents from other lands is school hours. Very few state schools have afternoon sessions. The standard average school day runs from 8:00 am–1:00 pm; deviations fall within a half hour of these points. The old rationale for this arrangement was that students would use the afternoons as well as the early evenings to tackle their burdensome homework, but this argument has grown increasingly stale as social mores change. The key point for parents is that a greater chunk of your day must involve making arrangements for your child's non-school activities.

Hold on, it gets even trickier. As students don't have to come into school if they have no first-period classes or wait around until school ends if they have no further classes, your child's schedule may be different everyday. Moreover, if a teacher is out for some reason and the school can't arrange a replacement (a more and more common occurrence), your child may be sent home mid-morning, without any prior warning to the parents. And if you have more than one child in school, chances are rather good that they will have different schedules most days and you'll have to make separate arrangements for each.

Arrangements should, in any case, always involve providing the kids with lunch at home, or a reasonable substitute. As lunch was never a part of the German school system, there are no school cafeterias in German state schools. Mid-morning snacks are generally available, either at local stores or from hawkers who ply the schoolyards with their wares during breaks. Unfortunately, these snacks are invariably low on nutrition and high on perdition. A nourishing, well-balanced lunch is therefore a recommended adjunct to the school day.

This compact school day highlights a key difference between the educational philosophies of the German and Anglo-Saxon traditions. Whereas American or British education tries to build the whole person by offering a spate of extra-curricular activities, German schools focus on academics or career training. German society leaves activities like sports, musical bands, and debating societies for clubs, church organisations and other non-school bodies.

Registering a Child for School

You don't have to worry about registering your children for school, because the system comes after you. If you and your children are officially registered as German residents (which all of you should be by this point), your local school will write to you some time before the start of the school year and ask you to come in and register your child for classes. You then drop by during official registration hours and fill out the necessary forms. Even if you have decided not to send your offspring to a state school, you must contact your local school and inform them, in written form, what alternative you have arranged. Of course, registering a child with any of the alternative institutions entails a direct registration with that particular school.

Alternative Education

There are a number of alternatives to the state system, some with instruction in German, others in foreign languages. In the first group are religious schools, Waldorf schools and Montessori schools.

Religious schools operate very much like German state schools, except that they, of course, put a much greater emphasis on religious and moral instruction. These schools are mainly Catholic, though the Lutheran Church also maintains a nationwide network of such institutions, and there are Jewish and Muslim schools as well. You needn't be a practising member of any of these faiths for your children to attend, but they must always show due respect for the religious views put forth at these institutions.

Waldorf schools are alternative schools based on the esoteric philosophy of Rudolf Steiner called Anthroposophy. These schools emphasise the development of creativity in the child and place arts in a central position in the curricula. The pedagogical techniques as well as some of the subject matter are strongly influenced by Steiner's philosophy, though his thought is not itself a part of the curriculum. Waldorf schools have spread around the world since the first one was founded in Stuttgart in 1919, but they are still most heavily concentrated in Germany, with 191 schools, where they are very highly regarded by a certain segment of the population.

Montessori schools are similar to Waldorf schools in that they place special emphasis on the encouragement of individual creativity and attempt to develop the student's personality through alternative instruction methods. They ordinarily run from kindergarten up through the lower grades.

Any decision to send your children to German schools depends on how well the kids have taken to the language and how successful you believe they'll be in tackling a German-language curriculum. Two friends of ours who had lived in Germany for almost a decade, and were quite content here, decided to return to America precisely at the point their daughter reached school age. I had predicted that move, as the daughter, though born and bred here, had acquired only a scattering of German words and phrases. The parents were afraid that the girl, though very bright, would perform badly in school and, 'be treated like an *Ausländer*'.

Foreign-Language Schools

There are, however, English-language alternatives if you are willing and able to pay the not-insubstantial fees. The most well-known and well-regarded are the International Schools, based largely on the American system, including a full program of extra-curricular activities. These schools run from preschool for four-year-olds through all grades, culminating in the American high school diploma and the International Baccalaureate diploma. There are year-round admissions and, for students whose English is a little weak, English-as-a-second-language (ESL) courses to bring them up to regular course level. Tuition and other costs, such as transport, registration and sundry other fees can run to just over 12,000 euros a year.

If you're still listening after hearing those costs, you should know there are International Schools in Berlin, as well as Berlin-Brandenburg; Bonn; Bremen; Dresden; Dusseldorf and Neuss, just across the river from Dusseldorf; Haimhausen in southern Bavaria; Hamburg, Hanover; Frankfurt-Sindlingen; two in Munich, Oberursel outside of Frankfurt, Potsdam near Berlin, Stuttgart. Residents of Berlin have a low-priced alternative, called the JFK School—a German state school with an American program offered in English.

There are also full-session Japanese language schools in Berlin, Dusseldorf, Frankfurt, Hamburg and Munich, with part-time schools operating in Bonn, Bremen, Frankfurt, Munich, Nuremberg and Stuttgart. These, not surprisingly, emulate the Japanese school system, and can put a dent in your wallet, though nowhere near as deep as the International Schools can.

And if you'd like to add some Gallic flavour to your children's education, French schools operate in Bonn, Dusseldorf, Frankfurt, Freiburg, Hamburg, Munich, Saarbrücken and Stuttgart. These schools transplant the entire French system to German soil and bear similar costs to the Japanese schools.

TEENAGERS

The teenage years in Germany are problematic, just as they are in most modern industrial societies. But to paraphrase Tolstoy, all unproblematic stories are alike while every problematic story is problematic in its own way. For both teenagers coming here from another country and the parents of these teenagers, it's certainly those differences in German problematics that are of most interest.

First of all, any foreign teenager coming here will be faced with all the difficulties mentioned in previous chapters, though young people in Germany tend to be more flexible and open than most of their elders. But all the trials of moving to a new environment and trying to fit yourself in could be more pronounced in Germany than in some other places, depending on your teenager's sensibilities.

One difference that many parents coming here may find troubling is the drinking age. Starting at 18, anyone can legally be served or purchase any and all alcoholic drinks. But in reality, youths two and three years younger are routinely served alcohol in clubs and discos, or buy it at a supermarket with no trouble whatsoever. Many teens, especially those coming from more restrictive societies, aren't able to handle this new freedom. But most of them will be encouraged by their peers to join in from time to time. As a parent, you'll have to do all you can to see that your teens handle this in a responsible manner.

NON-WORKING SPOUSES

In the last 30 years, Germany has become more and more a double-income domain. That makes it a little difficult for non-working spouses living here. This is compounded by the dearth of strong community or neighbourhood relations, except in the smallest towns and villages, as well as the locals' reluctance to embrace strangers of any nationality.

Actually, I know very few non-working spouses in the foreign community, as amongst most of our friends and acquaintances, both husbands and wives work. Even those who don't have a regular job with a German or foreign company have become self-employed or taken up some gainful employment, perhaps precisely because Germany provides so few options for non-working partners.

There are, nevertheless, some opportunities for spouses who remain outside the work force. A number of clubs for English-speaking women, focused on the needs of those who aren't in the work force, have operated for decades. These are concentrated in and around the major cities.

There are also other programmes for spouses staying at home, especially those who take care of the children. The catch is that almost all of these programmes are offered in German and the ones that aren't are often in Turkish or Serbo-Croatian. Undoubtedly, many of the people running these programmes will know some English and thus be able to bridge over some basic problems during the early going. But this merely indicates why learning the language is so important, especially for non-working spouses.

Most urban-dwelling, non-working spouses would recommend that other couples in their situation try to live within a major city, or at least on the edge of one. They all contrast their lives with those of women living in more remote suburbs, ensconced in small English-speaking enclaves, learning almost no German, removed from much of the activity going on around them and fittingly bored. This, they emphasise, is the one thing that non-working spouses here should strive to avoid.

PETS

The Germans love pets. In fact, if you hear that some German treats his wife or his kid like a dog, you know that he is a model husband and father; no human could want better treatment than that which the average German pet-owner lavishes upon his four-legged friend. Even if a Berlin court in early 2003 ruled against a 71-year-old driver whose vehicle was rear-ended when he slammed on his brakes to avoid a dachshund who had suddenly dashed out in front of him!

Unfortunately for foreigners relocating here, that affection seems to be reserved for the home-grown variety of pets. Regulations for bringing a pet from abroad are complex and forbidding and different for each country of origin.

Too Many Rules

When I went to the *Veterinäramt* (the state Veterinarian Department) here and asked about regulations for bringing in pets, the vet asked me how many volumes this book was supposed to be. He then escorted me into his office and pointed out the book stipulating all the German rules on pets—the book was about four inches thick, all of it filled with small, tight print.

So we'll just have to pass on this one and repeat the advice the good doctor at the *Veterinäramt* gave us when he suggested that you consult the German embassy or consulate in your home country about bringing pets here. They'll know the specific regulations for your land and will be able to advise you on the chances of getting that non-human member of your family into Germany.

TRANSPORTATION

Germany may seem fairly small to an American, Canadian or Australian and fairly big to a Singaporean, Korean or Hong Kong citizen. But no matter how you perceive it, Germany remains remarkably easy to get around in, due to an exemplary transportation system. Germans are more than a little proud of this system, and deservedly so.

Local Transport

There are few problems getting around within most German towns and cities. While public transport may not always bring you right to the door, you can usually get pretty close to where you want to go.

Brigades of buses criss-cross most urban centres, knitting the various parts of town together. In many of Germany's larger cities an extensive underground system, known as the U-Bahn, serves those travellers who want to get there faster and aren't devoted to seeing the city sights as they travel. Trams or streetcars augment both of these modes of transport and are especially prevalent in the new eastern areas of the country.

S-pecially Good Transport

A rather laudable feature of the German transport system is the S-Bahn, or suburban trains. These are high-speed lines linking larger towns and their major suburban communities. Most German metropolitan areas boast extensive S-Bahn networks, making it easy to get you into and out of the city centres.

S-Bahns generally travel underground when in the middle of town, rising to street level and beyond as they move out of the centre. Though quite convenient, they generally don't run as frequently as U-Bahns, so when it's possible to reach your destination through both means, the U-Bahn may be the surer bet. And as they cater primarily to suburban commuters, S-Bahn service is drastically reduced on Sundays, often to once an hour and sometimes dropped altogether.

Paying for the Service

When entering an S-Bahn or U-Bahn station, you may be surprised to see no ticket counters, no turnstiles, no gates, and wonder if this ride isn't free. It isn't; most local public transport in Germany runs on the honour system—and the dishonourable get punished rather harshly.

Every *Fahrgast* (traveller) is obliged to purchase his or her ticket from one of the coin-operated machines located strategically within the station before travelling. These machines are usually upstairs, so you have to get your ticket before proceeding to the trains.

No one will check your ticket when you climb aboard, but the trains, trams and buses are regularly visited by teams of *Kontrolleure* (ticket inspectors) who verify that you're travelling with a valid ticket. If not, the inspectors will dutifully impose a fine ranging from 25–40 euros, depending on the city.

A Fine Way to Travel

Don't try to talk your way out of a fine for not buying a ticket as the ticket inspectors have probably heard every excuse imaginable and they are trained to turn a deaf ear to even the sorriest of stories. And the least acceptable of all unacceptable excuses is that you simply didn't have change. The ticket-dispensing changes all give change for any coins, and most of them now also recognise and accept banknotes. The contention that you were in a rush and you faced a long queue at the machine will also immediately wither before the inflexible gaze of the *Kontrolleure*.

Those fines can cost 20–30 times the price of a ticket, so it's much wiser to buy the ticket. This holds true for trams and buses as well. Ticket-dispensing machines are usually located right next to every tram or bus stop. Bus drivers can be the great exception in being able to make change and sell tickets, though they usually baulk at breaking large bank notes. In many cities, you're required to enter the bus at the front door and either show the driver your ticket or buy one (some cities only have this requirement after 8:00 pm, supposedly after ticket inspectors have gone home for the day).

Ticket prices vary from city to city, although they generally run from 1–2.50 euros for a basic fare. Longer rides into the suburbs typically cost more, and most stations or stops feature a map showing various zones of travel and the price for each. Admittedly, these maps and fare zones can be confusing, even for native speakers, so don't hesitate to consult someone who looks like he or she knows more than you do.

If, on the other hand, your ride is a short one within the city, it may fall under the grace of the lower 'short distance' fare. Look on the ticket machine for the special button that reads *Kurzstrecke*. The machines will also usually display a list of stops that qualify as *Kurzstrecke* from that station.

Weeklies and Monthlies

You can save yourself all this bother by simply buying a weekly or monthly ticket, offered by most cities and sold at special counters in the main stations of the system. In addition to being convenient, these tickets can save you a good deal of money if you use public transport regularly during the period.

This all sounds nigh on wonderful, and it does hold for practically all bigger German cities. However, as the size of the towns shrink, so do the services provided. In the quieter hamlets, as well as most rural areas, public transport can be quite limited and then tends to disappear completely in the evening. Residents of these areas inevitably find themselves dependent on private cars or taxis.

As mentioned above, S-Bahn service often becomes thin as the evening progresses, but all public transport tapers off a bit after the early evening peak. Last trains and buses run somewhere between midnight and 1:00 am and begin appearing again from around 5:00 am. Berlin enjoys an all-night bus service, and cities like Frankfurt and Hamburg also put in a night owl bus service on weekends.

One recent unsettling development is the increase in crime on the public transport systems of larger cities. As a result, many travellers are reluctant to use the facilities in the evening, when most of this crime occurs. Teams of security personnel accompanied by malevolent-looking dogs now frequently patrol the trains and this has restored some passenger confidence. But as patrols are far too few to cover the whole system at any one time, transport authorities themselves warn evening passengers to sit in the first car of a train, as the driver commands telephone contact with security forces.

Taxis are Maxi

For many users of public transport, especially women, who tend to be the major victims of attacks, these measures still aren't reassuring enough, so they rely more and more on taxis for their evening transport. Taxis are usually plentiful and quite reliable in every German city and all but the smallest of towns.

One pleasant feature of German taxis is that most of the fleets are composed of white Mercedes, so you certainly ride in style when you're taxied around in Germany. On the other hand, you do pay for this touch of luxury, and many foreigners find taxi costs hereabouts a little on the expensive side.

But don't let me scare you off the evening trains, buses and trams. Recent trends are alarming to many Germans who remember when transport crime was virtually nonexistent, but levels still remain lower than in many other Western countries. I myself don't know a single person who's been a victim of transport crime here.

The National Rail System

For those travelling longer distances, the national railway is just the ticket. The network is extensive, with generally good connections—at least within the respective eastern and western domains. Remember that for over 40 years, east-west traffic was not exactly encouraged, so lines that crossed the border were hardly state of the art.

The best connections in the system are still those that run north and south, though there are thin patches of service even along this axis. Bigger towns and cities are well-covered, but smaller places become problematic or might even be totally ignored.

Connections between the West and Berlin were always relatively good, as the West German government obviously wanted to keep this link intact, and it has even improved in the last few years. But the whole east-west network should be sparkling in the near future, as the *Deutsche Bahn* (the German national railway) has been pouring tens of billions into revitalising the system.

Track density is, in fact, already higher in the eastern states, undoubtedly due to the lack of cars in the old DDR. And perhaps for the same reason, the easterners have traditionally relied on trains more than their western cousins. At least in terms of rail travel, the new eastern states should soon indeed be that 'blooming landscape' politicians keep talking about.

A Choice of Trains

The system features different types of trains, designated by a tricky array of letters. For shorter distances, you can hop on the *E-Zug* (*Eilzug*, or hurry train) or *D-Zug* (*Durchgangszug*, or through train). Lovers of paradox will appreciate that the 'hurry' train is by far the slower of the two.

The *D-Zug* is, however, to be avoided if at all possible when tackling longer distances, as there are much faster and much more comfortable alternatives such as the Inter-Regio, the IC (Intercity), and the flagship of the system—the ICE (Intercity Express). The ICE can reach speeds of 250–280 kmph (155.3–174 mph) on its fastest stretches and is conveniently fitted out with card-operated telephones, fax machines, fully equipped offices, videos in first-class, dining cars and snack cars featuring beer on tap. Paired with this last feature is a due supply of high-tech toilets.

Prices for the train are based on a uniform cost per kilometre throughout Germany, though a small surcharge is tacked on for IC, ICE and Inter-Regio. If you're a frequent rail traveller, it is wise to invest in a *BahnCard,* which now comes in three sizes and entitles you to 25 per cent off, half-price or free travel on almost all inter-German trips within a one-year period. The prices for these *BahnCard* deals run from 50 euros all the way up to 3,250 per year for second-class, 100 to 5,400 euros for first-class. All three cards allow up to four others to travel along at half-price under certain conditions.

Rail travel has always been a favoured form of transport in Germany, and all the new, improved services have only increased its popularity. Friday and Sunday afternoons and evenings and Monday morning travel can be quite busy indeed on the most heavily travelled lines, so it's highly advisable to reserve a seat for these times—probably a week in advance if that's possible. The aisles and sections between cars are filled with people who didn't.

Air Transport

The German rail network is well-connected to the likewise impressive rail systems of many other European countries, so getting around Europe by train can often be a convenient, cheaper alternative to flying. But if you have to travel longer distances, and most foreigners frequently do, German air transport is also exceedingly commendable.

Germany has 13 airports. The largest of these by far is Frankfurt/Main International. The Frankfurt facility is, in fact, the largest and busiest airport on the continent, as well as the leading air cargo centre for all of Europe. It also boasts a number of other major plus points, including prime shopping facilities, banks, an emergency clinic, and a top-notch conference centre. In the early 1990s, various polls rated Frankfurt as the best or second best airport in Europe. Despite opening a second, state-of-the-art terminal in the middle of that decade, Frankfurt's facility has dropped off the leading airports lists. But it's still pretty good.

The Other Airports

Much of Germany's international air traffic moves in and out of Frankfurt, though many charter flights prefer Dusseldorf, Germany's second leading airport. While planes out of Frankfurt travel to the four corners of the globe, some of the other airports are serviced only by intra-European flights. Berlin currently has three small and not very congenial airports. However, a consortium has set about expanding the current Schönefeld airfield in the eastern section into the Berlin Brandenburg International Airport. This world-class facility is now scheduled for opening in late 2007 or early 2008.

The Skytrax World Airport Awards 2005 (ranked by passengers) declared the newish Leipzig-Halle facility as the best airport in Eastern Europe, while Munich's airport was rated fourth best in the world, and Number One in Europe.

Unless you are travelling from Munich to Hamburg, or from far in the west to Berlin or another eastern city, it's possibly faster and certainly cheaper to travel within Germany by train. But if fly you must, Germany's air transport will take care of you nicely.

The Beloved Automobile

With all these wonderful forms of public transport, you might think that the private auto was an endangered species in Germany, but the truth is just the opposite. Car registrations have leaped from 8 million to over 40 million in the last 35 years, and the trend continues upward.

General Driving Rules

As you learned in Chapter 4 (*Refer to* 'Der Führerschein *(Driver's Licence)' on pages 92–94*) after you are officially registered, you need a German licence to drive here. An

The Deal with Wheels

So why would any sane human being opt for splintered nerves, traffic jams, a diabolically constructed maze of one-way streets and a serious lack of legal parking spots rather than jump on such excellent public transport? Actually, the reason is simple—it's always more convenient to hop into your own car, leave any time you want, and come back the moment you decide. You yourself may be swayed by these factors at some point, so I'll include just a few pointers for city driving here.

- Even if you have to drive part of the way, it's prudent to break before you reach the main bumper-to-bumper district, park the car in some legal spot, and take the final stretch with public transport. This saves nerves and probably even money.
- German motorists like to take off just as, or just before, the light turns green, and they are rather unforgiving of those who slowly move out from a stoplight. Moral: Don't dawdle at that light!
- On the other hand, don't shoot through red lights, as many traffic signals here are armed with low-level cameras that take lovely snaps of licence plates which have run the light. And the traffic police won't accept any plea that you were wrongly photographed.

international driver's licence is not valid in Germany if you are a German resident.

German road signs are sometimes unique to Germany, or to Europe, and you should master these before you go out on the road. You'll be tested on the signs when you get your licence transferred, but that doesn't always mean you have mastered the cryptography here.

In general, German traffic rules correlate with other European nations, though you should familiarise yourself with local differences. And watch out for cyclists! Most German cities have special paths for pedal bikes, and there

- Don't simply rely on a city map to get to your destination, unless that map indicates one-way streets and is no more than a year old. Otherwise, you are likely to find that the nearest path to your goal is blocked by a melange of one-way streets nefariously planned to keep you driving around in bizarre, infuriating patterns. If your map isn't up to the task, ask a local who knows street patterns, or confine yourself to larger, two-way streets.
- Many German residential areas have restrictive parking procedures, with 'residents only' sticker parking on one or both sides of the street. Be sure when you park on smaller streets that an unobtrusive sign (unfortunately, only in German) doesn't restrict parking or you may return from your business to find a nasty surprise waiting on your windscreen.
- In many German cities, some larger streets have a special *Bus Spur* (bus lane) reserved for buses and taxis. These lanes are *verboten* for private autos except when making right turns, and then only right before the turn. If you're zipping along down a nearly empty lane while rows of cars on your left are locked in a jam, there is very possibly a good reason for this.

are strict regulations for motorised bikes, but bike riders are wont to stray from their specially designated paths. Indeed, many two-wheeled travellers prove to be fearless daredevils when in heavy traffic.

City Driving

Most German downtown streets are clogged with rows of cars and choked by their dense exhaust during the day, neither of which lets up much until later in the evening. One recent study indicated that German motorists spend an average of 65 hours a year staring at either red lights or the gridlocked car in front of them. Some thoroughfares, such as Berlin's famed Kurfürstendamm, are packed until around midnight.

The Autobahn

The near legendary German Autobahn is the Taj Mahal, the Mecca, the Mount Everest, the El Dorado of the world's motorists. Every foreign driver has heard of it, been warned about it, been urged to dare it, and then suddenly, there you are—rolling along on the world's most famous highway. You may get your kicks on Route 66, but that Autobahn offers a transcendental motoring experience.

Foreigners hitting this world-renowned net of motorway usually have one of two reactions. For one group, there is an exhilarated joy as they race along, discovering in the boundless speed and freedom what they sense is the ultimate reason the automobile was invented. For the second group, there is a sense of horror and a desperate realisation that German motorists cannot drive to save their lives, but only to endanger those of everyone else on the road.

The Autobahn, begun by the Nazis in the 1930s as a massive public works project, now stretches almost 12,000 km (7,456.5 miles), spreading a glorious concrete cobweb over the whole country, east and west. The West German government was always rather generous with highway funds, so the Autobahns in the west and from there to Berlin are in rather good repair; those in the east have

A typical holiday period traffic jam on the Autobahn.

improved considerably, though amateur race drivers may still find a few rough patches in this part of the country.

But let's get to the enticing element here: most of the Autobahn has no speed limit; your velocity is limited only by the laws of aerodynamics and the capacity of your car. Speeds of 160–200 kmph (96–120 mph) are not unusual here, and certain super-models leave those slowpokes in the dust.

The Limits of Unlimited

Safety experts and environmentalists (feral speeding reputedly contributes to *Waldsterben,* the progressive extinction of Germany's famed forests) have pleaded for years for some overall limits, but politicians have up till now steadfastly resisted such pleas, fearing that imposing an overall Autobahn speed limit would be akin to restricting the consumption of beer to Wednesdays.

Nevertheless, a few concessions have been made. Certain select stretches of the Autobahn now bear posted speed limits, and the government 'recommends' that drivers keep their speed to an average of 130 kmph (78 mph). This recommendation is generally taken as an in-joke between German drivers and their leaders. However, particularly adverse weather conditions lead to impositions of temporary limits, which can go as low as 60 kmph (35 mph).

Autobahn Etiquette

While most of the Autobahn is free of speed limits, there are clear rules, regulations, and even a kind of etiquette, though this is pretty much the etiquette one finds in the more predatory parts of the jungle.

The left lanes are for passing only and passing on the right is *strengstens verboten*! (That is as forbidding as it sounds.) Now, it's not unknown that while you're zooming along in the left lane trying to overtake one or more vehicles, another car will suddenly zoom up behind you and let you know that you are taking too long overtaking.

By the way, flashing of headlights and beeping of horns to get someone out of the left lane is illegal. Don't pick up these habits just because they are daily routine for thousands of other drivers. If the police catch you doing it, none of those other flashing, beeping heroes will pull over to console you.

Braking the Fun

All of the above only applies under ideal conditions. At other times, long stretches of the Autobahn more closely resemble gargantuan parking lots. This happens especially at the beginning and end of holiday periods and, as Chapter 7: Enjoying Germany (*Refer to* 'Public Holidays' *on pages 198–204*) reveals, Germany has a good many of these. Delays of several hours on the most popular southern routes have become common at certain holiday times.

Large parts of the Autobahn still have only two lanes, and these can easily become clogged. Such cases can bring Autobahn traffic to a crawl—and very quickly so. Great danger can result when cars must suddenly go from 180–200 kmph (111.8–124.3 mph) to a creep in 10 seconds or less.

In fact, one traffic expert, Professor D. Uwe Loos of the VDI Society for Motor Vehicles and Traffic Technology, has calculated the average speed on the Autobahn in congested areas as 20 kmph (12.4 mph)—yes, that's the average!

There is a lesson here. Germany has a dreadfully high level of traffic fatality and many Autobahn crashes are large pile-up collisions. When television news reports on major road accidents, they frequently cite the cause as speeds too high for prevailing weather conditions. It's sadly clear that many drivers ignore posted emergency speed limits, and a test spin on most German highways during wet, slippery, or foggy conditions will quickly confirm this first-hand.

If weather, stress or tremendous holiday crowds give you any cause to reconsider travelling on the Autobahn, don't hesitate to lock up the car and transfer to that excellent train system. Or try to book one of those special low-price flights, usually in a package with hotel and assorted extras.

Remember, getting around in Germany, one way or another, is one of the very best things about the country.

FOOD AND ENTERTAINING

'Martin Luther convulsed Germany—but Francis Drake
calmed it down again. He gave us the potato.'
—Heinrich Heine

TRADITIONAL GERMAN FARE

The blunt, practical side of the German personality comes out unmistakably in traditional German food. It is a cuisine for a people who work hard, yet have a limited range of foodstuffs, frequently face an inhospitable climate, and are tight with their time. In other words, standard German fare consists of hearty foods prepared somewhat simply and prosaically. A typical German meal makes up in stuffing capacity what it lacks in sophistication. As one old joke had it, the only trouble with German food is that, a few days after eating it, you're hungry again.

CARNIVORES GALORE

Most Germans are dedicated meat-eaters. How dedicated? In the mid-to-late 1980s, when health concerns led many people to cut down on their meat intake, Germany was the only Western nation going in the opposite direction.

When German meat-eaters tuck into their favourite fare, they often like to have it in huge, generous chunks, such as *Schweinshaxe* or *Kalbshaxe* (shank of pork or veal). One major strain of German food culture, *gutbürgerliche Küche* (good bourgeois cuisine) features this stock plate arrangement: a sprawling slab of meat flanked by a modest portion of potatoes, noodles or dumplings and an even more modest serving of vegetable or salad. The ascendancy of *die gutbürgerliche Küche* (you'll see many restaurants in Germany proudly carrying this designation on their signs) was a phenomenon of the 1950s when, after long years of deprivation, during which time meat was a scarce commodity, it became available again and the people consumed it with a vengeance.

TRIGG.

The pig is the totem animal of the German kitchen. Not only is it relatively easy to raise, it provides needed nutrients and calories in large blocks at single servings. More interestingly, culinary historians report that going back centuries, Germans generally found pork to be the tastiest of all meats.

And as the old saying goes, German cooks make use of every part of the pig except its squeal. And they do a darn good job of it too. You have probably never seen as many different cuts or preparations of pork as you will in Germany. Plus, the price of pork is relatively low, vis-a-vis other meats.

Other popular meats include beef, chicken and turkey. Lamb has become more widespread of late, largely due to the growing Muslim population in Germany, though it is still more of an exotic diversion than a regular feature on German tables or menus. Duck is another bit of exotica, though it is a common feature in many Asian restaurants here. Goose still holds a special place of honour in the palates of some Germans, but then only as a ceremonial meal. The two big days for a traditional goose dinner are 11 November (St Martin's Day) and the big Christmas meal. But traditions can fade and most Germans I have known have switched to turkey or ham for Christmas and ignore St Martin's Day entirely.

Schnitzel

Probably the two most famous and widespread words out of the German kitchen, other than *sauerkraut*, are *schnitzel* and *wurst*. *Schnitzel* basically refers to the cut of meat, and this is more or less your standard cutlet.

As with the cutlet, the *schnitzel* is a thin slice of meat. In Germany, veal, chicken and turkey are all offered in schnitzel form but the most popular German *schnitzels* are—you guessed it—pork. Those of you familiar with *Wiener schnitzel* in its veal incarnation should be aware that here in Central Europe, your *Wiener schnitzel* will usually be of the pork persuasion.

Of Cutlets, Chops, Schnitzel and Kotelett

A quick culinary language note: *Schnitzel* is a direct translation of the English word 'cutlet', but there is a German word *Kotelett*, which is the English 'chop'. Sound confusing? Well, it does confuse many people, and English-speakers often err when they first come here, ordering what they think is a cutlet and getting a thick chop. Even more frequently, Germans will recommend something to you as a cutlet, using the obvious, but here incorrect, translation.

The *Wiener schnitzel* is a distinctive cutlet that gets pounded exceedingly thin, thus also stretching out its length in the process. In fact, in its hometown of Vienna (*Wien* in German, thus the name of the *schnitzel*), it is considered a travesty if the *schnitzel* doesn't lop over the side of the plate. This thinned cut is then fully breaded and pan-fried.

Types of Schnitzel

Other favoured *schnitzel* preparations are:

- *Holsteiner* (breaded and served with a fried egg and lemon wedge on top)
- *Jäger* (in a dark, mushroom sauce)
- *Zigeuner* (in a spicy sauce with tomatoes, bell peppers, and paprika)
- *Rahmschnitzel* (in a simple cream sauce)

Almost all German restaurants will offer at least a few of these schnitzels and at *gutbürgerliche* places, a full range is close to obligatory.

Wurst

Wurst is the German word for sausage. In parts of North America and Britain, *wurst* is used specifically to designate German sausages. Originally just a poor people's food because of its composition, the *wurst* has risen from its humble background to take a place of deep, enduring affection amongst the German public. Even though most Germans today can afford to pass up *wursts*, large segments of the population regularly tuck into these sausages with gusto.

The basics of wurst are minced raw meat (pork, beef, veal, chicken, rabbit or horse), combined with seasonings and, in rare cases, extenders such as cereal, then cooked in various ways. As the mincing process makes the meat largely unidentifiable in the final product, parts of the animal that would normally not be eaten in any other context get tossed into the production of the wurst. In fact, standard wursts are made with those parts of meat that would otherwise be thrown to undiscriminating animals.

The traditional casings of *wurst* were made from beef, pork or sheep intestines that had been first carefully cleaned and preserved in brine or salt. The modern age has introduced synthetic casings formed of plastic or hydrocellulose in some cases. Not all of the synthetic casings are edible and many have to be peeled off before consuming the sausage.

Wurst Case Scenario
Charles DeGaulle's famous quip about the difficulty of uniting and running a country that has 275 varieties of cheese makes one wonder how he would have felt if confronted with running a country like Germany, which has 1,500 different types of *wursts*.

The Germans actually distinguish between two forms of the *wurst*—the thicker ones that get sliced into cold cuts and eaten on plates or open-faced bread or rolls and the thinner ones, called *Würstchen*, or little sausages (*chen* being the standard German diminutive), which are consumed all at once. The *Würstchen* are probably what most of us think of when we hear the word *wurst* or sausage.

Many *wurst* and *Würstchen* types bear the names of the area where they were first produced, and the huge variations in spicing and composition of the minced goodies result in an appropriately wide range in terms of taste. German *wurst* cognoscenti argue that the most flavourful common *wursts* are the *Thüringer* (originally from Thuriginia) and the finger-sized *Nürnberger*, which hail from Nuremberg. The *Frankfurter*, my town's entry in the *wurst* sweepstakes and the direct ancestor of the American hot dog, is frequently judged over here to be one of the less exciting German sausages (though it is still fairly popular).

When they take it as a full meal, Germans like to eat their *Würstchen* with *sauerkraut* and potatoes or cold potato salad. Alternatively, they can be munched as a quick snack at a *Schnellimbiss* (*see* 'Der Schnellimbiss' *later in this chapter on pages 187–188*).

VEGETABLES

Traditionally, the Germans were culinary first cousins of the British—admittedly, a bit more inventive, a tad more resourceful and a lot more adventurous. This can be seen in the way both nations treat meat, or in the way they mistreated vegetables. As Germany's climate was not always that hospitable to things coming out of the ground, much of its native produce consisted of hearty vegetables that could withstand a good bout of winter.

Cabbage

The German word for cabbage is *Kraut*, so you can probably guess what a central role that particular vegetable played amongst the Kr... err, Germans. (Though it was never as bad as amongst the English, of whom Walter Page said, "They only have three vegetables, and two of them are cabbage.".) But cabbage got to be so ubiquitous in Germany that they even came up with a second word for it, *Kohl*, and this root appears in the names of many other vegetables whose heartiness grants them a long pedigree in the German kitchen: *Rotkohl* or Rotkraut (red cabbage), *Rosenkohl* (Brussel sprouts), *Blumenkohl* (cauliflower), *Grünkohl* (kale), *Kopfkohl, Sauerkohl, Weisskohl* and *Kohlrabi*.

The traditional German way of preparing vegetables was to boil and boil them until sure they could no longer attack you. (Well, attack you from inside, as many Germans insisted.) German tastes have now largely shifted in the direction of maintaining flavour and nutrients, so even the traditional German produce is today often served somewhat close to natural savour and structure, though the soggy, insipid versions still turn up all too often. The hard-line *gutbürgerliche* restaurants tend to favour this method of abuse, so watch out.

Potatoes

As Heine's quote at the beginning of this chapter suggests, the vegetable that appears most often on the German table is the humble potato (*Kartoffel*). Like most people in Europe, the Germans had to wait until the 16th century for the potato, but they took to it very quickly, no doubt partially aided by the praise lavished upon it by Prussia's redoubtable King Frederick the Great.

Germans take their potatoes in a variety of ways, though the most prevalent ways are boiled (*Salzkartoffeln*), pan-fried (*Bratkartoffeln*), mashed (*Püree*), or sliced into scrawny strips in the French manner and fried (the name also lifted from the French, *Pommes Frites*). Similar to the latter is a potato preparation with a much longer pedigree in Germany—potato pancakes (*Kartoffelpuffer*). These are strips of minced potato pounded into thin cakes, mixed with onion, and then fried. Germans like to serve them with apple-sauce (*Apfelmuss*), often in large servings as a meal unto itself. They are also a popular fixture at fairs and carnivals; the *Weihnachtsmarkt* (*see* 'Der Weihnachtsmarkt', *in* Chapter 7: Enjoying Germany *on page 211–213*) would be unthinkable without a few stands plying potato pancakes.

Potatoes are traditionally more associated with the north and south-east. The south-west favoured noodles, and you'll still find a preponderance of noodles served in the Swabian kitchen of the region. The flat noodles are standard, but a quite popular variation of this number is the Swabian *Spätzle*, which literally means 'little sparrows'. These are tightly whorled, bitey noodles that often accompany meat and fish down in the south-west. But they are also often served as the main event, a meal in itself, either with lentils or spiked with onions and covered with cheese. Vegetarians finding themselves in a traditional Swabian restaurant or café can skirt the parade of meat by ordering one of these tasty dishes.

A second, extremely popular German alternative to the steadfast potato is the formidable dumpling (*Kloss*, or *Klösse* in plural). These are large scoops of flour bound with such items as ground potatoes or bread, seasoned, formed into large balls, and then steeped in boiling water. As German dumplings are undeniably heavy items, you should order them only when you're packing a hearty appetite.

REGIONAL DISHES

In addition to some of the favourites listed above, there are a large number of regional dishes that merit trying at least once. Out of the literally thousands of local dishes or local variations, I have put together a short list comprising popular numbers that are readily available in their home regions, at least in season. Some of them have, in fact, become so popular that they are now regularly obtainable in most parts of the country.

- *Eisbein*
  Literally means 'ice-leg'. This Berlin favourite is actually a huge chunk of pickled shank of pork. It is almost always served with *sauerkraut* and *Erbsenpüree*, a mash of yellow peas.
- *Finkenwerder Scholle*
  Those of you who know the humble plaice only from fish 'n' chip shops will gain a new respect for the fish when you've had this Hamburg area treatment, which is a simple but masterful pan-frying with bacon bits. Usually served with an acidic potato salad along with green salad.
- *Gaisburger Marsch*
  A Württemberger stew composed of cubed brisket of beef, potato slices, *spätzle*, fried onion rings and sometimes a few other vegetables.
- *Grüne Sosse*
  A *Frankfurter* speciality, this is basically what its German name says it is—a green sauce, made of various herbs (every version is different, but regulars include chives, sorrel, parsley, sweet basil, chervil, cress, dill, estragon, and lovage), as well as cream. Sometimes, chopped boiled eggs are added, but more often the sauce is served over full boiled eggs and/or boiled potatoes. Meat eaters prefer it over boiled beef. At home, we discovered it goes extremely well with poultry *schnitzel* and various green vegetables. Generally available only in spring, summer and very early autumn. The winter version is not so tasty, as the herbs used are frozen.
- *Grünkohl* (or *Braunkohl*) *mit Pinkel*
  A most fitting specialty for those harsh Bremen winters, this dish is steamed kale with bits of bacon, pork belly and *Pinkelwurst*, a very fatty sausage. (You should always remain blissfully ignorant about what exactly goes into your *wurst*, but on this one, the butcher was apparently told, "Use your brain and show a lot of grit!") Many companies and clubs in the Bremen area will do weekend

outings in winter where restaurants specialising in this delight serve up heaping portions, after which, much *schnaps* (the German spelling drops a 'p') is gulped to cut the fat a little.

- *Kassler Rippchen*
  Originally from Berlin, this smoked pork chop is now available and beloved throughout Germany. Invariably served with *sauerkraut* and mashed potatoes.

- *Königsberger Klops*
  These are tasty meatballs, originally from East Prussia, which have spread throughout Germany since the disappearance of that province. They consist of ground beef, ground pork and ground salt herring, along with onion and stale roll crumbs. They are always served with a thick flour sauce enlivened by lemon juice and capers.

- *Labskaus*
  This one is a simple classic from Germany's northern port areas (i.e. Bremen, Hamburg, Lübeck, etc.) and though it started as a hearty fisherman's breakfast, most non-fishing folk take it as one of the day's main meals. A unique hash of puréed salt beef brisket, herring fillet, red beets, potatoes and salt pickles, it is obligatory to serve the *Labskaus* with a fried egg on top and a pickled herring on the side.

- *Leberkäse*
  This is a Bavarian speciality that has infiltrated the darkest corners of many a Prussian kitchen. Though the name means 'liver cheese', it is neither a cheese nor a liver product, but a steamed loaf of minced pork. It must always be partially baked so that it gets a crunchy crust. It is traditionally enjoyed with a strong mustard and *sauerkraut*.

- *Leipziger Allerlei*
  This bright mix of vegetables such as carrots, peas, cauliflower, green beans and morel mushrooms fried in butter, chicken broth and cream has spread from its Leipzig hometown to gain favour throughout Germany. It is either taken as a light meal unto itself or as the vitamin-rich accompaniment to a meat portion.

- *Maultaschen*
  This is a kind of Swabian ravioli, filled with minced veal, lean smoked bacon, minced pork and parsley, spiced with nutmeg, then served in a beef bouillon. They are sometimes offered *gesmeltzt*, which means cold slices of finger-sized *Maultaschen* strips fried in butter and topped with lightly beaten egg. The *geschmelzt* edition is usually accompanied by browned onion rings and Swabian potato salad. (Swabia, by the way, is in Germany's south-west, with Stuttgart at its heart.)

- *Rheinischer Sauerbraten*
  Sauerbraten is one of Germany's most famous dishes, and countless Germans tout this Rhineland version as the tops. Here, beef slices are marinated in a sweet-sour mix comprising redcurrant jam, cream, onions, grated *Lebkuchen* (*see* 'Sugar and Spice and Everything Nice', *in this chapter on page 179–180*), raisins, corinthians and red wine, then slowly braised. If it's served to you without red cabbage, someone is pulling a fast one on you. The second plate partner could be boiled potatoes, though dumplings are more common.

- *Weisswürste*
  These celebrated Bavarian white *wursts* are actually an unappetising off-white to pale grey in colour. Still, these boiled veal and herb sausages are eaten with ardour down south. They are actually supposed to be taken before noon, to assure absolute freshness. You're also supposed to order an odd number (they are definitely small enough to fit in more than one) and enjoy them with a Bavarian sweet mustard.

- *Rote Grütze*
  We jump out of alphabetical order for this one, as it is a fitting finish to the list, being a unique northern German dessert. It is essentially a cooked fruit pudding, the ingredients of which include various red fruits such as cherries, strawberries, raspberries and redcurrants as well as sago or tapioca. (Thus, *Grütze*, which means groats or grits.) After the fruits, juice and sago have been cooked together, the pudding is cooled and topped with either fluid cream or vanilla pudding.

This tasty, refreshing dessert is widely available in the towns of the far north, such as Hamburg and Bremen. Although the fruit is freshest and the dish thus tastes best in summer, *Rote Grütze* has grown so popular that it's now available year round in some places, thanks to the grace of freezing the fruits.

BAKED GOODS

Forget the tired propaganda about French pastries or Italian breads and cakes—German-speakers are the indisputable world masters of baked goods. If it's made of dough and comes from an oven, it generally comes best from a German, Austrian or Swiss oven. Fortunately, there has been a great deal of cross-fertilisation between these three baking powers, ensuring that almost all the baked treasures of each country are available in the other two.

German breads are wonderful and range from the light, almost white to the black. They are rarely puffed up with air to a cottony texture, so eating these breads and rolls is a sensual experience for your mouth and jaw as well as for your palate.

You should always buy your bread here directly from a bakery, and there is at least one in every German neighbourhood. Experiment with different types until you find your favourites. You will also probably discover that certain breads go better with certain foods, so you'll want to switch around every so often, depending on what you eat with it. If you come here and fall into the old habit of just popping into a supermarket to pick up a puffy loaf of white toast bread, you should be expelled from the country!

Sugar and Spice and Everything Nice

The selection of German cakes and pies is every bit as bountiful as that of rolls and breads, so I'll leave it to you to find your favourites. But I would be remiss in my duties here if I didn't point out that the Christmas season is a very special time for German bakers, who then turn out specialties only associated with this season. Again, the range of choices is nigh on exhilarating, but there are two you definitely must try in your first German autumn or winter: *Lebkuchen*, the richly spiced and splendidly composed German gingerbread, which usually starts appearing in stores or special *Lebkuchen* shops around early October; and *Stollen*, the German fruit cake, which begins turning up a little closer to Christmas itself.

Incidentally, German certification regulations distinguish between two types of oven master. A *Konditorei* can only make cakes, cookies, candies and pies while a *Bäckerei* is only certified to bake breads, rolls and the like. Many shops will carry the designation *Bäckerei-Konditorei*, indicating that the master baker is certified to turn out all manner of baked goods. But if you stroll into a *Konditorei* and ask for a pretzel or a loaf of bread, you'll walk out disappointed.

THE STRUCTURE OF GERMAN MEALS
While German eating habits have undergone a slight transformation over the last 50 years, they still retain a certain uniquely German flavour. For instance, rather than the standard three squares a day, the Germans have two other meals that they manage to squeeze into the programme.

The Formidable German Breakfasts
The day starts in Germany much as it does in most countries, with breakfast (or *Frühstück*, as it's called here). Standard features include bread and/or rolls, often lathered with butter, then topped with cheese, slices of cold meat or wurst and perhaps an egg. If the latter is included, it's more likely to be boiled (*gekochtes Ei*) or scrambled (*Rühreier*) rather than fried eggs (*Spiegeleier*) or an omelette.

Lighter treatments feature the standard rolls or bread topped with jam, honey or Nutella, an acquired-taste spread of rich chocolate and nuts, which is very popular amongst children. Inconceivably to many non-Germans, Nutella is also a favourite with many adults here. Rising health and diet concerns in recent decades have supplanted or supplemented some of this with muesli or fruit. This is all usually washed down with a few cups of coffee or tea (hot chocolate for the kids), with fruit juices often doing service as well.

It all sounds rather filling, and it is. But believe it or not, for many Germans it's not enough, and they slap another meal in between this one and lunch—*zweites Frühstück*, or second breakfast. If you are trying to keep the old figure in trim, you'll be happy to hear that this one is fully optional and, besides, it is only a fraction of the first breakfast. To provide the stomach with some ballast for the coffee or tea that is quaffed mid-morning, many Germans will down yet another roll with cheese or cold meat, perhaps a piece of cake, or maybe just a pretzel. In offices, this meal is often consumed right at the desks, or at a common Cafeteria, which in German simply means 'coffee room'.

Lunch

The *zweites Frühstück* manages to tide most Germans over until around noon or a little later. Traditionally, *das Mittagessen*, or midday meal, was the biggest German repast of the day. Children arrived home from school, fathers scooted home from the office or factory, and the whole family sat down together to a meal that probably commenced with a soup, proceeded on to the bountiful main course, then ended in dessert. Dessert would be a pudding, ice cream, perhaps fruit or a fruit salad, though never cake. That delight was being saved for its own special meal.

The Evening Meal

In the old scheme of things, the evening meal—*Abendessen* or *Abendbrot*—was noticeably smaller and lighter than the midday meal. The second of those German terms literally means 'evening bread', and bread indeed played a major role in the meal, alongside cheese, cold meats or wursts, perhaps with salad and assorted condiments. Germans believed, and many still do, that it wasn't all that healthy or waist-conscious to polish off a big meal in the evening and not allow the body enough time to digest and burn off the calories. True, as Germans generally eat their evening meal around 7:30 pm or 8:00 pm and trundle off to bed not too much later, there is less burning-off time than in some other cultures. Plus, keep in mind just how substantial those traditional German meals can get.

The Eating Wertewandel

The modern age has slowly been nudging German eating habits in the direction of British and American noshing, with a smaller lunch at midday and the main meal coming

Eating meals outside is not traditionally German but the sidewalk café is gaining popularity.

in the evening. The reasons for this are obvious: more and more people are out working and simply don't have the time to fix a big dinner around noon. Nor can workers usually make it home and back again to the office or factory on a shortened lunch-break.

Most company canteens still offer the traditional three-course meal for a reduced price, which many employees avail themselves of. Nonetheless, in recent years, I and many others have noticed that more and more white-collar workers waive the belly-busters for a salad plate, a *wurst* or two and maybe a sandwich. And more gets accomplished in the first two hours of the afternoon session—not coincidentally, we can surmise.

Though the modern business world has forced this change in German feeding practices, many Germans revert back to their old ways on weekends, especially on Sundays. That is why if you receive a Sunday invitation, it will probably be for the big midday repast, or for the following big Sunday meal, *der Kaffee*.

Der Kaffee

One early Sunday evening about a year after I had settled in Germany, I asked a young woman if she would like to join me for dinner, and she replied she wasn't at all hungry since she had just had *Kaffee*. I at first took this as a lame excuse for not going out until she explained to me that, in Germany, the term *Kaffee* often refers to a uniquely German meal served in the late afternoon. Somewhat akin to the British high tea, this affair is not only a delectable, hearty repast filling that gap between lunch and dinner, but also a measure of one's hospitality and sense of the finer things in life.

As the name suggests, a focus of the *Kaffee* is coffee, which

Herculean Coffee

A word about German coffee, a glory of the Teutonic kitchen: Germans demand a strong, full-flavoured brew in their cups. They moan that it's extremely difficult to find decent coffee in much of the world and virtually impossible in Britain or the United States. German coffee is ordinarily ground from a mix of beans to achieve that full, rich taste the Germans covet. The German roasting process also contributes to the strength of the local brew. If you are enamoured of the weaker concoction, be ready for a jolt of flavour and potency when you sip the German version is served in a pot and offered up in as many cups as the guests like. Recently, tea has appeared for non-coffee drinkers, and fruit juices or other soft drinks are usually provided for children. But unlike the British high tea with its dainty sandwiches, the main event here is cake and usually not just cake in the singular. It is commonly considered bad form to confine your guests to a single choice in this area, so expect to see two and sometimes three or four kinds of cakes at *Kaffee*.

EATING RITUALS

As befits a cuisine with such a humble background, there are few rituals attached to German meals. The few that still obtain are quite simple and easy to master quickly, which you should do to make the right impression with your German hosts. The most important of these is to wish *Guten Appetit* (good appetite). This is said at the beginning of every midday and evening meal, though not at the breakfasts or at *Kaffee*, and is intoned just after the first dish of the meal has been served to everyone and you are all about to start. It is in some sense the starting signal. It doesn't matter who says this first, but everyone at the table should repeat it—to not do so is considered antisocial.

A vaguely observed rule of etiquette that applies for large gatherings is that everyone waits for the hostess to unfold her napkin before they do likewise. Napkins, by the way, should sit in your lap during the meal, being brought up to your mouth as you need its services there. And at the end of a meal, the cloth napkin should be folded again (not balled up) and placed on the table.

Restaurant Protocol

Whether you are dining in a foreign or typically German restaurant, there are varying codes of conduct that one should be aware of. The sway of one code or the other depends more on the level of restaurant than its ethnic line.

One curious feature of many German restaurants and cafés is the practice of table sharing. This is especially curious amongst a people like the Germans, who otherwise strive to keep strangers at a safe distance. If you go into any café, or any but the more elegant restaurants and there are no free tables but free seats at other tables, you can sit down after asking, "*Ist hier noch frei?*" (Is this seat free?) Unless the person or persons at the table are waiting for someone else, they will probably nod, allowing you to join them.

You should do the same if you find yourself in the situation of occupying a table with free seats. One exception: I and many other people now ask if the new arrivals are smokers; if so, I explain that I react negatively to smoke. If they can make if through the meal without lighting up, they sit down. Otherwise, they go to look for another semi-occupied table. Even in Germany, this has become acceptable of late.

This sharing arrangement would seem to be an excellent way of making new acquaintances, except that it rarely works out that way. The Germans are so skilled at compartmentalising that they can sit at the same table, a few feet away from someone, and virtually ignore the person. Almost no words will be exchanged between strangers at a table, except for the obligatory *Guten Appetit* and a *Wiedersehen* when you or the other people leave. If you don't offer these wishes, you'll be considered rude or strange. But any attempt to strike up a further conversation will frequently be given a curt chop and the looks on the other faces alone will often tell you that no conversation is desired. Don't try to prove how friendly you are by forcing one, as this will usually go down rather badly.

Foreign Cuisines

The comment of one errant gourmet here that "German brass band music is the perfect accompaniment to German food" may be a trifle harsh, but many foreigners, even those fond of the cuisine's stolid charms, find they don't want to make a daily habit of it. But you don't really have to, as there are many delicious alternatives. The wide spectrum of immigration has provided Germany's larger cities with a bounty of foreign restaurants and grocery stores. And even the smallest town in all but the most remote stretches will have at least one Italian, Balkan or Turkish restaurant and sometimes all three.

In the late 1980s, Thai restaurants had become most fashionable in Germany, and it was hard to find a city of any size that didn't boast at least one. Now Germans seem to have returned to their first foreign culinary infatuation, Italian, with Greek not far behind, and Japanese coming up fast on the expensive outside lane. With younger people, Indian is very 'in' (as the Germans say) and younger professionals have taken to Mexican in the towns that have this type of restaurant. Chinese food is always a ready alternative for people wanting to go foreign, though sadly much of the Chinese cuisine offered in Germany has relinquished much of its brilliance to accommodate German palates.

Tipping

A dilemma for many Germans and most foreigners over here is the matter of tipping. Theoretically, tipping is not necessary as a service charge is included by law in all restaurant prices. Any waiter or waitress who tells you it isn't is deviously trying to squeeze more money out of you. This frequently happens at big tourist spots, particularly if you are speaking English or some other foreign language. You should duly teach these shysters a good lesson by ignoring the following advice and paying solely what is written on the bill.

Though tipping is strictly optional, it's also expected for any kind of half-decent service. But the protocol on tipping is very, very murky. A rough guide would go something like this:

- anything under 5 euros (the euro has replaced the Deutschemark in Germany since 2002), round it off to the nearest euro
- from 5–20 euros, top it off to the next euro; for truly good service, throw in another 1 or 2 euros
- between 20–50 euros, round it off to the nearest 5 or 10 euros, unless the tip is under 2 euros, at which point you should just add another 1 or 2 euros, but not more than 3 or 4 euros to the bill

- anything in the range of 50 euros to infinity, round it off to the nearest 10 euro plateau (20 euro if you're closer to infinity)

After a while, you'll develop a finer feel for this matter yourself, at which point you can move outside the guidelines suggested here.

Incidentally, in Germany a tip is not left on the table as you leave, but paid directly to the server. When you hand over your money, you should tell her or him the figure you've decided to pay and let the waiter or waitress subtract the total, with tip, from the cash you hand over. If the money you hand over exactly covers the tip and you don't expect any change, just say, "*Das stimmt so.*" Also, because of the murky rules and the practice of tip-sharing and such, many people paying with credit cards will still give the tip separately in cash, to ensure their server gets it.

Der Schnellimbiss

One reason that American fast food chains such as McDonalds, Burger King and Pizza Hut have flourished in Germany is that the country already had a solid fast food tradition in place, one stretching back at least into the pre-

The simple Schnellimbiss can be found on almost every corner in Germany.

war era. Stands and shops slinging a few basic kinds of *wurst*, *Frikadellen* (the native German hamburger, innocent of any bun) and drinks dotted the urban landscape in most German cities. The 1960s ushered in the waves of *Pommes frites* (French fried potatoes), the American style of hamburger, and fried chicken. Today, many of these stands (called *Buden* or *Schnellimbiss* in German) have chosen to ride the high wave of multiculturalism, and added items like *schashlik*, *lumpia* and *falafel* to their palette. But no matter what you choose, you can be pretty sure the food will be low-priced and embody the glory that is grease. The *Schnellimbiss* is the place for a cheap, quick meal; it is no haven for the health-conscious.

A warning to those of you hitting a *Schnellimbiss* for a *wurst*: if you expect your *wurst* to be served in a form-fitting bun, as it is back home, there is a little surprise waiting for you. The Germans are used to eating their *wursts* unbunned. When you order one of these goodies at most stands here, it will be served up on a long paper plate with a glob of mustard and a roundish roll on the side. Standard consumption habits hereabouts are to wrap a napkin around one end of the wurst, dip it into the mustard, then bite in, alternating this with chomps on the roll held in the other hand. For the last bit, you simply unroll the napkin, polish off the nub of the *wurst* and then wipe your greasy fingers with the napkin. (The consummately messy curry *wurst*, a *Schnellimbiss* classic, is eaten in slices, with a toothpick.)

DRINKS
Beer

Beer is not only the most popular drink in Germany, it's virtually recognised as a national treasure. And the more than 5,000 varieties of beer produced by the country's well over 1,200 breweries contribute to the treasure trove. Be assured all those breweries have to keep working hard too, as Germans have for years been amongst the world's champion beer drinkers, constantly holding their own against such determined challengers as the Australians, Belgians, Czechs, Danes, and the Irish. (In

recent years, the Czechs have surpassed the Germans in per capita consumption of brew.)

Now, you yourself may not be a beer drinker—yet. Your author very rarely touched the stuff until he arrived in Germany. Now I am a dedicated though, I hope, discerning fan of the brew. Drinking beer with friends, colleagues, customers and relatives is a basic social lubricant in Germany, perhaps even more so than sharing coffee. As someone once remarked to an un-beerable person at our table, "If you don't drink beer, what are you doing in Germany?"

The practice of drinking beer in Germany can be a pure delight; rather literally too, as Germany has a strict regulation for its breweries, called the German Purity Law (Deutsches Reinheitsgebot). This regulation, first established by a Bavarian duke in 1516, stipulates that beer can only be made from four ingredients—hops, barley or wheat malt, yeast and water. Not only does limiting the make-up of beer to these elements protect the purity of the beer's taste, it is presumably the added items that pad the paunch, cause headaches and sundry distempers of a most nasty sort.

For close to five centuries, you weren't even allowed to sell beer that deviated from these purity standards in Germany. But then, in the benighted 1980s, beer producers from other EC countries argued that such restrictions represented unfair trade barriers and thus violated European Community (now Union) regulations. Now it is legal to sell impure brew from other European Union lands here, though you almost never see them anywhere; after all, with more than 5,000 first-rate unsullied beers to choose from, why would anyone try anything else? (For the record, foreign beers that do conform to the Reinheitsgebot, such as the Czech original Budweiser and Pilsner Urquell or the Danish Tuborg and Carlsberg, have been ringing up impressive sales in Germany for quite some time.)

While there are thousands of individual beers here, they are not spread over the many different types that one sees in countries like Belgium. In fact, basically there are 20 types of beer in Germany. The most widely quaffed and most popular is *Pilsner* or *Pils*, a golden-coloured, light but full-flavoured beer that closely resembles the British lager. The *Pils'* milder sibling is the *Export*, whose taste is quite similar to, but more subdued than, the bitter *Pils*.

The next most common German beer is the *Alt*, a darker beer originally associated mainly with the Rhineland area, but now pretty much spread throughout the country. Its flavour is a bit more fruity and throaty than either the *Pils* or the *Export*.

A local rendition of the *Alt* is Cologne's *Kölsch*, served in its customary thin, narrow glass. Golden-hued *Kölsch* approximates the *Alt* flavour, though it is weaker in both taste and alcohol (3.7 per cent for the latter). *Kölsch* devotees claim that it's a more social libation since you can drink more of it without getting tired or drunk.

No similar claim can be made for the Bavarian *Weizen* beer. *Weizen* is German for wheat, and the addition of this grain to the usual barley malt is the main reason for this brew's distinctive taste. It comes in two varieties—the yeast-based version which has a cloudy golden colour, and the yeast-free (or *Krystal*) *Weizen* with its clear golden hues. The basic *Weizen* is stronger in both taste and alcoholic content than the standard *Pils*.

These represent the most common kinds of German beers, though there are others worth noting. Some of these are seasonal, such as the *Maibock*, a dark, very malty beer offered mainly in May although bottled versions are sold throughout the year. The *Weihnachtsbock* is similar to the potent *Maibock*, but only available at Christmas time. Others can be had all year round, though not all around the country. These include *Rauchbier* (smoked beer), *Berliner Weisse* (an acidic beer sweetened with either raspberry syrup or essence of woodruff and served in its characteristically wide-mouthed glass) and *Malzbier* (a sweet, minimal alcohol 'near-beer' often given to children or pregnant women).

As beer is such a popular drink in Germany, the major German breweries also turn out a line of reduced alcohol or non-alcoholic beers. The taste of these brews ranges from a weakened version of the *Export* to tap water that has picked up a few whiffs of real beer while in storage. At the high end of this taste register is *Clausthaler*, by far Germany's best selling alcohol-free beer and worldwide market leader in this field. If you are a group's designated driver and don't want to pass up the social graces of beer, you'll just have to go through the various non-alcoholic brews until you find one that suits you.

Important note: There is really no such thing as non-alcoholic beer on the market, as even those products with that designation have a very low alcohol content, usually under 1 per cent. Normal drinkers should have no worries about quaffing this product in large measures, as you would

Can I Have Some Food with my Beer?

If most people eat in order to live, while the French live in order to eat, one could argue that the Germans eat in order to have something to drink their beer with. But they hardly need the excuse of food to drink the stuff. In fact, many Germans refer to beer, only half-jokingly, as *flüssiges Brot* (liquid bread).

probably die of a burst bladder before you ever got drunk on the stuff.

However, it can be dangerous for recovering alcoholics, just as candy with alcohol fillings is. Just one bottle of this 'safe' brew can tip you off the wagon and back into old, bad ways.

Wine

Despite the preponderance of beer, the Germans, being good Europeans, also drink a good deal of wine. Some of it even comes from Germany! While few would rank Germany as one of the world's truly great wine producers, the country does produce some extremely fine whites. The most highly regarded wine areas are the Rheingau, the Nahe and the Mosel-Saar-Ruwer regions. The best wines from these areas are the majestic Rieslings, the Grauburgunders (the German version of Pinot Gris) and the Weissburgunders (Germany's answer to Pinot Blanc). Baden in the south-west (which also, as a rule, enjoys Germany's warmest climate) and the Franken region of Bavaria produce a number of good, popular wines, with the Müller-Thurgau varieties being the most prevalent.

If you're in a wine shop or supermarket buying wines (oh yes—German supermarkets are permitted to sell all kinds of alcoholic beverages) and you want to go native, the labels on German wines help those unfamiliar with the products by putting coloured seals on the bottle: yellow seals indicate dry wines, green seals semi-dry, while red seals denote sweet wines.

In the main, the best German wines are whites. In recent years, German producers have started turning out some admirable reds, though most Germans themselves turn to other European countries (or even California, Australia and Chile) when they want to go red. But even if you, too, are a red wine enthusiast, you needn't worry, as almost every wine outlet in the country offers a flurry of good wines from European neighbours such as France, Italy, Spain and Greece. And all these wines tend to be surprisingly cheap to anyone who is used to buying them outside of Europe (or under the crush of British sin-taxes).

In addition, Germany offers a most pleasant surprise for champagne lovers: Germany has its own domestic variation, called Sekt. (In Germany, as in most European countries, the name *champagne* can only be legally applied to the bubbly produced in the Champagne region of France.) The taste of Sekt compares favourably with standard French champagnes, although it bears a much lower price tag: full bottles of good Sekt cost about a third of a middling champagne's tariff. And all the major brands also put out pony bottles of their product for when you don't want to over-celebrate.

(A sad closing note for those of you who have grown fond of Blue Nun, probably the widest-selling German wine. "That white wine which is correct with everything" is not really available in Germany. As Germans are not particularly taken with this fruity *Liebfraumilch*, it's produced exclusively for export.)

Schnaps and Prost

A fitting footnote to this discussion of German alcoholic drinks is the *schnaps*, which is basically a strong spirit of various extractions. It is a footnote because *schnaps* is always drunk, if at all, at the end of a meal or the end of a pub visit.

Germans have two toasts when they raise their glasses: *zum Wohl* and *Prost*! (the more plebeian but also more common of the two). One of these is always offered when the drink is alcoholic, and almost never for non-alcoholic refreshments. The toast should always be offered at the first drink when everyone has received his or her glass. There is no protocol as to who should first prompt the toast, but once it has been prompted, everyone must reply in turn. Not to return a toast, or to commence drinking without offering one, is considered most antisocial.

Water, Water Everywhere

Of course, there are many people who don't care to drink alcohol with meals and certainly not between meals. So what are your alternatives over here? Well, not to change your habits, but Germans do find it extremely peculiar for adults to accompany serious meals with milk or soda. The abstemious here prefer water. But note well—when they say

water in a drinking context over here, they mean mineral water. Germans have a mild aversion to tap water, but they are virtually addicted to mineral waters, whose number of varieties seems to rival that of German beers. If you are in a restaurant and ask for plain old tap water (*Leitungswasser*), you are liable to get either funny looks or a short lecture on how unhealthy tap water is. (The first time I committed this faux pas, my lecture came from a waitress who kept darting back to her station to sneak drags from a cigarette).

The Germans' reservations about tap water are not without grounds. Most German water contains unappealing levels of calcium deposits. But no one in history has ever dropped dead of calcium deposit overdose. Much more to the point, mineral water does contain many healthy elements that the splash from the tap can't remotely match.

Unfortunately, after you've decided to adjust to German ways and start quaffing mineral water seriously, you'll again be subjected to what the Germans call *die Qual der Wahl* (the torture of choosing). There are easily hundreds of mineral waters on the German market. But all of these individual brands can be divided into two main categories: *Sprudel* (fizzy or carbonated) or *Stilles* (quiet or non-carbonated). The problem really lies in the fact that there are huge differences within each grouping. Because of the presence of different minerals and trace elements in the different waters, the variations in taste can be significant. Some are quite salty, others rather metallic in taste. And even among the *Stilles* group, some waters are more still than others.

Another jolting adjustment that some people moving to Germany will have to make is that water, juices and other soft drinks are rarely served with ice here. This doesn't mean they are served up warm, but many Germans find iced or excessively chilled drinks undrinkably frigid, as well as numbing to the palate. If you like ice cubes in your drink, you'll just have to ask for them and hope that the bar or restaurant keeps an emergency stock of ice. Or you could just order a cold beer—also served without ice, of course.

ENJOYING GERMANY

CHAPTER 7

'Idleness is the beginning of all vice.'
—Old German proverb

'Today I'm going to do exactly what I want to do—nothing.'
—Contemporary German advertising slogan

As you will discover in Chapter 9, those poor work-obsessed Germans actually put in fewer hours on the job than any people in the industrial or post-industrial world. So how do they manage that? And what do they do when they're not working? Read on. You're liable to like what you read.

GERMAN VACATION TIME

Upon arriving in the United States for holiday several years back, my wife was asked by an inquisitive passport control officer if she harboured any secret desires to settle in America. "What?" she replied incredulously, "And have to get by with only two weeks vacation every year?" Her short anxiety attack there was not at all atypical of her compatriots; one of the workers' rights Germans prize most highly is their vaunted six-weeks holiday or vacation time.

Actually, as stated in the standard work contract, every German worker is entitled to 30 days of holiday, to be broken up or taken in one lump as they prefer. What they often prefer is to set their holidays strategically so as to maximise the amount of consecutive free days they can get with it.

This is done by scheduling holidays around as many weekends as possible, or trying to wedge a legal holiday or two into the vacation block. For that reason, the months of May and June—when a string of legal holidays usually occur —are the most popular vacation times for Germans.

School Holidays

In scheduling your vacation, you have a clear advantage if you're not the parent of school-age children, as most parents are virtually forced to arrange vacations to coincide with official school holidays. If you are free to slot your vacations into other time periods, you have a much improved chance of getting exactly what you want.

To prevent the Autobahn and other major roads from becoming mere camping grounds during longer school holidays, the different German states try to stagger these holidays and thus allow some road relief, as well as continued functioning of the economy and social services. This means that your family may not be able to travel with friends living just across the state line, but it does give you less competition for the roads and preferred family vacation areas.

Public Holidays

In addition to the 30 days of paid vacation, Germany also features a number of fully paid legal holidays scattered strategically throughout the year. These holidays can be as many as 15 or as few as 12, depending on where you live: if you like these one-day breathers, it's better to live in a predominantly Catholic state, and the more predominantly Catholic the state, the more holidays it serves up. Here is a quick list of Germany's legal holidays:

- **Neujahr (New Year's Day)**
  1 January
  This day is mainly spent recovering from the long night before. Some people still uphold the old German tradition of eating either carp or pork with *sauerkraut* on this day.
- **Heilige Drei Könige (Feast of the Epiphany)**
  6 January
  This one is a legal holiday only in Baden-Württemberg and Bavaria. It celebrates the visit of the three kings to the Christ child.
- **Karfreitag (Good Friday)**
  A moveable feast, it can take place any time between mid-March and mid-April. It commemorates the death

by crucifixion of Jesus Christ. A number of solemn church services are held during the day.

- **Ostersonntag und Ostermontag (Easter Sunday & Monday)**
  The same as above, as Easter is always two days after Good Friday. It celebrates what Christians believe was Christ's resurrection from the dead. These days, it equally celebrates the triumphs of the German candy industry, as baskets full of candies and chocolate eggs are presented, mainly—though not exclusively—to children. Also popular are painted hard-boiled eggs. Easter egg hunts or egg runs are still held in a few areas, though they have become extremely rare.

- **Tag der Arbeit (Labour Day or May Day)**
  1 May
  Large parades culminating in uplifting or defiant speeches in praise of working people characterise this day. More and more, the evening before sees dances and parties (*Tanz in den Mai*) sponsored by groups with various social or political agendas.

- **Christi Himmelfahrt (Ascension Thursday)**
  Moveable feast celebrating the ascension of Christ into heaven, it falls 40 days after Easter, and thus is held between the middle of May and beginning of June. This day is also always Father's Day in Germany, which is generally not a family holiday. Father's Day German-style means fathers go out together and engage in a lot of male-bonding and fraternal drinking.

- **Pfingstsonntag und Montag (Whitsun or Pentecost)**
  Moveable feast. Celebrates the Holy Spirit descending on Christ's apostles with the gift of tongues. Always occurs in late May or early June, about ten days before the next holiday.

- **Fronleichnam (Corpus Christi)**
  Moveable feast. Celebrated in all the Catholic or quasi-Catholic states (i.e. the West's southern states and the Rhineland area). The highlights of this holiday are open-air masses followed by processions carrying the Eucharist through the streets—especially big in smaller towns and villages.

- **Maria Himmelfahrt (Feast of the Assumption)**
  15 August
  Celebrating the ascension to heaven of Mary, the Blessed Mother of Christ, it is a legal holiday only in the Saarland and parts of Bavaria.
- **Tag der Deutschen Einheit (Day of German Unity)**
  3 October
  This holiday celebrates that day in 1990 when the two German states again became one country. (It replaces the June 17 holiday, which you may still find listed in some older books.)
- **Reformationstag (Reformation Day)**
  31 October
  Celebrating Martin Luther's Reformation movement, it is a legal holiday only in the five new states, i.e. the former East German areas.
- **Allerheiligen (All Saint's Day)**
  1 November
  A Roman Catholic celebration of all saints recognised or non-recognised, it is a legal holiday in the predominantly Catholic states, as well as the heavily Catholic areas of Thuringia.
- **Buss-und-Bettag (Penace Day)**
  A moveable feast that always falls in mid-November, this Protestant holiday is now officially observed only in the state of Saxony. As the English name suggests, this is a day for atonement and penance for one's sins. This was a holiday throughout Germany until 1995, when it was dropped as official holiday everywhere except Saxony.
- **1 und 2 Weihnachtstag (1st and 2nd Christmas Day)**
  25 and 26 December
  In addition, many offices only work half a day, or not at all, on December 24. Stores also close earlier on that day. It's very important during the last week or so before the big day to wish everyone you greet (including shop salespeople) *Frohe Weihnachten* (Merry Christmas). This is expected even if you are not a Christian and to flout this rule is considered quite unfriendly. From the 26th until the 31st, you switch your ubiquitous greeting to

Guten Rutsch ins Neue Jahr, which literally means, 'Good slide into the New Year!'

- **Sylvester (New Year's Eve)**
31 December
This is generally celebrated by going to parties or a favourite restaurant. Many restaurants offer special meals and entertainment programs on this evening. At midnight, fireworks are set off in the streets, while children twirl sparklers and flares about. The fireworks often last the better part of an hour, after which people return to what they were doing before midnight, or somehow find their way home.

In addition to this full slate of legal holidays, there are a number of days and celebrations that you cannot ignore if you care to experience Germany fully. In fact, the practice of these days is much more important than some of the holidays listed above.

- **Nikolaus**
6 December
This is St Nicholas' Day, the day when little bags of candies are given to all children and most adults. If you want to maintain a good spirit in your office, be sure to give at least a couple of goodies to all the colleagues you work closest with. Bosses are expected to present bags of candies or a *Nikolaus* (a chocolate statue of the saint) to all their employees or subordinates.

- **Fasching or Karneval**
Fasching is often called Germany's fifth season. Its roots were pagan, when the ancient German tribes invoked its rituals to drive out the bad spirits of winter. After Germany's conversion, a thin Christian veneer was spread over this, to celebrate the last days of joy and merrymaking before Lent. A cursory look at the present-day celebration will convince you that the festival has remained truer to its pagan roots than its Christian calling.

Fasching begins officially on 11 November. (To be specific, the eleventh hour of the eleventh day of the eleventh month, but don't expect much on that day, which is also St Martin's Day and mainly features a lot of people eating roast goose and red cabbage.) Fasching really begins to pick up steam in February or early March, about a week or two before Lent starts, and peaks on the Monday and Tuesday before Ash Wednesday.

Fasching is also dubbed *die Tollen Tage* (the Crazy Days), and that pretty well catches the tone of the festivities. The German equivalent of Rio's Carnivale or Mardi Gras, Fasching sees people painting up their faces in strange ways or going whole hog and running around with wild costumes or disguises. Pubs and other drinking establishments do their best business of the year, as throngs of *Narren* (fools) stream in to celebrate what was once the end of all celebrating for 40 days. Organised clubs of musicians and other performers present the shows they have been rehearsing all year long. These musical and dance shows are interspersed with emcees or comics who tell terrible jokes spiked with even more terrible puns. And all of this fun is lubricated by drinking, drinking and more drinking. After which, they have one or two for the road.

Fasching, as one wag put it, is that time when the Germans try as hard as they can not to act German. This is the period when perfect strangers, usually protected by big rubber noses and fright wigs, will talk to you ebulliently on streetcars and underground trains; when other strangers, equally perfect, will hug you on the street or in a *Kneipe*, maybe even kiss you if they have had enough encouragement, liquid or otherwise.

Such carryings-on start to occur on the third weekend before the final stretch, pick up in frequency and intensity on the following two weekends and then reach lift-off stage the final two days. There are three key days in Fasching, and they each deserve a mention of their own.

- **Weiber Fasnacht**
  This celebration always falls on the Thursday before the last weekend of Karneval and comes from the darkest days of male chauvinism. It was supposedly that day when everything was reversed so that women were the bosses and called all the shots. As the balance

of power has shifted a little in recent years, the one remnant of this custom that you men should be aware of is that on this day, women are allowed to cut in half the ties of any man they see. In many offices, pubs and restaurants, this practice still goes on. So this is the day to wear that ghastly tie you were given as a present last Christmas.

- **Rosenmontag (Roses Monday)**
  This is usually the day for the big Karneval parades (though some cities hold them the day before). Hundreds of floats and marching battalions stream through the main thoroughfares, accompanied by loud music and wild screaming. Not a few of the spectators watching from the sidewalks are costumed as extravagantly as those in the parade. After the parades, people head off their separate ways, many of them to the big Karneval balls or their favourite pubs.

- **Fastnacht or Fasnacht (Night of Fasting)**
  This is probably the most misnamed day of the year, as it extends the whole day and not just after dark, plus the only fasting to be seen is when people pause from putting food or drink in their mouths long enough to laugh or shout '*Helau!*' (the standard Fasching battle cry). In many areas, it is the highest peak of the season and mainly involves the activities mentioned in the previous sentence. Like both Weiber Fasnacht and Rosenmontag, it is an unofficial holiday and all offices and shops are closed at least from midday on.

Now that we've gotten you all excited about Fasching, you should know that you won't find this level of celebration throughout the country. Since it was a Catholic festivity, the dour puritans of the Reformation decided to stamp out this diabolical remnant of Papist paganism. As you move into the predominantly Protestant areas of the north and the east, the festivities become rather muted or even non-existent. I once spent the last week of Karneval in Hamburg, and you wouldn't have known anything was happening. And except for colourful bunting in some restaurants and pubs, the same was true for

Berlin— though the average Berlin weekend resembles Karneval in most other cities anyway.

Karneval is celebrated most devoutly in the Rhineland area and Bavaria; the cities with the largest and wildest activities are Cologne, Mainz, Munich and Dusseldorf. If you want to see Fasching at its richest and fullest, you should be in one of those cities during the last days. But no matter where you are, all celebrating comes to an abrupt halt at midnight on Ash Wednesday, when all pubs and restaurants have to close by law and custom. (Until early the next day, that is.)

LEISURE ACTIVITIES

One might wonder what the Germans manage to do with so much leisure time. (The average German adult is estimated to have 2,500 hours of free time each year to fill.) The simple answer: they take ample advantage of it—and with typical German thoroughness.

Time on Their Hands

On average, adults in Germany have almost 2,500 hours of free time. They work on average 36.7 hours per week and have at their disposal three to four hours of leisure time per day as well as ten hours per day at the weekend and on public holidays. Annual leave is up to six weeks. Differences between the former West and East Germany are gradually being eliminated. For some time now, German households have spent between 10–15 per cent of their disposable income on free time. In total, Germans spend around 225 billion euros every year on free time activities.

Following the trimmed workday, they frequently rush home to tend to their flats or their houses. Those Germans with houses spend a great deal of time taking care of the abodes, doing renovations, puttering around in the garden and related activities.

A typical *Kleingärten* in the middle of the densely populated Schöneberg section of Berlin.

Kleingärten

For those who don't have their own house or garden, there is a uniquely German institution—the Kleingärten or Schrebergärten. These are a series of small, enclosed plots in a large common garden area, usually within or just at the edge of a city. The plots are usually rented by people who travel there from their homes and tend to the flowers, fruits or vegetables they grow there. They often have little sheds built on them, where furniture and tools are stored. They are especially popular as a weekend refuge from urban grime and grind.

Be a German and See the World

Perhaps understandably with all those longer paid holidays, the Germans love to travel. For a good many years now, Germany has led the world in foreign travel. And the further the better. It is not at all unusual here to encounter average workers who have visited Asia, North and South America, Africa or Australia. One advantage of this for us *ausländische Mitbürger* is that Germans, upon hearing where we come from, will often launch into recollections of their trips to our country. It is a good way to meet new people here, or to solidify relationships.

Vereine

Germans have a great many ways to fill the leisure time within their own borders too, and they often do so with zeal. A particularly German institution is the *Verein*, or club. Germans seem driven to organise themselves into these officially registered clubs for any number of activities—or just to search for activities.

Most of the clubs are legal entities, and as such have their own club constitution and by-laws. Membership dues are usually minimal and few people will be scared off by these costs. In addition, many clubs allow non-members to participate in a specific event, sometimes even on a regular basis, with the payment of a modest fee for each participation.

Sports are a common pursuit of many *Vereiners*, and for many people at the amateur level, *ein Verein* is the only possibility—or affordable possibility—to take part in sports activities. The clubs have their own facilities, or use of community facilities, as well as basic equipment. Uniforms and other accessories are usually the responsibility of the members themselves.

But sports are not the only activity organised into the *Verein* structure, and amongst the some 300,000 officially registered *Vereine* in Germany are clubs engaged in such pursuits as amateur theatre, card-playing, conversing in English or some other foreign language, promotion of ethnic cultures, discussion of political or cultural affairs, shooting of guns, stamp collecting and trading, breeding dogs and so on. In other words, if you're a joiner, you are sure to find some *Verein* to suit your needs.

A Passion for Sports

As is true of most advanced nations, more people in Germany are fascinated by sports than actively participate in them. Armchair experts are legion hereabouts, with the airwaves

Players from around the world star in the Bundesliga, Germany's premier football league.

full of sports shows, sports reports, and live broadcasts of sporting events. Indeed, two cable television channels devote themselves exclusively to the glorification of athletics, in various pedigrees.

As befits the nation that has appeared in more World Cup football finals than any other, and taken that coveted cup three times (only the legendary Brazilian team has claimed more World Cup titles), Germany's greatest sports passions are poured into football (soccer). World Cup appearances by the national team turn many German villages and whole sections of larger cities into virtual ghost towns. The eerie silence pervading these areas gets shattered periodically by buildings rocking with cheers or shuddering with a collective moan; solitary pedestrians know then that the German team has scored, or suffered some painful setback.

A milder form of World Cup fever spreads during important matches in the premier professional league (the Bundesliga) or when the German side takes the field in the European Cup. The streets are a bit more populated at these times, but pubs and clubs without television sets see noticeable drops in custom on evenings with big games.

A Cornucopia of Sports

But if soccer is not your cup of tea, you certainly won't be left out in the cold sports-wise in Germany. The country has become a passionate pack of tennis watchers, especially since the ascendancy of such domestically bred world stars as Steffi Graf, Boris Becker, Anke Huber and Michael Stich. Golf has also become fairly popular, thanks partly to local hero Bernard Langer, though it still lags behind such hot numbers as basketball—both the local product and, particularly, the real stuff from the NBA—skiing and ice-skating.

American-style football has become very 'in' of late, with NFL exhibition games drawing sell-out crowds in larger cities. Germany has become the centre of the marginally big-league National Football League—Europe with teams in Berlin, Cologne, Dusseldorf, Hamburg and Frankfurt. In fact, there's only one non-German team (Amsterdam) now left in a league that once stretched from all the way from Scotland to northern Spain. Meanwhile, delayed broadcasts of NFL and American college games are offered on the two sports cable channels, and football junkies needn't worry about Super Bowl withdrawal agonies—the 'Big One' is broadcast live on a pay-television network, and one of the ordinary sports channels presents highlights a few days after the event.

But if your particular tastes in sports flow a bit out of the mainstream, don't despair. A sampling of recent offerings by the cable sports channels as well as the publicly-funded networks turned up presentations of bowling, surfing, handball, volleyball, wrestling and boxing, billiards, car and motorcycle racing, horse riding, weightlifting, rock and roll and ballroom dancing championships, martial arts titles, aerobics, the European electronic darts championship and even American Gladiator contests. Slower paced sports such as baseball and cricket which depend on a cultural knowledge of their rituals and psychological components haven't caught on in Germany. But with these few exceptions, if you are a sports addict, Germany can offer you a large number of fixes.

Sports enjoy a social value over and above their own virtues. Discussing sports is a good way to quickly integrate yourself into German society, or at least into some parts of German society. Your colleagues in the office or the factory will often warm up to you faster if you display a working knowledge of the major sports events of the day. (*For a quick introduction to these events and personalities, see* Chapter 10: Fast Facts *on pages 277–288.*)

THE KNEIPEN CULTURE

As an indispensable antidote to indulgence in organised sport or other strenuous physical activity, the Germans have achieved a highly developed pub culture, where various alcoholic libations can loosen the tongue, warm the heart, and soothe a troubled mind. Sports are not necessarily excluded here, and many a key game has been endlessly replayed here, with all the advantages of distance.

Pub-popping is a favourite activity across all levels of German society, and can be a good way to meet new people or solidify relations already begun. Representatives of various nationalities make their way to their favourite pubs (called *Kneipen* in German) regularly.

The Serious Business of Drinking

Our small theatre company often had trouble drawing an audience, and when we asked members of the company why their friends and colleagues didn't turn up, we were told they preferred going out drinking —and we mainly performed in a pub!

But you should set out on your search for the perfect pub with this warning: the democratic mixing that characterises pubs in many other countries is more the exception than the rule here, where the old German principle of compartmentalisation holds sway. Most German *Kneipen* have their own specific clientele, and outsiders are not especially welcome. Thus, you are apt to see neighbourhood pubs where only established neighbour status counts; pubs for certain national groups; yuppie pubs; student pubs; and perhaps the most exclusionary of all, *Szene* pubs, where only members of the local 'In-scene' are appreciated. (Sorry, I forgot the neo-Nazi pubs, which are easily the most exclusionary of all, but no one reading this book should stroll anywhere near these places.)

You will quickly recognise that you have wandered into one of these establishments, and you shouldn't expect much camaraderie here, unless you are accompanied by a member of the accepted group. Still, there are a good many pubs where strangers are accorded a warm welcome and brought into conversation quickly. I have generally found this to be true of pubs in working-class areas, or the more down-market *Kneipen*. But then again, you should not dress up when coming to these places, or you will be snubbed rather ostentatiously. The more upmarket places tend to be less receptive no matter how one is dressed. And in 'ethnic' pubs, you are effectively boxed out of the conversation unless you speak the language in charge.

STRASSENFESTE

Another favourite way for Germans to amuse themselves is the *Strassenfest* (street or block party). These are pleasant events organised and sponsored by local governments and businesses. Though these celebrations differ greatly in size and sprawl, they more typically spread over several streets, sometimes a mile or so along river banks (such as Frankfurt's famed *Mainuferfest*). These fests feature stands hawking various kinds of food and drink, games, and public relations or informational services. The larger *Strassenfeste* also feature amusements for the kids, and everything is accompanied by lively bursts of live and/or recorded music.

Most of the thousands of *Strassenfeste* around the country take place in the summer months when organisers can take advantage of the nice weather and thus ensure the best turnout. A special type of *Strassenfest* that occurs a little later in the year, as the first harvests start coming in, are the various *Weinfeste*. These fests take place primarily in small towns and villages in the German wine-growing areas. The music, good cheer and food here are similar to the *Strassenfest*, though as the name suggests, most of the stands at a *Weinfest* offer the latest products of the wine crop, with many vintners maintaining their own stands.

Oktoberfest

Germany's most famous *Weinfest* isn't really a Weinfest at all, but a *Bierfest*. We're referring, of course, to Munich's world renowned Oktoberfest. Not only is the Oktoberfest the largest of all these events, sprawling over several acres of a fairground at the edge of town, but it is also the longest, running for two weeks—most of that time actually not in October, but in September.

The Oktoberfest offers rows and rows of stands selling their wares. But the key feature is the huge tents where the major local breweries set up makeshift beer halls. The suds flow ceaselessly for most of the fortnight, served up in the huge litre glasses typical of Bavaria, and is quaffed by the tens of thousands of visitors who sit at long tables and benches and try to keep their conversation a few decibels

A slow night in one of the beer tents thrown up for the world-famous Oktoberfest in Munich.

above the Bavarian bands that fill the tents with their deep barrelled music.

The mood can be like Fasching, with perfect strangers suddenly becoming intimate in a way totally out of character for German society. Yet I know many people, Germans and foreigners, who were quite disappointed by the Oktoberfest, finding it too big, too noisy and too commercialised. Others love the event and travel there every year. Your chances of having a good time are certainly optimised if you like drinking plenty of beer and know German fairly well—especially the Bavarian variant. (Though visitors come from all over the world for this one, and you are sure to run into countless English-speakers too.)

Der Weihnachtsmarkt

One of the most impressive and lively mutants of the *Strassenfest* is *Weihnachtsmarkt* or *Christkindelmarkt* (Christmas market). Actually, the *Weihnachtsmarkt* pre-dates the *Strassenfest* fashion by several centuries. Originally, they were markets set up in major towns to allow craftspeople to sell their wares before Christmas.

This origin is preserved in today's *Weihnachtsmarkt*, where one finds numerous small stands offering a vast array of small and large craft items. Fittingly enough, the *Weihnachtsmarkt* is where you will find the best selections of and best buys on Christmas decorations. (And remember that Germans started the Christmas tree tradition). But there are also stands selling pottery, woodcrafts and hand-crafted jewellery. In addition, there are frequently rows of stalls selling various other wintry articles at sharply reduced prices. Over the years, I bought a few lovely cashmere scarves at the *Weihnachtsmarkt* that would have cost me almost twice as much in a department or clothing store.

Weihnachtsmärkte are usually found in a large central square, a wide pedestrian zone, or sometimes just along a few small streets. The largest and most famous are to be found in Nuremberg, Rothenburg ob der Tauber (*see* Chapter 2: Overview of Land and History *on page 12*) and Munich. They usually open in late November, running for about four

Germany's largest and most famous *Weihnachtsmarkt* (Christmas Market) in Nuremberg.

weeks. But plan your visits carefully! *Weihnachtsmärkte* usually close down a few days before Christmas, so if you run over to your local *Weihnachtsmarkt* on the 23rd or 24th with some last minute shopping in mind, you're liable to end up with just an unpleasant surprise.

THE MEDIA

Germans have no shortage of opportunities to keep themselves informed and entertained, especially if you can read as well as ingest visual images: there are over 10,000 daily, weekly or monthly newspapers and magazines in Germany, including the many trade and specialised journals. Most of these publications are, of course, in German, though German-based publications in Turkish, Italian, Polish and Serbo-Croatian also fill many news-stands, providing reports from the homeland or stories on the life of that particular ethnic community in Germany.

Likewise, there is a gaggle of English-language publications sold in most parts of Germany. Probably the best known and most accessible is the Paris-based *International Herald Tribune*. In fact, Germany is the Tribune's second largest market, with a circulation of over 30,000. The venerable 'Trib' is now printed in Frankfurt, making it available at news-stands in all major German cities from early in the morning, or even for timely home delivery. It plies readers with a stout mix of American news and hard and soft coverage of the rest of the world.

Most of the larger British newspapers, such as *The Times*, *The Guardian* and the *Daily Telegraph* are available on a regular basis, as are magazines like *The Economist* and European editions of *Time* and *Newsweek*. American institutions such as the *Wall Street Journal* and *USA Today* have also begun gracing German news-stands regularly. As you can see, you will have no problem keeping yourself informed of what's transpiring in the English-speaking world.

The German Press

Of course, none of these publications will keep you as well informed about Germany as the German journals, and if your

German is good enough, you should try dipping into some of these occasionally. Germany's biggest newspaper by far is the *Bild Zeitung*, with a daily circulation of over four million. The *Bild* is also the easiest to read (these two facts may not be entirely unrelated) and is for that reason often preferred by foreigners whose German is still a bit shaky. *Bild* is German for 'picture' which already tells you a lot about this paper. Large photos, sometimes of scantily clad or unclad women, augment the columns of shrill prose that present any story in its simplest black and white tones. The *Bild* may be a cut above Britain's notorious *Sun* newspaper, but no one has ever accused it of being a respected journal.

That accolade has, however, been accorded to Germany's second-largest newspaper (with roughly one-tenth the circulation of the *Bild*)—*Die Zeit*, a rigorous Hamburg weekly. The next largest newspapers are the highly respected *Frankfurt Allgemeine Zeitung* (commonly clipped to FAZ); the *Berliner Zeitung*, similar to the *Bild*; the *Süddeutsche Zeitung* of Munich; Hamburg's *Die Welt*; the *Frankfurter Rundschau*; and the *Handelsblatt* out of Dusseldorf, Germany's most popular exclusively business and financial sheet.

> One curious phenomenon of the German print media landscape is the lack of any serious Sunday newspaper culture. While there is no complete absence of Sunday papers (the FAZ, *Bild* and *Die Welt* all put out thin, paltry Sunday editions), that great British or North American tradition of hefty Sunday papers just doesn't exist here. In Germany, Sundays are for other things, such as families and overeating.

Amongst the deluge of glossy German news magazines, the best are the formidable *Der Spiegel*, *Der Stern* and *Focus*, a relative newcomer modelled on *Newsweek*. Many of the others serve up a curious mix of informative articles, nude photos, tantalising recipes, challenging sexual positions, helpful household tips and ads for everything from male potency pills to quick, question-free loans.

The Almighty Tube

While not as ubiquitous or incessant as in America, television has expanded greatly in Germany within the last 20 years, due to the growth of cable and satellite channels and the competition they present to the publicly funded stations. If you are cabled (or satellite-dished), you can currently receive about 35 channels and media moguls are still expecting that number to increase significantly in the near future. (On the other hand, one high profile cable venture of the late 1980s folded in the early 1990s and at least one other company has been struggling mightily to survive almost from its inception.) The major cable station here, RTL, also happens to be Europe's largest TV programmer.

Not too long ago, television in Germany began cranking up in mid-morning, and the airwaves all went dark after 1:00 am or 2:00 am. Now all-night programming bumps into breakfast-television shows, and even the most persistent insomniacs have a modest choice of shows through the roll of wee hours.

Public Broadcasting

The solid pillars of the German television system are still the government-funded stations. These include the two large national networks (ARD and ZDF), as well as a group of so-called third channels. The third channels are connected to a particular state, such as Bavaria, Hesse, or North Rhine-Westphalia. The smaller states combine their resources to form regional third channels, such as Southwest Television, North German Television and Central German Television. These third channels have traditionally been known for their more challenging programming, though of late even these stations have bent their principles a bit to squeeze in broadly popular shows.

The ratio of public to private stations is reversed when one turns from television to radio, but one thing holds for both media—all owners of television sets or radios are required to pay a small annual users fee, which fund the public stations. As soon as you purchase either a television or home radio, you are required to go to any bank or post office and pick up a GEZ (*Gebühreneinzugszentrale*) registration form. After you fill out this form, the GEZ will withdraw the fees from your bank account. (At present, the monthly fees are 5.52 euros for radio, 17.03 euros for TV, 17.03 euros for both.) This registration can now also be done online through the GEZ website.

While this again seems to work on the honour system, don't think you can just skip the registration and enjoy absolutely free entertainment. The GEZ folks have trucks driving around with electronic devices that detect the number of television sets or radios in a building. If they discover yours and it hasn't been registered, you can find yourself with a little fine tacked on to your monthly fee.

Cable Television

The Telekom is also responsible for cabling, and you must pay them an additional monthly fee if you are cabled. Those living in single homes must go to the Telekom office themselves to arrange this service; residents of a building with more than one housing unit are dependent upon the will of the other residents, or the landlord. Here the landlord or landlady has to apply for the cabling, and pass along the monthly fee. If you do live in a multi-family building, you can't go your own way on this matter. If you are the only one who wants cable, you won't get it. But this is something you shouldn't worry about as most Germans are rather enamoured of cable television.

Watching television is a great way to learn the language. (That was the excuse I always tossed out when I would get caught watching some stupid TV show.) But those who are cabled also have a number of opportunities to view English-language programming. Currently available on German cable are the ubiquitous CNN, NBC Super Channel, and the European edition of MTV, from Britain.

The other German channels are much like the airwaves in most of the world—a steady glut of Hollywood films and American television shows. Although the vast majority are dubbed into German, some are presented in the original language with German subtitles, and others are broadcast in two-channel sound for those with stereo television sets—by pressing a button you can switch back and forth between the German version and the original.

If your immediate neighbours or your geographical location make getting cabled too difficult, you can always get your home fitted out with a satellite dish. To do so, just look up the companies offering satellite dish services in your area and find the best deal. Actually, satellite television is in many ways preferable to cable, in that dished-out service provides more stations (including some from back home) and can be cheaper if you're planning to stay for two years or more. (As they are still free from monthly charges, satellite reception systems will only cost you the price of purchase for the dish itself and a one-time installation fee.)

Satellite television is one area of life where foreigners in Germany actually hold an advantage over natives. Most residents of rented housing must get permission from the landlord or owner to install a dish and this can be denied on grounds of possible damage to the property or merely that it makes the property unsightly. But a court ruling in the early 1990s declared that foreign residents have a right to satellite dishes so that they can maintain television contact with their homelands.

THE ARTS

With this deluge of television offerings, you might think that people would rarely venture outside their own homes for entertainment and culture, but this is far from the truth. For well over a century, Germans have proudly enjoyed wearing the tag '*ein Kulturvolk*' (a cultural people) that has been hung on them, and they often pack their concert halls, cinemas, museums and theatres.

The Theatre

It is certainly true that many theatrical productions are less than inspiring, or comprehensible, and the prevailing system of subvention clearly plays a major role in this. The *Stadttheater* (municipal theatres) are top heavy in their distribution of government largesse, resulting in a superficially impressive glitz and much stretching room for the artists' imaginations, no matter how excessive.

For example, some of the productions at big theatres suffer greatly from self-indulgence. Go and judge for yourself, but be aware that a big German production of one of the classics of world drama might be quite different from what you had expected. One good thing about these self-indulgent extravaganzas is that you can be visually amused even if you don't catch all the language.

If your German is less than functional, that doesn't necessarily mean that you have to starve yourself of the joys of legitimate theatre while here. English-language productions turn up from time to time in many cities, and even some smaller suburban communities occasionally see *Gastspiele* (guest performances) in English. A number of cities even have more or less ongoing English-language theatre companies. Nevertheless, it is not always that easy to catch theatre performances in the language of Shakespeare and Shaw.

Patron of the Arts

The German government provides more money to the arts, per capita, than just about any government in the world. The result is a flourishing cultural scene in both large and small cities that embraces visual and performing arts of all varieties. While private company sponsorship is still relatively meagre, it does occasionally add to the amount available for productions or exhibitions.

The quantity is certainly there, as the fantastically wide number of offerings in bigger cities such as Berlin, Munich, Hamburg, Stuttgart, Cologne and Frankfurt attest to, and in these places the biggest dilemma for most culture vultures is often what to see and what to skip. But many professional and amateur critics question what quality all that tax money is buying.

Museums

Germans are also dedicated museum-goers. Today, there are over 6,000 museums and the number is growing. (Two hundred new museums opened in the year 2000 alone.) More significantly, attendance at the museums also continues to grow: Germany's museums now draw upwards of 110 million visitors annually. That 6,000 plus number is quite impressive for a medium-sized country and the good news on this front is that the 6,000 are distributed somewhat evenly around the country. While the major cities boast the largest concentration of museums, even many small towns or villages will have a bantam museum housed in a church or town hall.

There are art museums in abundance, but there are also quite a number of historical and ethnological museums, as well as museums of music and musical instruments, wine production, chocolate, toys, optical appliances, and even a bread museum in Ulm. Perhaps the most visited museum in all of Germany is Munich's celebrated Deutsches Museum, a science and technology treasure trove that allows visitors to see the development of many machines and appliances through both originals and models.

Museums in and of themselves are Germany's medieval or early Modern Age churches and cathedrals. Though many of these were severely damaged in the war, almost all have been restored to their former glory—and not a few are glorious indeed. Most remain open for public viewing at certain times. But all of these beautiful churches still function as houses of worship, so kindly observe the signs they hang out during services and refrain from ogling while others are at prayer. Sightseeing during a service is considered exceptionally

ill-mannered and will usually earn you a harsh reprimand, maybe even a request to leave the building.

Cinema

In the last year of the Great War, the German government, realising that it was losing the war on the home front more than on the battlefield, decided that what they really needed was more effective propaganda. They therefore funded and founded a super film studio, the Ufa in Neubabelsberg, a Berlin suburb. A year later, that government was gone, but the lavish film studio it had built was just cranking up to produce its greatest work.

The German cinema was, without a doubt, one of the world's greatest between 1919–1933. Classics like *The Cabinet of Dr. Caligari*, *Metropolis*, *Nosferatu*, *The Last Laugh*, *The Blue Angel*, the *Dr Mabuse* series and *M* are standard fare in any film history course. But the fleshpots of Hollywood began to lure some of Germany's best talent in the late 1920s, and many of the remaining great talents were forced or chose to flee when the Nazis came to power in 1933. The German film has never quite recovered from these two shocks, and the glories of Ufa's Golden Era have remained beyond the grasp of Teutonic filmmakers ever since.

The Nazis were also quite enamoured of film, and the German film industry boasted quite a large output between 1933–1945. But history has judged most of this product to be not worth keeping. Curiously, not too many of these films were heavy with Nazi philosophy; they were more often just a lot of fluff and schlock.

The film industry got rolling again in the late 1940's, but German films of the next two decades fell far short of the quality evidenced in the cinemas of France, Italy, the United States, Britain, Japan or Sweden. It wasn't until the 1970's that excitement again sprang up around German filmmaking, as many people started talking about *Das Neue Deutsche Kino* (the new German cinema). For the first time since the Nazis had seized power, the names of German filmmakers, working in Germany, were being talked about by serious filmgoers in other nations. The names being mentioned were Rainer

Maria Fassbinder, Wim Wenders, Werner Herzog, Volker Schlöndorff and Margarethe von Trotta, Schlöndorff's wife in those days. Some even went so far as to speak of a new Babelsberg and predicted that the German cinema would soon be the world's number one.

Today's talk is more of the deep crisis in German cinema, and from time to time you hear people asking whether the German film is dead. Certainly not, but neither is it in the very best of health. A few German films of the last 25 years have managed to become international hits, such as Wolfgang Peterson's *Das Boot* (*The Boat*), Doris Dörrie's *Männer* (*Men*), Wim Wenders' *Wings of Desire*, Tom Tykwer's *Lola Rennt* (*Run, Lola, Run*) and *Goodbye, Lenin*. But the overwhelmingly vast majority of the local product is confined to limited local consumption and, if very lucky, a limited afterlife on German television.

As is true with many countries, the fare at most German movie houses consists overwhelmingly of Hollywood products: over 80 per cent of the offerings in the commercial houses comes from America. Some of these films are presented in the original with subtitles, but as the German dubbing industry is clearly one of the world's best, most cinema product gets dubbed into the local lingo before being turned loose on audiences.

Cities like Frankfurt, Hamburg, Berlin and Munich now even boast video shops whose offerings are either partially or wholly made up of English-language films. Unfortunately, I haven't yet run across a single middle-sized or smaller town where the English originals in video are offered to the public.

Spoilt for Choice

All the above is, of necessity, only a broad survey. The lesson behind it all is that even with all the leisure time Germany can heap upon you, you would have to work very hard to be bored during your free time. As one of our friends said about the major benefits of living here, in most German cities, you always have a lot to do.

LEARNING THE LANGUAGE

CHAPTER 8

'I speak Spanish to God, Italian to women,
French to diplomats, English to businessmen,
and German to my horse.'
—Attributed to Emperor Karl V

WHEN CANVASSING MY FOREIGN FRIENDS and acquaintances about their experiences in Germany, I often raised the question, "What should one do to get along well in Germany?" I admit I was surprised to find one answer which kept coming back amongst their first suggestions—learn the language!

This advice, in some ways, runs against the grain because for English-language speakers living in Germany, it is all too easy not to learn the language. Easy, but not wise—forget what you read in the guidebooks about every German speaking excellent English. There are millions of German residents who can't navigate one complete sentence in English, and though there are millions more who can function in English, a great many people (including myself) have for years earned a respectable living teaching English to Germans whose command of our tongue was considerably less than excellent.

Still, it is certainly possible to survive in Germany with just English, and I've known more than a few English-speakers who, having lived here for ten or 12 years, have managed to master about one word for every year of their stay. But you remain sadly limited if you know almost no German and you cut yourself off from a certain level of conversation, communication and general participation in the life of this country. You needn't become a virtuoso in the labyrinthine structures of advanced German, but you should learn at least enough to get along in daily intercourse.

GOOD NEWS AND BAD NEWS

Let's start with the good news. As an English-speaker, you have a big head start in learning the local lingo, as the two languages share abundant similarities in their vocabulary. Indeed, as soon as you have grasped a very simple pronunciation shift, you will discover that you have instantly acquired quite a huge store of German words. The 'i-o-n' package is just one good model here and the following examples of similar English and German words will get you started.

- Situation
- Definition
- Manipulation
- Diskussion
- Motivation
- Zivilisation

Following this shift, you just have to stretch a little more to transform some English words into their German equivalent.

Orientation	*Orientierung*
Modernisation	*Modernisierung*
Consolidation	*Konsolidierung*
Stimulation	*Stimulierung.*

In addition, many newer German terms are lifted directly from English.

- Computer
- Service
- Know-how
- Recycling
- Lifestyle
- Team
- Baby
- Business
- Software
- Chips
- Timing
- Singles
- Hobby
- Teamwork
- Manager
- Last but not least

After a few days of rapid language acquisition, you may even think that you will be fluent in German by the end of the week—don't! German is a rather difficult language to learn, especially when it comes to the structure of any but the simplest sentences. (These fall into place pretty much like their English equivalents.) Plus, all German nouns have gender, and the German language doesn't always assign things the same gender that nature did. To top it all off, German has four cases, so the words before those nouns change their form, depending on the function of the noun in that sentence. And by simply using the wrong case, you can change the meaning of the whole sentence.

HOW TO LEARN THE LANGUAGE

That was the bad news, but I hope it convinced you that one must make a serious effort to learn German. Don't think that you will pick the language up off the street like it was second nature; many elements in German are totally unnatural for English speakers. Unless you are satisfied speaking a stumbling, bumbling pidgin German that may even make a worse impression than no German at all, you

A little language can be a useful skill in situations such as this.

have got to approach the task systematically, at least at the beginning. Afterwards, you can expand your knowledge with such painless methods as watching television or listening to radio, or just walking out on the streets, where you will be bombarded by German in both written and spoken forms.

One reliable, systematic approach is to get a good, easy-to-follow book. (A few recommendations can be found at the end of this book.) Books do have their limitations, however—they can't answer questions, nor can they check on your pronunciation. Attending a course or two is the preferred solution.

The Professor

One American university professor we knew was convinced he could learn German with one formidable phrase book supplemented by what he could pick up off the streets. At the end of his stay nine months later, he was still seeking help in translating simple instructions and phrases.

School Daze

There are a great many opportunities to take a German course within Germany. If you are very lucky, you will find a German speaker willing to give you private lessons. Some people even offer these in exchange for English lessons. If not, you can study cheaply at a *Volkshochschule*. The drawback with these adult education schools is that classes always start out with large groups, so you rarely get the individual attention you may need. Moreover, you are confined to the learning ability and speed of the rest of the group. And finally, you are absolutely dependent on the teacher you get. Some are quite good, others quite bad.

My two experiences with the Volkshochschule were mixed. My first course dragged along for several weeks and picked up tempo when the slower members of the class dropped out. However, when the participants had dwindled down to a dedicated few, the teacher himself suddenly disappeared. And we had no recourse with the Volkshochschule, not even getting part of our money back. The second course did make it to the end of the term, but the journey was sometimes a little bumpy.

If you don't want to take these risks with the *Volkshochschule*, you can always go to one of the numerous language schools that are a fixture of German society. The class size is invariably smaller here and you even have the opportunity for individual instruction. The schools will almost always see to it that you get all the lessons you paid for. But perhaps not with the same teacher! As some schools treat their teaching staff poorly, there can be a high level of dissatisfaction, which can result in either a haphazard teaching performance, or the departure of the teacher before the course comes to an end. I've known people who have had three different teachers for one short-term course, and they did not find this at all advantageous. And don't forget that you may pay considerably more money at these private schools than at the *Volkshochschule*.

The Goethe Instituts

Probably the safest way to take a German course is through the Goethe Institut. This is a non-profit organisation authorised and partially funded by the German government to promote German culture and language. Their standards are commendably high, teachers must meet certain criteria and the courses follow an established method that emphasises learning. All in all, the Goethe Instituts enjoy the best reputation for teaching German outside of the regular school system. Unfortunately, they are also usually the most expensive institution. As with so many things, you just have to balance cost against quality in this matter. One acquaintance of mine who went the Goethe Institut route confirmed that the course of instruction was top-notch, but questioned whether it was quite worth the tab.

Accessibility may be another factor in your decision. While just about every German town of any significant size has a *Volkshochschule*, and many of them also have at least one language school, the Goethe Instituts are located in only 16 German cities. On the other hand, if you are thinking about learning some basic German before coming to

Small-group instruction at a Goethe Institut, the most famous school for German-language teaching.

Germany, the Goethe Institut is a worldwide organisation with 126 institutes in 77 countries. Any questions about the Goethe Institut programs in your own country can be addressed to the Central Administration at:

Goethe-Institut Inter Nationes
Dachauer Strasse 122
80637 München (Munich)

NAMES AND TITLES

One part of learning the German language involves the proper use of German names and titles. We have already mentioned in Chapter 4 (*refer to the section* 'Public Selves, Private Selves' *from pages 105–107*) how you should address people in your own immediate environment. Now you are ready to learn how to address people in the larger world.

Herr, Frau & Fräulein

The three basic terms placed before a person's family name are: *Herr* (Mister), *Frau* (Miss, Ms and Mrs) and *Fräulein* (Miss). A female automatically progresses from the *Fräulein* to the *Frau* stage when she reaches the age of about 18. Unlike English, the two terms have nothing to do with marital status. Interestingly, by adding the definite article (*die Frau* and *der Herr*) these terms double for 'the lady' and 'the gentleman'.

Professional Titles

These three terms would do nicely to cover all meetings and greetings, except that Germans have an abiding fascination for further titles. As evidence, you need merely flip through any German telephone book, where many a name is followed by such educational attainments as: *Diplom* (the first college degree) in Engineering, *Diplom* in Business or Economics, *Diplom* in Biology.

None of these achievements is ever appended to a name greeting, but the *Doktor* appellation definitely is. Someone who has earned the doctor's title in any field expects others to acknowledge that fact whenever possible. This means never greeting such a personality with a measly *Frau* or *Herr,* but rather *Frau Doktor* or *Herr Doktor.* In addition, some holders of a position such as professor, director, or *Chefarzt* (head doctor, usually also a professor of medicine) count on being addressed with those titles appended to the *Herr* and *Frau*, certainly when they are performing their official duties.

Nobility

Although the political privileges of Germany's nobility were officially abolished in 1919, there are still quite a few people strutting around with the defunct titles they inherited from their noble forebears. Thus, we today find in our midst the *Prinz* and *Prinzessin* von Thurn und Taxis, the *Herzog* and *Herzogin* (Duke and Duchess) von Somewhere Else and scores of *Graf* this and *Gräfin* that (Count and Countess). The system may be defunct, but if you ever cross paths with one of these august personalities, you should include their titles in your greeting. Not to do so is considered extremely poor form by many people—not least of all by the bearers of these titles.

Twain's Pains

One last word of advice: there is a wonderful little essay by Mark Twain, 'The Awful German Language', that you should try to get your hands on. In describing his own tortured attempts to master German, Twain has sweetened the process for the rest of us with his usual wit. But don't read this piece until you have already made some progress in your own learning curve, or you may take Twain's exaggerations, feigned contortions and comic distortions as straight fact and abandon the whole project before you even get started.

More importantly, after you have penetrated the arcane depths of German a bit, you will be able to enjoy Twain's account that much more, and savour little gems like his direct translation of this German exchange: "Where is the turnip?"—"She is in the kitchen"; and "Where is the beautiful English girl?"—"It has gone to the opera," which Twain submits as proof of the high regard Germans have for turnips, and the low regard they have for beautiful girls.

DOING BUSINESS
IN GERMANY

CHAPTER 9

'Germany is, and will remain, the dynamic engine
of the integrated European economy.'
—Report for the European Union

ALMOST EVERY FOREIGNER I'VE EVER TALKED TO HERE has given one of two reasons why they set up in Germany: (1) because a lover or spouse was living here, or (2) to earn a living in the plush, promising fields of the German economy. I hate to dash your romantic illusions, but members of this latter, more mercenary group clearly make up the bulk of relocated foreigners. The chances are therefore pretty good that you, too, have come to Germany because of its economic promise. If so, then there are some things you ought to know to make sure you get full delivery on that promise.

Chances are also pretty good that you're not actually planning to set up a business of your own here. Those who are aspiring entrepreneurs will be given their just due later in the chapter. But let's start off addressing those of you who've been sent here by your companies or who plan to land a juicy job in the German economy.

A POSITIVE WORK ENVIRONMENT

A major factor behind many decisions to move or stay here is the improved morale the general work environment provides. For example, a number of Asian, European and North American émigrés working here point out that in Germany, no matter what your job is, you earn respect for that job if you do it well. One Briton who worked in a German hotel throughout the 1990s asserted, "Here you're judged on what you do, not on how you speak, where you live, or what your family background is." And most Germans and foreign workers would probably agree: here your accomplishments are recognised and rewarded—often handsomely. In fact, repeated polls indicate that a large majority of 'gainfully employed persons' in Germany are 'at least satisfied' with their jobs.

In the Fitting Into Germany chapter on pages 74–121, we talked about securing your work permit and job-finding assistance. Now let's look at how things actually function in the working world of Germany.

THE WORK ETHIC

Certainly one of the most enduring of all national stereotypes is that of the hard-working German. Almost everyone outside Germany is firmly convinced that this is a nation of workaholics.

Brace yourself for a little shock: Germans, those world-class workaholics, work less—nay, far less—than any other people in the industrial world. Official statistics from the last available year (1998) found German workers putting in only 1,560 hours of work a year, compared to

around 1,889 hours for Japanese workers and 1,996 hours for US Americans.

And the trend may even be downward for hours worked, though more than a decade of government and management finger-wagging shows a few tortured signs of reversing this trend. National leaders can still get themselves in a lather over this subject, as former Chancellor Kohl did some years ago when he warned that the country was in danger of turning into an enormous leisure park. Now that was a good, crunchy sound bite, even if it brought more heat than light to the discussion.

The Working Day

Those 1,560 hours would translate neatly into 195 eight-hour days, except that an eight-hour day is much more the exception than the rule in a country where the average legal work week only runs to 37.5 hours. (Though lawmakers more and more permit certain industries and professions to insist on a draconian 40-hour week or longer.) Nevertheless, people here still work a little over half the days in the year—but on those days, they are generally expected to really work. People coming from more relaxed cultures may be jolted at first to find the other expectations bosses and colleagues place upon them.

For example, the typical work day in Germany starts earlier than in most countries—and ends earlier as well. Don't be too shocked if your company expects you to start the daily grind at the ungodly hour of 7:00 am, though 8:00 am is probably a little more common, and many companies simply split the difference and get rolling at 7:30 am.

At the other end of this early-bird arrangement lies the good news that you'll ordinarily get off at a time many workers around the world would consider the middle of the afternoon. Depending on the length of the lunch break, you may be heading home at around 3:00 pm or 3:30 pm; certainly 4:00 pm is pushing the level of endurance. (This all assumes you're not putting in overtime, a most unpopular but increasingly prevalent phenomenon in today's Germany.)

Do Your Business Early

But within such a system, one person's fortune is another's misfortune: it's rather unlikely that you'll ever reach someone at the office after 4:00 pm, so any important business should be taken care of well before this time. (And don't dare phone or drop in at quarter to four or later! Your partner will most likely be packing up to go—at least mentally—by that point.) Furthermore, this last call should be cut by at least an hour on Fridays, when most workers avail themselves of the opportunity to extend their weekend into most of Friday afternoon.

Service on the Civil Side

I myself have often been frustrated in attempts to reach key people in private companies after 2:00 pm on Friday, and you're floating in pure fantasy if you expect to get any business done at a government agency after noon on that day. You also have to shave an hour or two off the time to do any official government business on the other four workdays. Civil servants (and Germany has armies of them) are often the brunt of jokes because of their limited availability. One favourite appeared in the late 1980s when unions and management were grappling over demands for a 35-hour week. The report was that the civil servants' federation adamantly opposed this suggestion—their members would never stand for having their work week doubled!

THE BASICS OF THE GERMAN ECONOMY

Earlier starting and quitting times are results of custom and preference, but the shorter work week is just one more accomplishment of Germany's mighty unions. Although actual union membership in Germany has dropped in recent years (as it has in most countries around the globe) to just under 30 per cent, the unions here still exercise considerable clout, far exceeding their numbers. (A lot of this clout comes from one big power, IG Metall, which, with some 2.8 million members, is still the single largest labour union in the world.) The unions as a group form one of the cornerstones of the fabled German *Soziale Marktwirtschaft* (social free market system).

Essentially, the *Soziale Marktwirtschaft* (of which you'll hear so much) is little more than the capitalist welfare state that developed in many Western nations following World War II, though the Germans like to view their own model as a fairly unique form. As they see it, this is capitalism with a rigorous social conscience.

The basic principles of this system were embraced by most forces in the economy after the war, when it was apparent that the economy needed the fullest cooperation from all forces in order to get things rolling again and build up the nation. Indeed, the 'economic miracle' that transformed post-war Germany from a devastated, defeated nation that could barely feed, shelter or heat itself into one of the world's most powerful economies was fashioned out of these principles and probably wouldn't have been so miraculous without them.

Social Partners and Their Social Pact
One of the main principles is the hallowed 'social pact' between the major employers and the major unions. Rather than staking out strong adversarial positions that could lead to social unrest and repeated widespread spells of that one great dreaded ogre, Insecurity, labour and management (often tellingly referred to in Germany as the 'social partners') have for decades generally sought compromises and concessions that would lead to long periods of industrial peace. To this laudable end, as many guarantees of industrial peace as possible have been built into the system.

As a result of this general understanding, Germany has become something of a model for workers' rights as well as workers' input. Part of this victory for workers is the shorter work week and the many holidays; on the other side of the bargain, there have been far fewer days lost to strikes than in some more contentious countries. While no system is perfect and Germany has suffered a certain number of disruptive strikes, slow-downs and work stoppages, the whole thing has functioned commendably well over the decades.

Hiring and Firing
Elimination of departments and forced reduction in personnel raises another important matter. Chances are, you've heard

Scene from a 1992 strike by Germany's public-sector employees.

from different sources that it's virtually impossible to fire anyone in Germany. This, however, is just another gross distortion of complex German regulations. The truth is more like this: Germany does have a number of strong regulations regarding dismissal of workers, but they are more involved in braking than in preventing the operations of the hire-and-fire carousel.

Any employee in Germany can be given *eine fristlose Kündigung* (dismissal without notice) for good reason. 'Good reason' in Germany includes things like stealing, repeated lateness, using violence or making threats against employers or fellow workers, or passing on business secrets to a competitor. However, the company works council has to approve the firing, and the employee can still fight the dismissal by appealing to an *Arbeitsgericht* (labour court). There the employer will have to present evidence that the dismissal was justified. If not, the worker is reinstated or receives a generous settlement for wrongful dismissal.

If business is bad, employees can also be let go through an *ordentliche Kündiging* (proper dismissal). These must be given within six weeks of the end of a quarter (i.e. the end of March, June, September or December). They also require approval by the works council and are also subject to labour-court appeals. More importantly, even if they are accepted by the workers or deemed justified by a court, the workers involved are entitled to a statutory settlement.

But there's an easier way to get rid of people within the *ordentlich* catch. At the beginning of any legal employment, there's what is called a *Probezeit* (trial period). This period allows employers to see if they like the new employee and to let the employee see if he or she likes the job. During *die Probezeit*, either side can terminate the employment contract at any time, without reason, if they so choose.

Traditionally, *die Probezeit* ran for three months, as this was considered to provide the best protection to both employers and employees. Recently, however, there has been a pronounced tendency to ratchet up the length of time to six months. This increase is viewed by many as giving hire-and-fire prone employers more breathing space to see if they really want a worker or how much they might need him or her. One computer programmer I know turned down a job offer several years ago largely because he was leery of the six-month *Probezeit* attached to it.

Regardless of whether you have a three- or six-month trial period, it's most important that you make a special effort to show what you can do during that period. Otherwise, you may be back out on the street as quickly as in any traditional hire-and-fire society.

Finally, if someone tries to sell you that musty bill of goods about the impossibility of firing someone in Germany, remember anyone can be fired at any time, as long as the employer is willing to pay the final settlement. (In many cases, they find the payment well worth it.)

German Thoroughness

Even if it does look a tad shopworn these days, Germany's 'social pact' for preserving industrial peace has held for quite a long period—even as the Germans have managed to maintain their reputation for high-quality work. One major reason they have, even under the pinch of shorter working time, is their undamaged tradition of thoroughness. As alluded to above, when Germans work, they usually work

Until recently, sloppiness of work and shoddy performance was quite simply not tolerated in German factories or offices. The famed apprenticeship programme maintained by most big companies trained factory workers, office workers and future management hopefuls alike in the type of work expected at that company—and it was invariably serious, first-class work.

hard. Indeed, more than one objective observer has pegged that appraisal one notch higher and noted that they pursue a level of thoroughness which many would find bordering on over-zealous.

And necessarily so, as almost all German economic calculations since the dawn of the Industrial Revolution have been infused with this fundamental truth: that Germany, being a land with precious few natural resources, has always had to rely primarily on the ingenuity and industriousness of its people—both citizens and foreigners—for only the high quality of their work would allow the nation a high degree of economic success. Since the early 19th century, German industry has primarily proceeded on the basis of importing raw materials from abroad, transforming them through the alchemy of the expertise and polished skills of its workers, then sending them out again at a significantly higher, 'value-added' price.

The tag 'Made in Germany', which by the 1920s had already become an unmistakable sign of quality worldwide despite the country's meagre store of natural resources, could only retain its cachet if that typical German thoroughness in production and administration lost none of its shine.

Regrettably, over the last decade it has indeed lost some of its lustre in certain fields. Yes, the notorious *Wertewandel* has even penetrated traditional German work habits, making that vaunted Teutonic thoroughness not quite as thorough as it once was. These days, even the Germans' fabled drive occasionally gets stalled in neutral. Small wonder that for over a decade now, executives and older employees in Germany have been wringing their hands over the future of the country, seeing in the weakening of the work ethic, particularly among the young, a process of rushing the country to hell in a handbasket.

But more sober-minded observers insist that reports of the death of the German work ethic are greatly exaggerated. Of course, the hard stuff that rebuilt the nation from rubble after the war into a major economic power has been diluted more than somewhat, but such a development was almost predictable, considering trends here and around the world. Even so, for many societies, just the diluted version of German application could stand as an ideal of thoroughness.

Probably the fairest summation here? Yes, the Germans are still quite industrious; no, they're not as hard-working as they used to be. (And you won't find that work ethic to be of equal concentration amongst all workers or in all branches of endeavour; the dropping-off seems to be especially true the younger they are.) But regardless of age, there's still a strong commitment to thoroughness ingrained in Germans. For some strong evidence, think of these names: BMW, Mercedes, Merck pharmaceuticals, Zeiss opticals, Siemens medical technology, Solingen steel cutlery, Braun electrical appliances. And that's just a start. The enduring blue-chip reputation for high quality of many German products indicates how potent the German work ethic still is. Enough people still put a high value on work to keep the engines of the economy at something close to full force. And that's quite a force indeed.

Also keep in mind that as an *Ausländer*, you're liable to be judged by how closely you fit the ideal rather than the deviation from that ideal. They will certainly make many allowances for you, especially during the early going, but then you'll also probably have to give that extra bit and a half just to demonstrate that your concept of thoroughness is thorough enough to meet the exacting German standards.

Thoroughness—In Its Own Good Time

But thoroughness takes time—even for a people so well-schooled in it. And many foreigners get dismayed by how long this thoroughness can take in Germany. This is particularly true when a decision has to be made. Whereas in other societies, a company or supplier may decide the matter somewhat quickly and then work out the details of that decision later, in Germany it's more likely that many of the details will have to be worked out before any decision is reached.

This can be frustrating for many foreigners, especially for North Americans or those from other dynamically based societies. This frustration can even come up within your own company when you're involved in a project where you feel that enough information has been gathered to reach a decision and press ahead with the next phase. Unfortunately, you're apt to discover that your colleagues or boss believe that more work, more study, more tests are required before that all-important final decision is made.

Just as likely, you may encounter frustration while waiting for a reply from a company you're hoping to do business with or even hoping to join. It is, of course, always possible that incompetence lurks behind the delay or that the company has simply put your matter on its back burner. More probable, though, is that they want to investigate a number of aspects more thoroughly before moving ahead. The up-side of this slow grind is that when you do get informed of the company's decision, much of the next stage of the transaction—working out the details—will have already been attended to by that other company'.

APPLYING FOR JOBS

As we have now touched on the matter of job application, remember the importance of planning and be aware that very rarely do German companies hire someone for an immediate opening or even for a job about to begin soon. Notice from either employer or employee must be tendered six weeks from the end of a quarter, so the job you're interviewing for today may only open up a quarter of a year later.

Also, if your talents happen to lie more in the way of craftsmanship than business acumen, don't forget the German emphasis on trained craftspeople and their insistence that practitioners of many fields be properly trained. Be sure to bring along all your certification when you come to Germany, and just pray that it's accepted; often, it won't be. And if the German authorities don't buy your credentials, you'll have to take a training program here (which for EU citizens as well as non-EU members with established residence here can be completely funded by the government). Remember, no matter how good you are at what you do, you won't be able to do it here unless you have that magic piece of paper.

SERVICE(?) INDUSTRIES

Having heard the moans of some doomsayers on the slipping of the German work ethic, we can now turn to one area where that ethic has not slipped any—primarily because it was standing at a pretty low level to begin with.

Yes, we're talking about the German service industries. Remember some of those curious aspects of German service industries from previous chapters: the absence of a number system for service; the near absence of few-items lines in big stores; the crying lack of friendliness amongst all too many salespeople? Let's now quickly pop in yet another one that has sometimes stung me: when a mistake is made or something goes wrong in a way that inconveniences or penalises a customer, the German business will simply reimburse the customer, perhaps with a perfunctory note of regret tacked on. Almost never will the company throw in a little extra benefit—to show the customers its goodwill and retain (or regain) their loyalty—or swallow all the costs for any correction, even though the company itself was largely at fault.

These four elements point up something unique in the very concept of service in this country: service as an ideal in and of itself (with its corollary of concern for the customer) is just not as important as it is in other countries. In Germany, service to the customer is defined chiefly in terms of providing customers with good, reliable products and good follow-up repair or service where needed. As far as making the very act of shopping or dealing a somewhat pleasant experience in itself... well, this is one area where the Germans lag far behind some other peoples.

The most baffling thing here is, German consumers themselves don't seem to demand those amenities that come standard in many other nations. Why? The answer seems to lie in the culture itself, with the shortcomings in German service perpetuating themselves through the spins of a vicious circle: customer-friendly service is not provided, so it's not expected by customers; therefore, customers don't complain that much or demand better service; therefore, service industries see no reason to provide or improve their service; therefore, customer-friendly service is not... ahh, you get the point.

Oh sure, Germans do their fair share of complaining about poor service and poor operation of stores, but they rarely do it openly. They'll either mumble to themselves, grouse to the customer behind them, or roil behind a stoic frown—then complain more back home or out with friends. In the stores themselves, they're more apt to assign blame to the slow-moving customer at the front of the line than to the sclerotic system itself. In fact, Germans seem to complain about poor service the way they complain about bad weather: as something to be sorely regretted, but which one can't really do anything about.

That's the bad news on the service front. The good news (well, half-good) is that as long as you don't expect service with a smile, the service industries here aren't all that bad. Whether it entails making deliveries or repairing appliances, furniture or the home itself, the people providing such services do tend to get the basic job done well (even though it can sometimes take a little longer than in some more service-oriented societies).

In the worst case, service in crowded restaurants and cafés can be almost comically slow. (And German comedians do, in fact, have a field day with waiters and waitresses.) But in those branches of the service industry where competence, speed and efficiency are vital, dispensers of such won't let you down very often. That good old German thoroughness from other industries seems to have rubbed off a little on these service folks.

THE GERMAN BUSINESS CHARACTER

Working or doing business in Germany entails a good deal more than just shifting your work day forward an hour or two and making extra efforts to keep your nose to the grindstone. Just as German society evidences a dominant character, there's a certain specific character to German business. And whether you join that majority who are 'at least satisfied' with their jobs may depend on your adapting to this character. As opposed to many Asian and Latin cultures, which are relations-oriented, German culture is resoundingly task-oriented. This orientation manifests itself particularly in the business world, where relations are much less important than the task to be accomplished. If you do come from one of the more relations-oriented societies, you may find the German fixation on tasks and the marginalisation of relations in the business world takes a rather wrenching adjustment.

Related to task-orientation is the fact that Germany is a problem-oriented society. Germans tend to approach most tasks as problems. In the business context, this means they often wait for some task to manifest itself as a problem and then set themselves to solving that problem with standard Teutonic thoroughness (which, of course, means the process of problem-solving can be quite intense indeed).

All this reflects another part of the German character—the fact that Germans are reactive rather than proactive. They're not risk-takers; they're not pioneers. They rarely define a problem on their own and then stalk a solution to it the way some Asians and North Americans might. When problems arise, Germans mobilise vigorously to solve them, but they don't show a lot of initiative in taking on problems in the early stage.

Same Procedure As Always
The Germans are, however, great devotees of procedure—they always want to know the rules of the game and want these rules on paper, or at least clearly stated. One American consultant who has worked on a number of key projects with big German companies reports on encountering difficulties in the first day or two because he had failed to make a clear statement of exactly how the project was going to proceed. Few Germans take kindly to the notion of allowing a project, or much else, to develop

This paper fetish comes through most clearly in the way Germans deal with business contracts. They see contracts as the final word, the end of negotiations. When they start work on a project, the contract for that project is like holy writ. But for many peoples, especially those from Asian cultures, the contract is just the start of serious negotiations. Many of my students, along with people from other major German companies, have expressed extreme frustration or irritation with clients from Middle Eastern and Asian firms whom the Germans felt were trying to re-jig the signed contract—something the Germans have a great deal of difficulty dealing with.

Because of this fixation on procedure, Germans are also 'paper fetishists'. They like to see things set down on paper, which then takes on a certain authority in and of itself, thus providing that security Germans so crave.

Of course, this could all just reflect the fact that many Germans in key positions are simply not too comfortable with negotiations, because they represent a phase where things are not clearly defined, where borders are shifting, fine distinctions blurred. German business boasts many first-rate negotiators, though often people whose talents lie in other areas are sent to do the negotiating. And a good many of these people, be they senior engineers or project managers, would prefer seeing the negotiations ended as soon as possible and then getting down to the 'real task' of carrying out the project.

A Heart for Charts

Another aspect of that German 'paper fetishism' is their love of charts. It's a rare German firm that doesn't have its proud collection of charts, and the companies virtually function based on these charts. One British banker earning his crust in a senior position at one of Germany's largest private banks admitted that he was at first somewhat knocked off stride by what he calls the 'numerical framework' way of thinking prevalent here.

He explained this further by recounting that while financial analysts in Britain and other countries will often look at various factors and then make a judgement based on these factors, the Germans often just have a list of key categories that might affect the decision. They then give the matter a rating in each category and finally count it all up to reach a total figure. That alternative with the highest final figure is the decision they make.

Structure First

But if the Germans are, in fact, 'paper fetishists', they might also be described as 'structure fetishists'. They like to make sure well-functioning structures are in place before launching into the work. Organisational structure therefore often takes precedence over goals. At first blush, this might seem to be in conflict with their 'task-oriented' nature, but for many German companies, the organisational structuring is the first task they have to set themselves to.

GERMAN CORPORATE/BUSINESS STRUCTURE

The basic German business structure is an Eiffel Tower (or pyramid) structure—highly, relentlessly hierarchical. This rigid hierarchy is bolstered by strongly defined roles and delegation within and between those roles. Responsibility within a firm is clearly defined. So clearly defined that, from top to bottom, you'll often encounter workers who choose to close themselves off into the roles designated to them. (This is often literally true. Just walk along the corridors of most German office buildings. You'll be struck by the fact that all or almost all the doors are closed. Germans, in general, are rather averse to the 'open office' principle popular in North America and some other societies.)

That critical lack of flexibility in the German character, seen in so many aspects elsewhere in the book, comes into play here as well. Once Germans have their roles within the work context, they endeavour to stay within those roles. That's why it's so difficult to get workers here—be they salespeople in a big store, guards at a building, tellers at a bank, clerks in an office, all the way up through those in middle and even upper management positions—to perform some activity, some service that falls outside their defined roles. Germans certainly have no problem with moving up to a higher job, but while still within a specific job, they seem to tear when they bend.

Management Knows Best

There's an old joke about a German desk jockey who arrives for work early one morning to find a tack on his chair. He's stopped short for a moment, then gingerly lowers himself onto the tack, confident that management must have had a reason for the tack being there.

This joke catches a certain truth about the traditional German business culture. Apparently, it hasn't lost too much of its truth, except that today he (though today it would just as likely be she) would probably slide the tack furtively to the edge of the chair before sitting down with a forced wince, suggesting that the tack had been dutifully mounted. These days, many German workers are more sceptical about top managerial decisions and less loyal to the firm itself. But they still go along with the basic structural procedures.

Bringschuld and Holschuld

This is all reflected in two key terms that describe major functions within the German business culture: *Bringschuld* (roughly translated, the obligation to bring something) and *Holschuld* (the obligation to fetch or collect something). *Bringschuld* represents the dominant force in most German firms: employees are expected to bring information up the ladder. Once top management collects and assembles all this information, it then makes its decisions.

And though there's a lot of information going up the ladder, it's usually stripped of strong recommendations or policy re-orientation. Command in German companies is much more a top-down than a bottom-up affair. Senior management makes its decisions and passes them down the chain of command; those below are empowered to carry out policy rather than formulate it.

Or to put it another way, senior management makes the strategic decisions, while middle and lower management are responsible for operational day-to-day management. And then the work teams carry out these operational decisions.

WOMEN IN THE WORKING WORLD

James Brown might have written the theme song for present-day German business: 'This is a man's world, this is a man's world, but it would be nothing, nothing at all without a woman...' Without women actually. Many women, in fact. Roughly 50 percent of labour force participation is by women, and their labour keeps many sectors of the German economy humming right along. But the system is rife with inequalities. While there was no sexual breakdown on that minority opinion within the work force that isn't 'at least satisfied', it's a safe bet that women are over-represented in that group.

A main source of dissatisfaction would seem to be salary disparities. In 2002, official government statistics indicated that the salaries of women in the private sector were just 73 per cent that of men, while even the pay cheques of working women in the public sector were just 77 per cent as hefty as those of their male colleagues. And repeated studies have suggested that women are rarely paid as much as men for comparable work. (One study found that women in top executive positions are paid at least 25 per cent less than men in exactly the same job.)

While a great many key positions throughout the German economy are manned by women, numerous observers, both in the trenches and in the research institutes, report that there's a glass ceiling for females; and in Germany, that ceiling is hung distressingly low. A 2002 survey found that 6.4 per cent of male German workers were classified as managers or executives, though only 3 per cent of working women were so classified. And this dismal percentage had held more or less steady since the first study of its sort, way back in 1963.

So what are the grounds for these disparities? Actually, some of the reasons sound quite convincing, as well as justified. For example, in an economy like Germany's, where engineering and technical expertise have long been so important, top positions have traditionally been filled by people who have strong engineering or technical backgrounds. And this just happens to be an area where the presence of women has been miserable.

As one of my English-language students (a trained engineer in an important managerial post who professes a certain sympathy for the plight of women) pointed out, in his first-year engineering class at college, only four of over 200 students were female; by graduation time, that number had dropped to zero. Such percentages do not bode well for successful climbing to the top in German industry.

But many observers, including not a few self-professed victims, see something more nefarious afoot in the unsatisfactory position of women—and the name they give it is male discrimination. A kind of corporate male bonding seems to play a significant determining role in who moves where within German business. Many men get sold short through this process, but women start out with an almost insurmountable burden in terms of proceeding smoothly through the corridors of power.

What the Men Say

A few quotes from male employers can give you an idea of the attitude some of them have (we'll let you judge their accuracy):

- 'Women are inadequately or inappropriately qualified.'
- 'Women cannot lead.'
- 'Women are too emotional. They cannot impose their will.'
- 'Women are short on self-assurance.'

And the old reliable objection: "Women aren't dedicated to their careers. If they have to make a choice, they sacrifice their career for a family. It's not worth investing personnel development on women."

Or as one German executive vice-president of a major multinational corporation said to me some 15 years ago, "I'd rather buy a machine than hire a woman. At least machines don't get pregnant." (Of course, machines don't get sick either, but that advantage didn't stop this executive from hiring men.)

In many of my Business English seminars, I noted that women participants whose English was obviously superior to most of their male fellows turn somewhat reticent in class. They become almost apologetic when they offer the correct answer after most of the men have failed to hit it. And when the class is broken up into smaller groups for role plays, women (even some with responsible positions in the company plus a good command of English) are given less important roles to carry out—which they then seem to accept!

From personal experience as well as from many reports by both men and women, I would say that at least one of these points is accurate in so far as it relates to women in the German business world: women here are short on self-assurance, though the cause may have more to do with negative feedback from male colleagues and bosses than with hormones.

As we'll see below, the ability to project self-assurance is a mighty powerful weapon in the German business world, and its lack may be one cause of some women's problems: they may simply be victims of their own self-doubt. Or victims of the self-doubt drilled into them by a male-dominated business world resistant to giving up its privileges.

Whatever the cause, women coming here to work should be aware of these barriers you have to push your way through. It's quite possible that you won't be judged entirely on your achievements and skills; you may have to run very hard just to walk like a man in this man's business world.

STARTING A BUSINESS

You know that old wheeze about a broken heart for every light on Broadway? Well, there must be at least as many broken hearts for every well-thumbed file at German Handels-und-Industrie Kammer (Chambers of Commerce).

Legions of multinational corporations and energetic entrepreneurs have looked at Germany and started drooling. One of the world's largest economies, smack in the middle of the new Europe—main engine of the EU's rapidly expanding single market to boot; a huge and prosperous domestic market; a highly trained work force; an exemplary infrastructure—how can one fail in such a promising economic environment? Well, many of those multinationals and twinkly-eyed entrepreneurs have found out how, and they've joined that long roll of broken hearts.

Beyond a doubt, Germany is a most promising economic environment. But at the same time, it's a pretty tough nut to crack. If you hope to do business here, you just can't come running in expecting all the doors to be flung wide open to you. If you're not aware of the many pitfalls, your failure here is as good as sealed.

The Nuts and Bolts of Getting Started

If you've done your preliminary surveillance work and are still convinced that Germany is indeed the place for your business, the first thing you'll want to do is set up as a legal entity. The two most common corporate structures in Germany are the GmbH (limited company) and the AG (public limited company). Of the two, you'll almost certainly want to choose the former; the AG is costly, encumbered with compulsory boards, compulsory audits, disclosures, etc., and finally doesn't provide any significant commercial advantages over the GmbH (except that you can sell shares on the open stock market with the AG). Most foreign companies of various sizes opt for the GmbH, and you probably should too. (In fact, many of Germany's major corporations are now reorganising into smaller GmbH units to sidestep the drawbacks of the AG structure.)

Interestingly enough, the procedure for setting up as a GmbH is less lumbered with regulations than it is in many countries, principally those operating under the scope of common law jurisdictions. The drafting of your corporate charter can be framed in relatively simple general language, without any need for lengthy purpose clauses detailing all possible corporate activities. Moreover, in a GmbH, you have no nationality requirements for shareholders or company heads and no compulsory boards.

What you do need is a minimum capital of 25,000 euros and a *Notar* (notary public) who can certify the organisation of your company. With the *Notar*'s seal on your registry papers, you then head off to the *Handelsregister* (commercial registry) at the municipal court of your company's official seat. All business units in Germany must be registered with these *Handelsregister*, where a registrar who is also a judge will examine your papers and then order registration. The register of the company is then open to public inspection.

An Important Cautionary Note

Until your company is officially registered, it exists simply as a civil partnership with unlimited liability—which in German corporate life is like bungee jumping with a pair of long rubber bands.

THE ROLE OF BANKS

In the Chapter Five, we talked about individual banking. But German banking in a business context is quite a different matter, and one that any would-be entrepreneurs must get acquainted and engaged with very quickly.

Business Week once wrote about Germany's 'antediluvian banking customs'. You're likely to find your own experiences with German banks to be mixed. On the negative side of the ledger, remember that German bankers are almost uniformly conservative and would rather place safe bets on established businesses and in proven fields. If your particular venture falls outside of these parameters, you shouldn't expect to find many sympathetic ears in the German banking community. In fact, a clutch of successful businesses here actually had to raise capital from banks or investors outside German borders in their early stages of operation.

But there's a plus side to this story as well. German banks provide more than just financial assistance and advice. They can also be vast repositories of information about the industry you're in, and they can arrange key introductions and important contacts (including some with government agencies where that's helpful).

Banks here employ experts who can assist you in every facet of setting up a company. In general, German banks are more involved in business than are the banks in most other countries (many of them being major shareholders themselves). In fact, if invited to, some bankers will even help you out in finding appropriate managers and other key personnel.

Banking in Germany being so intractable an 'old boy' system (with many of the negatives and positives accruing to such a system), if you're looking to set up an operation here or significantly expand an existing one, your best step might be to ask a friend in the same field to recommend an appropriate bank and a contact person there. Going in cold will all too often get you an even colder reception.

GOING ALONG WITH THE SYSTEM

You probably already know that there are a great many rules and regulations determining the operation of the German economy. These both bolster that prized industrial peace and incorporate a frustrating inflexibility into the system. If you're trying to establish a business here, you might find the rigidities most frustrating indeed as you get tangled up in the many regulations and unwritten rules. But always remember that it was precisely this rigid system that helped West Germany achieve its post-war 'economic miracle'.

That which makes Germany a most appealing place for employees can make it a rather unappealing place for employers. As an employer, you just have to realise that the shoe is now on the other foot, and you may discover that it pinches rather sorely over there. Now you see why Germany is not the entrepreneurs' paradise it seemed at first blush to be.

In fact, Germany is easily the most expensive country in the world in which to employ someone, and projections indicate that it will continue to hold this unenviable title through at least the year 2010. The high average wages would only land Germany in fourth place among the dearest countries; it's those extras that put Deutschland out of reach of even its most expensive rivals. Employers are required to pay half of their workers health, pension and old-age care insurance. They must also often cover their salary during the 30 required days of vacation as well as on all legal holidays. though more and more contracts are cutting back or even eliminating this. (Though as of early 2002, workers' costs in the five new eastern states were still only 69 per cent of their western cousins. Conversely, unit labour costs over in the east were 25 per cent higher.)

Now, if you think you can save a little by bargaining down the basic wages, you may have another surprise waiting for you there. Depending on the field you operate in, you may discover that the wages and salaries you must pay have already been determined in the *Manteltarifvertrag* (umbrella wage and benefits agreements) worked out by the large union and the manufacturers' or business association in your industry. If you hire any trained workers in this group, you must go along with the regulations, which could just include, among other goodies, a 13th month salary, paid in December as a fat Christmas bonus.

CRACKING THE MARKET

So just why is Germany that tough nut to crack mentioned earlier? One major factor was already taken up in Chapter Two: Germans, you'll recall, are not risk-takers. While there are a large number of risk-takers within the German population, they are not much encouraged by their environment. Companies and banks always seek to avoid risk as much as possible, and many locals—from workers on the assembly line up to highly imaginative management sorts—prefer the safety of a steady job with all its legal benefits and protections to striking out on their own. The entrepreneurial spirit isn't very spirited amongst these folks.

Although the German government does serve up a heap of tax advantages for small businesses trying to start up, enterprises both large and small can find the going tough because of resistance elsewhere along the system. For example, venture capital is still quiet, German bankers are almost uniformly conservative and would rather place safe bets on established businesses, and the listing of new shares on the stock exchange is very strict.

And if you should get past these hurdles, there are more waiting for you over on the consumer end. Germans display a great deal of product loyalty; if something works for them, they stay with it—doggedly. There's little of that 'well, maybe we'll give this one a try this week' attitude you find in many other cultures (especially those of North America).

This is not to say that German consumers never switch; they will, and very quickly, if you give them good reasons to do so. For example, concern for the environment led many shoppers to abandon detergents and other cleaning products that

The Disappearing Coffee Filters

And I was amazed how rapidly white coffee filters disappeared from store shelves when reports hinted that they might be harmful to health as well as added an unwanted side-taste to the brew itself. This nation of devout coffee drinkers first swept to small producers of brown, unbleached filters and ultimately drove all the major companies in this field to drop their own production of white filters for the domestic market had served their families for generations in favour of more environmentally sound offerings.

In short: to penetrate the German market, you not only have to build a better mousetrap, you have to convince the public that the old mousetrap will no longer do the job.

A MOST TAXING PROBLEM

Just above, we mentioned the raft of tax advantages the German government offers to starting businesses. This applies, in fact, not only to standard business ventures, but also to the multitude of officially 'self-employed' breadwinners here. But to take advantage of these tax breaks, you've got to know about them all. You never will, so—this is Germany, remember—you've got to turn to the services of an expert in the matter.

If you are in any way, shape or form *selbstständig* (the German designation for 'self-employed'), you'll be doing yourself a big favour to find a good *Steuerberater* (tax consultant) as soon as possible. These people can guide you safely through the intricate labyrinth of the German tax code and find the best solutions for you. (Look, even Roman Herzog, Germany's former president and a one-time justice of the German Supreme Court, admits that he can't fathom his tax forms.) As many of these people are financial as well as tax consultants, they can also pass along some valuable business advice as they steer you through the murky swamps of your tax conundra.

The problem is, good *Steuerberater* can be more difficult to find than good doctors, and their appointment books are certainly more filled than fine medical practitioners'. In fact, some of the most coveted ones won't even accept new clients unless they come with a strong recommendation from old, loyal clients. The only reliable way to turn up a good *Steuerberater* is to ask friends or associates who are also involved in self-employed activities. Skimming through the yellow pages for one is like trying to pluck a pointed snowflake from the winds of a snowstorm.

TUSSLES WITH BRUSSELS

Now that you've (hopefully) digested all of the above, you should know that it all has to be further viewed against the backdrop of new pressures continually put on the German economy and German regulatory authorities by the European Union. As members of the Union slouch more and more towards full integration, at least in the economic sphere, new rules and regulations coming from Brussels (the Union's headquarters) will have even greater impact upon German ways of doing business.

It may come as a surprise to others, particularly Britons, to learn that Germany has its own army of dedicated 'Eurosceptics': large numbers of Germans already grumble about rulings issued by what they affectionately call 'the dictatorship in Brussels', and a string of polls show a majority in Deutschland filled with misgivings about what major changes EU decisions may bring about in the German economy and German work relations (even as most other EU nations worry that the EU Commission's decisions are largely dictated by German and French interests).

DEUTSCHMARK, ADIEU!

Actually, the greatest fears that many Germans had about the 'unelected mandarins in Brussels' revolved around the dire consequences which might follow upon the loss of their beloved and trusted Deutschmark. But when the D-mark finally disappeared at the beginning of 2002, most of these fears proved unfounded.

True, there were some dislocations and glitches or hiccups in introducing the new EU currency, the euro. And throughout the summer and autumn, there were still grumbles heard daily about the costs of the currency switch. Most of these grumbles blamed the switch for the nasty spike in prices that occurred after the euro was introduced. Blame for this spike was assigned alternately to the euro itself and to unscrupulous merchants who grossly increased their profit margins to take advantage of the new legal tender. (The euro has almost twice the value of the defunct D-mark, so consumers were actually forking out fewer euros, though the buying power of their total incomes may have shrunk slightly.)

But the changeover was nowhere near the calamity or price-gouging exercise the biggest Eurosceptics said it would be. It has even proved a boon for coin collectors who now have a new and an old currency to put in their hoards. Evidently, most Germans now view the introduction of the euro like a trip to the dentist: sure, there was some discomfort, maybe even pain, but it was nowhere as bad as they had imagined it would be. Moreover, in the long run, it will probably help them significantly.

Arranging for Change

We already know how warmly Germans take to insecurity, so don't expect any of these changes to take effect with breakneck speed. While it's inevitable that change, compelled by developments on the international economic scene, will come to the German way of doing business, it's also pretty sure that the Germans' inbred insecurity will kick in to minimise these changes—or at least to slow their advance. Some of what's written in this chapter may change somewhat over the next five to ten years, but not as much as it would in a people more receptive to change.

A GERMAN BUSINESS DO-IT-YOURSELF

In addition to all the information piled on you above, let me throw in a quick do-it-yourself to the German business world that you may find quite valuable in moving through this scene.

Tough And Fair

One foreigner who has been doing business here for quite a few years said of his German partners, customers and suppliers, "These guys really play hardball. But they do play fair." This seems to be a widely-held opinion among those who have done business with the Germans. Don't expect major concessions from German customers or suppliers; they know that you only get ahead in the business world by being tough, usually with a capital 'T'. On the other hand, you needn't worry that you're going to get gouged by these associates: the long-established, reliable companies pride themselves on being fair and offering customers or contractors what they consider fair deals.

Making the Right First Impressions

That basic conservatism rooted in the German personality can be seen in the fact that German businesses, like most German customers, rarely do any 'shopping around' for services, suppliers, or managers. They procure their supplies and services from established partners, and managers are chiefly recruited from within their own ranks. It's therefore important to impress with your abilities or the quality of your products right from the start. Once German businesses establish a relationship with you, you'll have to do something truly egregious before they drop you and start looking for someone or something else. (Warning: in today's cost-conscious environment, jacking up your prices too much or too quickly can qualify as 'truly egregious'.)

Therefore, it's most important that you work even harder than usual to provide the best service or product you can with new customers. Put that extra effort into meeting your delivery dates; if there's going to be some problem, tell your customers why and when they can expect the later delivery. But try not to let such things happen at all; if you prove yourself early, customers will more readily forgive later slips and problems.

Of course, you often have to make a first impression even before you start doing business—for example, when interviewing for a job or negotiating a contract. While Germans are very task-oriented, they also often judge by appearances, so the right appearance can be the clincher to a deal or a job offer. The most outer layer of one's appearance gets its own look just below; perhaps more important is the impression your behaviour makes.

As might be expected in a society that suffers from so much fundamental insecurity, it's immensely helpful if you yourself project an image of self-assurance. Of course, you need something to back up that image, as many German employers and executives are quick to detect the hollow beneath the swagger. Don't leave any room for doubt: make sure you know your facts; come prepared for every interview and business meeting; and always be sure to follow through on what you promise.

If you remember from Chapter Three, Germans also have a need to be credible, to be believed (*wahrgenommen werden*). This is especially true in a business context where a failure to be credible may cost you your customer, your promotion, your job perhaps. Thus, the physical signs of security are also important.

Remember what we said in Chapter Four? Always look people in the eye, and offer others a firm handshake when you meet? These things are even more important in a business context. And it holds for women as well as men, though a woman's handshake needn't be as firm as her male colleague's. Most especially, don't look down or away from your partner; in Germany, this is read not as deference but as weakness or untrustworthiness. Here, you must somehow convey the impression of being strong and aware of your subordinate position simultaneously.

Dressing for Success

There are actually a number of different, shifting dress codes in German business, and your adherence to one or the other will probably be determined by where you work or do business. In most standard business situations (which includes all the major German companies, along with other traditional businesses), standard business attire is called for. This ordinarily means, for men, a dark suit, light-toned shirt with tie or sweater, and polished shoes.

As in many countries today, women are afforded a broader range of choice in this particular area. But it is far from 'anything goes'. Pants suits are acceptable in all but the most hidebound traditionalist firms, and brighter colours often come to the fore.

But whether you are male or female (and especially if you're the former), don't wear clothing in the office that makes too strong or extroverted a fashion statement. German companies prefer the company itself to be in the spotlight, not any of its individual employees.

But then there are a number of 'alternative' offices and businesses currently prospering in Germany, and if you find yourself doing business in these circles, you're much freer as to what you can wear. In fact, practically the only things that aren't acceptable are those styles prescribed in the paragraph above.

There are also a large number of companies that fall somewhere in between. You probably would not be expected to wear the same outfit at an advertising agency or a computer software firm as you would when working in a bank.

Dressing Down, Everyday

One American computer programmer based here recounted the policy in his firm, where short pants and T-shirts were perfectly acceptable uniforms in warm weather—as long as there were no clients about. When a client was coming, the word went out a day or two before that everyone had to be in jacket and tie.

Perhaps the best rule is to look around when you first start working somewhere and follow the style of dress that prevails.

The Right Tone

The right tone—of voice, topic, approach, seriousness— plays a major role in German business, and you should strive to find that right tone for you and your customer, client or employer. German voices, for instance, tend to operate in a deeper register than do many voices in the English-speaking world. If your voice is somewhat high-pitched, you might try to pitch it a little lower when doing business in Germany. This goes for women too, though it's mainly with men that a high-pitched voice can prove a serious liability.

Speaking of serious, remember that Germans take their business very seriously. Don't ever be too informal in discussions or meetings, or try to prove what a wonderful sense of humour you have. You'll find that most jokes in a serious discussion fall crushingly flat. And don't ever call a German business partner, associate or colleague by first name unless you've established a very close business relationship.

The Language of Business

Related to this is the question of language. We just saw in the last chapter how important it is to learn some German. But the simple, unassailable fact is that the advantage in any negotiations clearly rests with people speaking their mother tongue, or at least a language in which they're fairly conversant. Unless and until your German is somewhat accomplished and you, in fact, feel fairly comfortable speaking it, you'd be well-advised to see if the discussion can't proceed in English.

Many successful people working here do speak mainly English on the job, as many German businesspeople can handle English reasonably well, and not a few take a special pride in their English-language abilities. Even so, it can help considerably if you do master a few key German phrases and drop them into the discussion where appropriate. This will show your partner that you're making some effort to learn his or her language.

Training

A main pillar of the German economy's success is the high level of investment in human capital within many firms. For instance, almost all of Germany's big companies—and many of the smaller ones too—feature an expansive apprenticeship programme (*Ausbildung*) that benefits the companies as well as the *Azubis* (nickname for the trainees). While the young people learn a valuable trade and broadly marketable skills, the companies themselves acquire a steady pool of well-trained workers already familiar with the corporate culture.

In addition, there are a multitude of skills-upgrading courses that hone the skills of employees already established with the company, making them more able to compete in the new world markets. As many as 95 per cent of all German companies are said to offer their employees such further training opportunities. You yourself

More and more young women are training as apprentices in traditional 'men's professions'.

may, at some point, be advised to take one or more of these courses. They can be very profitable to your job performance and career. Many experts inside and outside Germany credit these programmes, especially the apprenticeship programme, with helping make and keep Germany the economic powerhouse it is.

Pressure Plays

Don't try to squeeze a raise out of your employer by threatening to take a better offer that you've received—this will almost certainly backfire in Germany. First, it indicates a lack of discretion on your part in even revealing this other offer, and German firms value discretion (first cousin of security) highly. Second, German managers don't take kindly to being threatened; except in rare cases, they would rather see a worker go than submit to psychological arm-twisting.

Getting Down to Business

Germany is a notoriously low-context culture (they don't need to know much about the people they're dealing with), and German businesses are plainly concerned with time, so long preliminaries are not appreciated here. The typical German wants you to 'get right down to business' after exchanging the minimum of pleasantries. And once you do get down to business, this same typical German doesn't like straying too far off track. He or she might even inform you that 'we're losing the *rote Faden* (main thread) of this discussion'. But don't even let it reach this stage: you can usually see that you're straining your partners' patience in the standard terms of body language: tapping of the fingers, energetic swinging of the foot, pronounced nodding of the head when you haven't really said anything that merits that much affirmation. This all means 'get back to the main topic', even perhaps 'let's wrap things up'.

By the way, this does not mean that German business discussions are stripped of all niceties and amenities. In fact, standard practice for any but the shortest of meetings is to offer the visitor coffee or mineral water (juice, if it's available). You should be especially aware of this when you're hosting some business partner or associate and always be prepared to make such an offer.

Business Gifts

The question of business gifts is a very, very tricky matter requiring a good measure of that old German salve of *Fingerspitzengefühl* (extremely careful instincts, literally 'fingertip feeling').

The matter is brutally simple when it comes to *Beamter* (civil servants). People in these positions are strictly prohibited from accepting so much as a ballpoint pen from government contractors. Of course, stories of corruption float frequently through the media showing that some *Beamter* accept a lot more than pens. But the fact that these accounts are always treated as scandals and that the recipient can be fired from his life-long cushy job or even receive a light jail sentence for this transgression indicates its hazards. The guidelines for gifts to civil servants are therefore drawn quite clearly: don't even think about it!

The matter fogs up a bit when it comes to private businesses, however. Here the situation reflects more that split nature in the German character. Theoretically, no German business accepts bribes; Germans find bribes demeaning, insulting and indecent. On the other hand, Germans are also humans, so they do occasionally like receiving gifts, if only to show appreciation for loyalty or a job well done.

How, then, to navigate the murky waters between the Scylla of not showing appreciation to special customers and the Charybdis of boldly offering bribes? One way is to make sure that the gift clearly resembles a gift. Money payments are strictly *verboten*. And there's, of course, a proper time and place for gifts: most are presented around Christmas time.

One exception arises when there are a number of problems on the site of a large project. Should the clients themselves go to a lot of extra trouble to clear the way or make concessions outside the contract, it is considered quite appropriate for the main contact person in the contracting firm to go to the clients and give them a little thank-you token for their help or understanding: something like a bottle of wine or Sekt, the German version of champagne.

Wine, Sekt, cognac, brandy, *schnaps*: these are all appropriate acknowledgements of a satisfying business relationship. Others might include flowers, boxes of candy, fruit or food baskets, or a small but useful product of the company making the gift. The key here is that since Germans rarely give presents to people they're not that close to, business gifts must keep within the bounds of reason and propriety. A good rule of thumb in this situation is that 'small is dutiful'. Many firms today limit themselves to the obligatory Christmas card to customers, though the widespread presentation of calendars—either in wall, desk or pocket size—is accepted as no more offensive than a Christmas card.

A special subdivision of the business gift is business entertaining. A potential big customer who travels to your plant, office or, especially, city probably expects that after a long session of negotiations, you will take him or her out to lunch or dinner, possibly even for a short guided tour of the town's major points of interest. Such entertaining is not only acceptable, it is budgeted for by most companies and blessed as tax-deductible by the German government.

But a closing note should reiterate this key point: the best gift you can give to a German client or customer is to do a good job, deliver a good product, and provide good service. Little more beyond that is expected; anything less than that is unacceptable.

FAST FACTS

CHAPTER 10

'Anybody who knows everything
should be told a thing or two.'
—Franklin P Jones

Hopefully, you now know a lot more about this elephant (*see* Introduction *on page vi–vii*)) than you did at the beginning of the book. But elephants can be cumbersome and ungainly, and there are some items which certainly bear mentioning but didn't quite fit in anywhere else in the book. Let's cover some of these items now, to give us an even better picture of our elephant.

ABOUT THE COUNTRY
Official Name
Bundesrepublik Deutschland
(Federal Republic of Germany)

Capital
Berlin

Flag
Three thick horizontal stripes in the colours black, red and gold, in descending order.

National Anthem
Das Deutschland-Lied ('The Germany Song')
Music is by Joseph Hayden and words by August Heinrich Hoffmann von Fallersleben.

Time and Time Again

Germany lies entirely within the Central European time zone, putting it one hour ahead of Greenwich Mean Time—but only during the autumn and winter months. Summer time goes into effect for the entire country around the last Sunday in March when all clocks are pushed ahead by one hour. This is reversed, usually on the last Sunday in September, with the clocks getting turned back an hour. As the country lies fairly north and in the western half of its time zone, it can stay light as late as 9:30–10:00 pm in the middle of June, though it never gets dark before 4:30–5:00 pm even in the depths of December.

Telephone Country Code

49

Land

Located in central Europe, Germany shares borders with nine countries. It has a coastline of 2,389 km (1,484.5 miles) with the Baltic and North Seas at its northern rim.

Location

Germany lies between the 6th and 15th longitudes and 55th and 47th latitudes. It is a member in very good standing of the European Union (EU), having in fact been one of the original five members of the EU's precursor, the European Common Market. (Many people assert that the initial impulse for the Common Market was to preclude another war between France and Germany.) As the EU member with the largest population, Germany sends the largest delegation to the European Parliament—99 members (out of 732). The European Bank, the EU's central bank, opened in 1995 in Frankfurt.

Area

total: 357,021 sq km (137,846.6 sq miles)
land: 349,223 sq km (134,835.8 sq miles)
water: 7,798 sq km (3,010.8 sq miles)

Highest Point

Zugspitze (2,963 m / 9,721.1 ft)

Major Rivers

Danube River, Elbe River, Isar River, Lahn River, Main River, Moselle River, Neckar River, Oder-Neisse River, Rhine River, Spree River, Weser River

Climate

Temperate and marine with cool, cloudy and wet winters, plus warm and wet summers. There is an occasional mountain wind called the *Fön*.

Natural Resources

Arable land, coal, copper, iron ore, lignite, natural gas, nickel, potash, salt, construction materials, timber, uranium

Population

82,425,000 (July 2004 estimate)

Ethnic Groups

Germans make up 91.5 per cent; other large groups include Turks, Greeks, Italians, Poles, Croats and Serbs.

Major Religions

Evangelish (Lutheran Protestant), Roman Catholic, *Frei Evangelishe Kirche* (a somewhat Calvinist variation of *Evangelisch*)

Languages and Dialects

German (various dialects, the leading ones being Bavarian, Swabian and Plattdeutsch)

Government

Germany is a democratic republic, with the right to vote granted to all German citizens age 18 or over. They are tasked with electing most public officials, from the local level up to members of the *Bundestag*, the larger and more important of the German Parliament's two houses. A *Bundestag* election must take place at least every four years.

The *Bundestag* is responsible for all national legislation as well as formulating and executing foreign policy. It is composed of 603 members, more members than in both houses of the United States Congress. The leader of the government is the *Bundeskanzler*, or federal chancellor. He (and through late 2005, it always has been a he), is usually the designated head of the largest party in the ruling coalition. The chancellor selects his cabinet after consultation with members of the coalition partners.

In choosing a *Bundestag*, each voter has two votes. Roughly half of the members are directly elected by the voters in their constituency, in the so-called first vote. The second vote on every ballot is the party vote. Voters cast a ballot for a specific party, and the remaining half of the *Bundestag* seats are then distributed to the parties according to the percentage of second votes they receive. The parties themselves fill these seats from a predetermined list of candidates.

The *Bundestag*'s smaller and less powerful sibling is the *Bundesrat*, composed of representatives appointed by the *Landtag*, or state legislatures, and reflecting the composition of the ruling group in that state's *Landtag*. Roughly half of all *Bundestag* legislation requires the endorsement of the

A session of the *Bundestag,* the major house of the German Federal Parliament.

Bundesrat, especially laws directly affecting the states. In matters where the states are directly responsible for legislation (i.e. education, law and order, etc.), the *Bundesrat* even claims the power of veto.

Der Bundespresident (The Federal President)

The German federal presidency is largely a ceremonial post, embracing more symbol than power. This too reflects the fears that framers of the West German Constitution had of repeating the Weimar Republic's mistakes, as it is widely believed the Weimar president enjoyed too much discretion in dissolving parliaments and appointing chancellors (especially in light of the last Weimar president's perverse choice of Adolf Hitler as saviour of the Republic). While the Federal Republic's presidents exercise nowhere near as much power as their Weimar antecedents, their symbolic functions as the representative embodiment of the nation can be quite significant.

The federal president is elected not by popular vote, but is selected by members of the Federal Assembly, a body of *Bundestag* and *Bundesrat* members who gather solely for this function.

Administrative Divisions

The symbol † signifies city-states, which have no capital as such.

The 'Old' Federal States (formerly West Germany)

- Baden-Württemberg, capital Stuttgart
- Bayern (Bavaria), capital Munich
- Berlin (†)
- Bremen (†)
- Hamburg (†)
- Hessen (Hesse), capital Wiesbaden
- Niedersachsen (Lower Saxony), capital Hanover
- Rheinland-Pfalz (Rhineland-Palatinate), capital Mainz
- Saarland, capital Saarbrücken
- Schleswig-Holstein, capital Kiel

The 'New' Federal States (formerly East Germany)
- Brandenburg, capital Potsdam
- Mecklenburg-Vorpommern (also called Western Pomerania), capital Schwerin
- Sachsen (Saxony), capital Dresden
- Sachsen-Anhalt (Saxony-Anhalt), capital Magdeburg
- Thüringen (Thuringia), capital Erfurt

The Judicial System

In addition to the legislative and executive branches, Germany possesses an effective judicial system. The German judiciary is largely regarded as independent although the judges in most parts of the system owe their posts to political appointment. But as their continuing employment does not depend on adhering to any particular political line, once seated on the bench, their independence is rarely challenged. Germany's highest court sits in Karlsruhe and is composed of 16 judges, who rule mainly on the constitutionality of laws passed by the parliament or on difficult cases that beg varying interpretations of the constitution.

Currency

Euro (€)

Gross Domestic Product (GDP)

US$ 2.271 trillion (2003 est)

Agricultural Products

Barley, cabbages, fruit, potatoes, sugar beets, wheat

Other Products

Cattle, pigs, poultry

Industries

Germany stands among the world's largest and most technologically advanced producers of iron, steel, coal, cement, chemicals, machinery, vehicles, machine tools, electronics, shipbuilding, food and beverages and textiles

Exports
Automotive vehicles, chemicals, electronics, foodstuffs, machinery and equipment, metals, textiles

Imports
Chemicals, foodstuffs, machinery, metals, textiles, vehicles

Ports and Harbours
Bremen and Bremerhaven, Cuxhaven, Hamburg, Kiel, Lübeck, Rostock, Wilhelmshaven
(inland) Brake, Duisburg, Cologne, Heiligenhafen, Frankfurt am Main, Leer, Wismar

Airports
Counting functional airfields, there are 613, of which 544 are paved

Railways
More than 44,000 km (27,340.3 miles) of railway lines in the public system, with an additional 3,465 km (2,153.1 miles) of private industrial or excursion track

Telling Time
We have already learned how obsessed Germans are with time, so now we should listen to them when they tell us how to tell time. The Germans use the 24-hour clock, starting at Null Uhr (zero hour)—our midnight. 20:30h is *zwanzig Uhr dreissig*, or 8:30 pm to those of the English-speaking persuasion. Germans don't only write time this way, they say it too. They may even translate it directly into English, if they haven't been drilled in their ante and post meridiems. While they have no real pm, something like 9:00 am is often rendered as *neun Uhr früh*, or 'nine o'clock early'.

There is another German oddity in telling time, though here it could be said that the Germans get it right: as 8:30 is actually half of nine o'clock, they call it *halb neun*, not the half-eight of British English. So whereas you may be used to referring to this time as half past eight, the Germans refer

to 'half before nine'. Again be aware that German friends, colleagues and customers may translate the German system directly into English when making appointments. If they should suggest half-nine, ask for the long version just to make sure you are both in the same hour.

Dates

Germans don't like to use the month's name, preferring the number instead, and then presenting it in the following order: day, month, year, with points in between. It's easy to see that, in the German system, 31.12.99 is the last day of the last century, but be aware that 06.05. is the 6th of May and not June 5. (Germans almost always write dates this way and often say them this way too.)

Numbers

Numbers and how they work are the same the world over, but Germans like to write them differently from the rest of us. In Germany, decimal fractions just don't get the point; they get a decimal comma instead. The solid point is saved for indicating thousands, millions and so on. For instance: 98,6 is a healthy ninety-eight point six, while 4,25 is four and a quarter and so on; 1.200 is one thousand, two hundred; 5.500.310 is five million, five hundred thousand, three hundred and ten. You will pick this up quickly, but just be careful when you start writing your first cheques and bank transfers. In fact, be very careful.

Another peculiarity that could give you trouble at first: when handwritten, German 'ones' feature a little tail on their upper left sides which often makes them look more like a very fatigued seven or a four that never got finished. To help you identify the 'one', remember that Germans always like to finish things, so it can't be a four, and the handwritten seven always has another slash across its middle so that you can distinguish it from the number one.

Electricity

230 volts and 50 Hertz. All plugs are two-pinned, but with round prongs. If your appliances are also so pinned, you can bring them along and buy a converter. These converters often carry the danger of blowing a fuse, but blown fuses are very easily remedied in Germany—literally by throwing a switch. An adapter plug (*Zwischenstecker*), which makes yours compatible with German round-holed sockets, is much cheaper and easy to get.

For videophiles and television lovers: Germans invented the PAL system, which is standard for the country, though some of the eastern areas still use the inferior Secam system. These systems are totally incompatible with NTSC (the standard system in the United States, Canada, Korea, Taiwan, the Philippines and Japan). If your VCR or TV set is based solely on NTSC, you can leave it at home. Don't believe what dealers or 'well-informed' friends tell you—it simply will not work in Germany. (Multi-system recorders will, however.)

NAME DROPPING

The following names and profiles will help you in your conversations with the people around you. Such points of reference are important to allow you to participate and also help to put your German friends and colleagues at ease with you as a part of the group.

Konrad Adenauer

He was the first post-war German chancellor, and an architect of West German democracy. Adenauer's stature and integrity played a major part in restoring Germany's position in the community of nations.

Michael Ballack

Another one of the many former East Germans who have excelled in the new united Deutschland, Ballack was one of the stars of the last soccer World Cup and looks set to again play a hero's role in the upcoming World Cup, the first ever on German soil. Even German football legend Franz Beckenbauer has called Ballack the best young midfielder in Europe. After a short but stellar career with Bayer Leverkusen, Ballack transferred to Bayern München, where he bagged the German Footballer of the Year awards in 2001–2002 and 2002–2003 and again paced Bayern to the German championship in 2005. Tall and stocky, Ballack makes an imposing figure on the field which both intimidates opponents and inspires his team-mates.

Boris Becker

One of Germany's sports legends, Becker became the youngest person to win the Wimbledon tennis title when he took that coveted honour as a teenager in the mid-1980's. He subsequently won two further Wimbledon titles and more than once finished amongst the top-ranked male players in the world.

In recent years, Becker has kept his name in the press with exploits in another kind of court—a very messy divorce (he'd taken up with a Russian beauty queen) and a multi-million Deutschmark tax evasion case. (In the latter, he pleaded guilty and paid a humongous fine, narrowly escaping a prison term.)

(Pope) Benedict XVI

Born Josef Ratzinger in Bavaria, this powerful figure in April 2005 became the first German elected pope in almost 500 years. Known as an arch-conservative, the future pontiff gained the nickname 'God's Rottweiler' when he headed the Catholic Church's Office of Doctrine. As cardinal, he offended many liberal German Catholics, but Protestants even more so with some of his rigid pronouncements and treatment of dissident thinkers within the Church. However, he has promised as pope to reach out to people of all beliefs, and he has certainly become an instant hero in his home state of Bavaria.

Joseph Beuys

A multimedia artist who was as famous for his apocalyptic political and social vision as for his art. His artworks still draw worldwide attention, partly because of his use of unlikely materials: shredded metal, cloth, sticks and, in particular, globs of animal fat.

Heinrich Böll

In 1972, Böll became the first German to win the Nobel Prize in Literature since before the Nazis came to power, and his influence quickly spread far beyond his devoted readership. Known chiefly for his broad social and political commitments, Böll's numerous stories, novels and essays deal primarily with the Nazi era and the Nazi legacy in the first decades of the post-war period.

Willi Brandt

A towering political and moral figure through some of the most trying times in Germany's post-war history, Brandt was West Berlin's mayor from 1957 through the early 60's, which made him mayor when the Wall was built. He served as foreign minister from 1966–1969, then became the first SPD chancellor of Germany's post-war period. As chancellor, he became famous for his policy of opening up relations with Eastern Bloc nations and impressed millions by falling to his knees in remorse at the Warsaw Ghetto memorial.

Forced to resign in 1974 upon discovery that one of his personal secretaries was an East German spy, Brandt remained as SPD party chairman for the next decade, during which he continued to exert strong influence both in that post and as head of a number of international bodies.

Sabine Christiansen

A former Lufthansa flight attendant, Christiansen made the move into broadcasting in the mid-80's, and anchored Germany's most respected and most watched evening news for ten years. In 1997, she got her own Sunday night talk show, simply called *Sabine Christiansen*, which has since become a must-see for many and a focal point of office conversation the following day. Described by *Die Welt* newspaper as 'the only conversation of political weight on German TV', Christiansen's show also earns praise as a weekly forum that makes key political issues palatable to a wide viewing public.

Joschka Fischer

German foreign minister as well as a leading figure in the Grünen party, Fischer has emerged as one of the more engaging leaders on the German political scene—largely because of his finely-honed humour. A high-school dropout, 'Joschka', as he is usually called, was one of the leaders of the Realo faction which pushed the Grünen in the direction of the political mainstream in the 1980's. In that decade, he made history when he became the first state parliament cabinet member to take his oath of office wearing sneakers.

In the 1990's, now more mainstream in his dress, Fischer again made history by becoming the first Greens politician to head the foreign ministry, the second most important post in the German government. His efforts and successes as an international mediator and long-distance diplomat have enhanced his stature on the world stage as well as helped his party to increase its vote and the ruling coalition to stay in power in the 2002 election. While a scandal in early 2005 over the lavish granting of visas to Ukrainian prostitutes and criminals tarnished his reputation somewhat (and knocked him from his long-held position as Germany's most popular politician), Fischer still remains a potent force in German politics. However, an anticipated loss by the 'Red-Green' coalition in September 2005 will find Fischer out of his job as Foreign Minister, maybe even shunted off to the fringes of political influence.

Thomas Gottschalk

Another TV star and talk-show host, the affable mop-top Gottschalk is a standard fixture of German television. He hosts the highly popular game/talk show hybrid *Wetten Dass..?* and has had four variety-talk shows of his own. Known for his broad, wide-eyed comedy, Gottschalk is a little too light for many people's tastes, but he enjoys a wide following in Germany and his popularity stretches across all age groups. He turns up in a battery of TV commercials and charity benefits, both of which enhance his profile and popularity.

Steffi Graf

Quite simply the greatest female tennis player of all time, Graf dominated the game from the early 1980s until she retired in 1999. Along the way, she won all four Grand Slam events at least four times each and spent a record 377 weeks as the world number one female player, part of that reign an amazing 186 consecutive weeks on top. Though now retired as an active player, Graf seems set to found a tennis dynasty with her husband, the ageless wonder Andre Agassi. The pair are already the proud parents of two young children.

Günter Grass

Along with Heinrich Böll, Grass is one of Germany's most famous post-war writers. As with Böll, Grass became a major personality in his homeland for his social and political involvements as well as his writings. His themes are also similar to Böll's. Grass' most famous novel, *The Tin Drum*, was later made into a film which won the 1980 Oscar for Best Foreign Film. In 2000, he joined Böll as the only Germans to win a Literature Nobel Prize in the post-war period.

Oliver Kahn

One of Germany's top-of-the-list football heroes, Kahn captained the German 2002 World Cup squad, which lost the championship game to Brazil. While his team came out second, Kahn himself handsomely defeated runner-up Ronaldo of Brazil as the winner of that World Cup's top player trophy, thus becoming the first goalie ever to take this honour.

A member of the German national team since 1993, Kahn has helped his regular-season side, Bayern München, to four *Bundesliga* titles since joining them in the 1994 season. In 2000, his stellar performances in the net earned Kahn two coveted awards—Top Player in the *Bundesliga* and European Goalie of the Year.

Neo Rauch

One of Germany's leading contemporary artists, this native of Leipzig has become something of an international star in recent years—his works sell almost as well in America as in Germany. Characterised by dense images that often evoke the inner conflicts of the figures, Rauch's paintings convey a gloomy surface atmosphere brightened by his masterful command of colour and technique.

Anselm Kiefer

Kiefer is another of the major German names in the international art world and one of the most famous living German artists. He is best known for his giant constructions, principally out of lead, and what he calls picture-bodies, since the works are often affixed with dust, flower petals, ashes and assorted roots. In recent years, Kiefer has moved into themes which reference ancient Egyptian and Hebrew history and expanded his base of devoted admirers.

Jürgen Klinsmann

Replacement of his former team-mate Rudi Völler as coach of the German national team in 2004, Klinsmann will lead the team into the first German World Cup. Although he brought no professional coaching experience to the post, the personable and telegenic Klinsmann was one of the stars of German soccer for over a decade, having excelled in their 1990 World Cup title and been chosen German footballer of the year in 1988 and 1994. After he skipped to Tottenham in the English league, he finished second as European Footballer of the year in 1995, but came back to star for the German national teams in the 1996 European championship and the 1998 World cup.

Helmut Kohl

West German chancellor from 1982–1990, then chancellor of all Germany until 1998, Kohl still ranks as the juggernaut of post-war German politics. Constantly underestimated by his legions of rivals in the early part of his career, Kohl continually confounded his detractors and served longer than any

Two of the world's mst famous contemporary Germans, Boris Becker (left) and Helmut Kohl (right), exchange views at a children's festival in Boon during much happier times for both of them.

German chancellor, except for the legendary Bismarck. He's primarily known as the 'Unification Chancellor' for his skills at seizing the right moment to push through the unification of the two German states. His inability, or refusal, to read the many signs in the political winds led to a humiliating defeat for Kohl and his party in the 1998 national elections. Kohl's involvement in a number of tawdry financial scandals during his time as chancellor, combined with his mulish stonewalling on recent investigations of these scandals, have further tarnished the 'Eternal Chancellor's' reputation more than a little.

Horst Köhler

Also a member of the CDU, Köhler has been the German federal president since July 2004, replacing Johannes Rau of the SPD. A doctor of Economics and Political Science, Köhler headed the International Monetary Fund from 2000 until May 2004, when he stepped down to vie for the president's post. Described as 'an enlightened patriot', Köhler argues that 'Germany should become a land of ideas' and cautiously embraces globalisation.

Angela Merkel

The top female in Germany's political jungle, Merkel is the much-honoured head of the opposition CDU, the first woman to ever lead a major political party in Germany.

Born in Hamburg in West Germany, Merkel moved as a toddler to East Germany, where she grew up and became a physicist and chemist. When the Communist regime collapsed in 1990, Merkel ran for East Germany's first and only democratically elected parliament and took a key post in the new government. She joined the CDU later that year and, after unification, became a powerful member of the new, enlarged German Bundestag, holding two key cabinet posts throughout most of the 1990s. She was first elected CDU chairperson in 1998, then re-elected in November 2002 with 93.7 per cent of the vote. Though she wisely deferred to the Bavarian governor as the Union parties' top candidate in the 2002 national election, she headed up the centre-right coalition's challenge to Chancellor Schröder in the next election of September 2005. If she does win, as most polls have indicated, she'll be the first female as well as the first former East German to run for, let alone become, chancellor.

Otto Rehagel

Just as the German Cardinal Ratzinger became a top figure in Rome, Otto Rehagel has become a demi-god in Greece, whose soccer team he helmed to a shock European Cup title in 2004 ('the miracle of Lisbon'). A highly respected coach in the German *Bundesliga*, especially for Werder Bremen, Rehagel was unceremoniously dumped by Bayern München in 1996 after leading them to second place in the league and a UEFA Cup final. He became the Greek national coach in 2001, and after what has been described as 'perfect' coaching in the 2004 European championship, he was offered—and turned down— the job as German national coach to stay with the Greek team. He will certainly remain a hot topic over the next year or so.

Gerhard Schröder

Elected chancellor in 1998, Schröder is the first Social Democrat to hold that post since Helmut Schmidt in 1982. Praised for his astute political skills, Schröder capped a successful stint as governor of the key industrial state of Lower Saxony by leading the SPD back to national power in the 1998 *Bundestag* election and then tugging his left-of-centre cohorts closer to centrist positions. He's now hailed as one of the principal 'Third Way' leaders on the international scene, seeking a workable path between old-school socialism and the cruelties of advanced capitalism. While it looked for a time as if Schröder would lose his re-election bid in 2002, he proved a much stronger campaigner than his rival Edmund Stoiber, governor of Bavaria, and led his coalition to a narrow victory. However, at the time of this writing, continued erosion of support for his policies made it look more and more like he was facing an inescapable defeat in the upcoming national elections of September 2005.

Michael Schumacher

Germany's leading race car driver and well established as a national sporting hero. Starting with the German national championship in 1989, Schumacher has piled up a stack of racing records in shooting to the top of the world's greatest Formula One race car drivers ever.

Schumacher has taken the overall Driver's Championship a record seven times, two more than any other driver in history. These racing titles include the last five, going back from 2004, itself a record. ('Schummi's' first two titles came in 1994 and 1995.) A slow start in the 2005 season suggest his title streak may come to an end soon.

Schumacher's also a fixture in many television commercials, particularly those that have to do with four-wheeled vehicles. Small wonder he earns US$ 80 million a year, much of it from endorsement deals.

Jan Ullrich

A star cyclist, Ullrich became a national hero in 1997 when he became the first German to win the prestigious Tour de France competition. Only 23 years old then, Ullrich was also the youngest person ever to win that coveted prize. His stock as a national hero rose when he took both silver and gold medals at the 2000 Summer Olympics. However, a drunk-driving incident that cost him his driver's licence and a positive testing for banned drugs in August 2002 severely hurt his image. The drug charge threatened to keep the fallen hero out of many major international races, but he escaped the career gallows by going clean and started buffing up his tarnished image with good shows in the Athens Olympics and a thrilling one-second win in the prestigious 2004 Tour de Suisse. His respectable fourth-place finish in the 2004 Tour de France was his lowest finish ever in that race. (His German team-mate Andreas Kloden finished second to Lance Armstrong in that event, which furnished him hero's credentials of his own in Germany.)

MAJOR TOPICS OF CONVERSATION

An acquaintance with these issues will enable you to intergrate more easily and may even help prevent a case of 'foot-in-mouth disease.'

Die Rechtscreibungsreform

Die Rechtscreibungsreform, or German spelling reform, has already spawned a great deal of controversy and consternation, and this should continue at least up through its full implementation in August 2005 and beyond..

In the mid-1990's, the Culture Ministries of the various states, who are responsible for—amongst other tasks—schools, decided that German spelling was a little too complicated. They decided to simplify the spelling to make it easier for schoolchildren. While some critics charge that this was an unwarranted example of 'dumbing down the language', others claim that the new prescribed spelling rules are actually more confusing and difficult than the old rules.

The wide-reaching changes were officially introduced in 1998, but a 'transitional period' was established, during which the new spellings were to gradually take over. By 31 July 2005, the new spelling is supposed to be the only acceptable one in all schools and government agencies. (Until then, students who use the old spelling are corrected for these 'mistakes', but teachers are not allowed to take any points off their spelling scores.)

The opposition is pretty strong. A poll released in August 2002 found that 56 per cent of German citizens characterised themselves as opponents of the reform, while only 2 per cent totally accepted the sweeping changes as a positive development. And it's not just a bunch of ignorant linguistic troglodytes who reject the reform: many of the country's most prominent writers, including Nobel Prize-winner Günter Grass, continue to write German in the old way and insist that their publishers publish their works that way. Even most of Germany's younger authors have lined up with Grass at the barricades. Moreover, the *Frankfurter Allgemeine*, probably Germany's most respected daily newspaper, announced in August 2000 that after experimenting with the deformed reform, they were going back to the old style of spelling and intended to stay with that style.

The reform's most famous opponent, linguist Theodor Ickler, points out that even the Reform mandarins have abandoned some of their own reforms and gone back to the old way. Nevertheless. the German Supreme Court rejected an appeal to stop the reform in June 2005, and what was left of it was to be fully implemented from August 2005.

Flensburg 'Punktekonto' (Points Account)

Flensburg, far in the north of Germany, is where they keep the *Verkehrssünderkartei* (traffic sinners' file). These official files tally the points that drivers pick up for traffic violations. Most moving violations carry a specific number of points. When you have collected enough points, you either have your licence revoked or are ordered to attend make-up driving classes. So, when someone gets photographed shooting through a red light, you might hear a witness say, "He just added a few to his *Flensburg Punktekonto!*"

The German Fashion Wave

During the first post-war decades, if you heard someone yoke German and fashion together, you could be pretty sure it was the beginning of some joke. But following Germany's rapid rise to the pinnacles of technological and economic achievement, a home-grown fashion industry also started to draw notice. In the 1980's, a new fashion wave led by designers of international caché such as Hugo Boss, Wolfgang Joop, Karl Lagerfeld and Jil Sander hit the world fashion stage with a resounding boom and became yet another source of German pride. Part of that wave included Lagerfeld's favourite showcase for his designs, supermodel Claudia Schiffer.

Masters of the Football World

It would take you some time to master the arcana of German football (soccer), but you will definitely impress your associates if you are at least conversant with Germany's three World Cup championships. (Especially as the first World Cup on German soil is to be played in 2006.)

The first was in 1954 in Switzerland, where the surprise German team tanked the heavily favoured Hungarian side in the so-called 'Miracle of Bern'. Exactly 20 years later, the Germans repeated their success by beating the home team Dutch nationals in Amsterdam. This one was known as 'The Kaiser's Crown' because Franz Beckenbauer, nicknamed the Kaiser, was the German team's captain and star player. In 1990, Beckenbauer was the German coach as they slipped by Argentina 1–0 in the Rome final to again take the title. (By the way, the German team has finished as runners-up in the World Cup more than any other national team.)

Stasi

The 'affectionate' nickname of the former East German secret police (shortened form of *Staats Sicherheits Polizei*, or State Security Police). Almost universally despised during the days of the DDR, the Stasi continues to stay in the news long after its demise because of the pervasive influence it had in the East, as well as the sea of charges and counter-charges regarding which East German citizens cooperated with the Stasi and to what extent they cooperated.

CULTURE QUIZ

ARE YOU READY?

By this stage you will have a much clearer idea of what Geman society has to offer. If you are prepared to persevere and break through the barriers which confront you, a rich and rewarding cultural experience awaits you. Often you will feel like a tightrope walker, precariously balancing the new demands of life in Germany, but in time you will be able to blend more easily into your new surroundings. To test your mettle, the following questions will help you to assess your competence in a number of specifically German social situations.

SITUATION 1

It's your birthday, and word has somehow gotten out at the office. Should you:

A Ignore the whole matter. If people wish you 'Happy birthday' throw them a quizzical look as if you don't understand what they are talking about.

B Send out, or rush out at the first opportunity, for some cakes or rolls and cold cuts, some soft drinks, perhaps a bottle of Sekt. Make sure there is enough for everyone in the office, as well as any regulars who might drop in.

C Smile and explain to everyone that where you come from, it's the birthday boy or girl who is treated, so you don't feel right in providing a little spread for everyone else.

D Invite everyone else in the office out for dinner or drinks at the end of the workday.

Comments

B is clearly the best choice, though you should always assume somebody is going to find out somehow that it's your birthday, so always come to work prepared with the appropriate goodies.

D is a desperate way out which, while appropriate, could wind up costing you a wad of money (you would be expected to pay for repeated drinks for everyone) and is not that effective as some people, being good Germans, will want to rush home or do shopping right after work.

A is most likely to cause confusion, mistrust and bad feelings, and is probably the worst choice here. But **C** is also a very bad choice and illustrates a key principle of living in Germany as a foreigner: while you won't be expected to fully assimilate into German society, you are expected to observe the major customs and practices of the society. Trying to act 'just like back home' on every occasion will brand you as very unsociable and/or unpleasant.

SITUATION 2

You happen to be deeply religious, and soon after arrival you attach yourself to a congregation sharing your beliefs. You notice that the congregation has a number of pamphlets in different languages. You:

A Take a few to put in your bag on the very off-chance that your beliefs may come up in conversation somewhere, and you can pull one out and offer it to the other person.

B Take a tidy pile of the pamphlets. Pass them out to people in your building, at neighbourhood shops, at clubs and at your place of work. Tell people you are ready to answer any questions they have about the content.

C Take a smaller pile of the pamphlets and only pass them out to people in your building or neighbourhood you feel are close to you, and at work only to colleagues you get along especially well with.

D Ignore the pamphlets. Keep your religious beliefs a closely guarded matter while residing in Germany.

Comments

The best answers are **A** and **D**. Options **B** and **C** will get you branded very quickly as a religious fanatic with any group you pass the pamphlets to. Even with **C** you risk alienating the close acquaintance or colleague, as most people here do not like having religion pushed on them.

Whether the best answer is **Ⓐ** or **Ⓓ** depends on your personality and the strength of your beliefs. **Ⓓ** is the absolute safest, as **Ⓐ** always carries the danger that people will be mildly curious about your religion, but turned off after reading the pamphlets or even by the mere appearance of the pamphlets in conversation. But if you feel that the people are seriously interested in the matter, you might offer one of the pamphlets. Just remember that active proselytising is looked upon askance in Germany.

SITUATION 3

You walk into a popular medium-priced restaurant at lunch, or a popular café late in the afternoon. A quick look around convinces you that every table is taken, though you notice that there are some individual seats available. You:

Ⓐ Wait for the waiter or waitress to seat you, or until a table is free.

Ⓑ Sit down unobtrusively in one of the free seats. Ignore the others at the table as these people are all strangers, even to each other apparently.

Ⓒ Go over to one of the free seats, ask the diners at the table if the seat is free, sit down and observe all the formalities. Don't engage in conversation unless it's started up by someone else at the table.

Ⓓ Leave and look for another restaurant or café where you can get a table to yourself.

Comments

Ⓓ is the easiest response, though probably not the best one. If it's a busy time, you may find all the places in the area packed, or have to settle for one where the quality of food is not very good.

Ⓐ wouldn't work in this situation, as only the more expensive restaurants have a head waiter (called *Herr Ober*). If you wait for a table to become free, you might be waiting for a very long time.

Ⓑ is a little awkward as it's hard to be unobtrusive in this situation. Although the Germans themselves may be reticent with strangers in some areas, your actions in this case could be seen as rude.

The best choice here is **C**. You should always ask permission before sitting down, and then don't forget the other formalities: immediately wish everyone eating at the table *'Guten Appetit'* or do so when their food arrives. In addition, when they leave or you leave, don't forget your *'Auf Wiedersehen'*.

SITUATION 4

Waking one morning with pain, you go to your local doctor's office, arriving right in the middle of morning visiting hours. There are several people ahead of you. You wait as patiently as you can, though you are in some discomfort. Then you notice that two people who entered the waiting room after you are called in to see the doctor before you. You:

A Go up to the receptionist and complain. After all, fair is fair.

B Go up to the receptionist and remind her of how much pain you are in. Tell her that it is important you be seen right away.

C Grit your teeth and bear it. It is quite possible that the two people you thought were jumping the queue actually had appointments for that time, or had even returned to the waiting room following the initial stage of some treatment.

D If you can bear the pain, simply leave and find another doctor. Any health care providers who treat their patients so thoughtlessly don't deserve their patients.

Comments

The only correct answer here is **C**. The two reasons given there are often why people are called in to the doctor ahead of other patients.

B may sound convincing from your perspective, but remember that in a busy practice, there are many patients who deserve immediate attention and neither the doctor nor the receptionist can handle everyone at the same time.

If you are in extreme pain, make this known the moment you come in, and you may be taken in sooner.

Considering the likelihood of **❻** being right, it's self explanatory why **❹** and **❶** just won't do.

SITUATION 5

You've been invited to a friend or colleague's home for dinner. The day before—or even that morning—you suddenly remember that you haven't informed your hosts that, for either religious or health reasons, you and your spouse don't eat pork. You decide to:

❹ Not worry about it. Although pork is the most popular meat in Germany, your hosts will probably take your religious background into account and serve something else.

❸ Not say anything and just hope that pork won't be served. If it is served, you'll come up with some strange excuse as to why you're not hungry enough to eat the whole meal.

❻ Call your colleague and inform him/her about your problem with pork. It may be late, but it's better to do that and so save everyone involved from major embarrassment later.

❶ To avoid embarrassment altogether, you come up with an excuse of sudden illness to get out of the invitation. Sometime in the future, you ask your hosts what they had been planning to serve.

Comments

The correct answer is **❻**. Although this does entail a certain amount of embarrassment, it does save the much greater embarrassment (and hunger pangs of) option **❸**. Answer **❶** can cause your hosts more trouble than **❻** and, they may someday discover you were telling them a white lie, which will lead to a sharp downgrading of your relationship.

Answer **❹** assumes a cultural awareness in an area where Germans sometimes have a glaring cultural blind spot. In fact, at an official reception given for the survivors of the Dachau concentration camp on the 50th anniversary of the camp's liberation, the organisers served roast pork even though many of the invited guests were Jewish!

SITUATION 6

You've been invited by a colleague to his/her home for coffee or dinner. While there, you see a CD that you've been trying to locate for some time, with no success. In fact, you've been told at a couple of shops that it's no longer available. You:

A Ask the colleague if you can borrow the CD so you can make a copy back home.

B Explain the situation and ask the colleague if he/she would mind making a copy for you. Quickly add that you'll bring a blank CD to work the next day for the copying.

C Ask the colleague if he or she would go to the store where he or she bought the CD and find out there if it really is no longer available.

D Don't say anything. You know how Germans dislike lending things out to people they don't know, and you don't want to put your colleague in an embarrassing position.

Comments

D is, of course the easiest, though probably not the best answer. **A** is not a good solution, because you probably will put your colleague in an embarrassing situation (it's very German to get embarrassed at such things) and **C** might not help you out at all.

B is the best answer, as your colleague probably won't mind making the copy for you. But you definitely should give that colleague a small gift in gratitude for doing the copying.

DO'S AND DON'TS

DO'S

- Do greet people in your building every time you see them. Usually that greeting includes *Herr* or *Frau* followed by the family name, not the first name.
- Do say *Guten Tag* or *Guten Abend* when entering a small shop.
- Do bring along a small gift when invited to someone's home. Flowers, a bottle of wine or some small souvenir from your homeland are considered most appropriate.
- Do inform your hosts beforehand if there are certain foods (especially pork) or drinks that you can't have.
- Do look people in the eyes when you speak to them.
- Do practise a firm handshake.
- Do give subordinates and colleagues a small candy or something similar on Nikolaus Tag (St Nicholas Day, on 6 December).
- Do give your seat to the elderly or infirm without being asked if you happen to be riding in one of those specially designated seats on public transport.
- Do close the toilet door behind you when you leave.
- Do give sincere compliments when you can. Even Germans love getting deserved praise, but they can also be deeply suspicious of false praise or anything that sounds false to their ears.
- Do drive in the far-right lane on the Autobahn unless you're trying to pass or going at very high speeds.
- Do learn to appreciate the glories of beer, if you can.

DON'TS

- Don't call people after 10:00 pm unless you've arranged to do so.
- Don't drop in on people, even friends, unexpectedly. (Dropping in on relatives unannounced at Christmas time is one acceptable exception to this rule.)
- Don't rest against someone's car. Cars are near sacred in Germany.

- Don't loiter in front of a residential address that isn't yours. The owners or residents may think you're up to no good.
- Don't be the first one to switch to the *Du* form or to first names. Always let your German counterpart take the lead on this one.
- Don't bring roses when invited to someone's home— unless you want the indelibly romantic association these flowers carry in Germany.
- Don't ogle at or approach people engaged in public nude bathing.
- Don't initiate a discussion on the two world wars or the Nazi period. You'll find many Germans quite willing to discuss the topic, but, again, let them be the ones to bring it up.
- Don't be overly friendly to strangers. Germans will assume that you're trying to get something out of them or that you're a little unstable.
- Don't eat or drink anything (other than water possibly) on public transport. Although you'll see many in Germany who do such things, it is generally considered lower-class.
- Don't eat solid foods, other than desserts, with a spoon. Most Germans consider this behaviour something done only by young children.
- Don't give a birthday present before the actual day. If you can't be there, it's best to give your present after the day. (Giving a present before a birthday is considered an act of tempting the fates.)
- Don't brag if you enjoy special tax privileges as foreign talent. Germans aren't all that happy about the high taxes they have to pay, but they deeply believe that everyone should share in paying them equally.

GLOSSARY

SOME USEFUL WORDS AND PHRASES

Even before you enrol in a German-language class, there are some extremely useful words and phrases you might want to master. The following group can make your initial adjustment to German society a lot smoother:

The Basics

- *Danke* and *Nein, Danke*—'Thank you' and 'No, thank you'
  These very basic expressions will carry you a surprisingly long way during your early period in Germany.

- *Bitte*
  This one does double service as both 'Please' and 'You're welcome'. Again, just a little bit of politeness that can smooth your way considerably at the beginning. (By the way, its double role explains why many Germans will answer your English 'Thank you' with 'Please!')

- *Entschuldigung*—'Excuse me'
  This is primarily used when disturbing someone to ask for information. Theoretically, it is also to be employed when you accidentally bump into someone, though a more common practice hereabouts is just to pretend it never happened. Somewhat tellingly, the English word 'Sorry' is heard more and more as a quick apology for unintentional bumps or disturbances.

- *Guten Morgen, Guten Tag, Guten Abend, Gute Nacht*
  —'Good morning', 'Good afternoon', 'Good evening', 'Good night'
  In Germany's southern areas as well as Austria, there's an all-purpose greeting for any time of day: *Grüss Gott* ('Greet God').

- *Wie geht's*—'How are you?' or 'How's it going?'
  There are more complicated additions to this but this simple formulation always does the job. And if someone poses this question to you, a simple, effective answer is, *Es geht mir gut* or *Es geht mir schlecht* ('I'm doing fine' or 'I'm doing badly').

Food and Drink

- ***Ich habe Hunger*** and ***Ich habe Durst***—'I'm hungry' and 'I'm thirsty'
- ***Frühstück, Mittagessen, Abendessen***—Breakfast, lunch, dinner.
  Essen means both 'to eat' and, in its noun form *das Essen*, 'the food'.
- ***Speisekarte***—A menu or bill of fare.
  Be careful here: if you go into a restaurant and ask for '*das Menü'*, they'll smile and bring you the set meal of the day, with all three or four courses. The *Speisekarte* will very likely be divided into two sections—*Speisen* (food) and *Getränke* (drinks).
- ***Bezahlen, bitte***—'I'd like to pay' or 'Bill, please'.
  When you ask for the bill at the end of the meal, your waiter or waitress is likely to inquire *Zusammen oder getrennt?* ('All together or separate bills?')
- ***Bitte, wo ist … ?***—'Please, where is… ?' (fill in whatever you're looking for.)
  If what you are looking for is easy to describe, you may hear as a reply, *Nach rechts* (right), *Nach links* (left) or *Geradeaus* (straight ahead).
- ***Das gefällt mir*** and ***Das gefällt mir nicht***—'I like that' and 'I don't like that'

Signs

Offen	Open
Geschlossen	Closed
Eingang	Entrance
Ausgang	Exit
Drücken	Push
Ziehen	Pull
Gefahr	Danger
Vorsicht!	Caution
Umleitung	Detour or Diversion
Fahrkarten	Tickets

Abfahrt	Departure
Ankunft	Arrival
Damen	Ladies' Room
Herren	Gents/Men's Room
Besetzt	Occupied
Frei	Free
Heiss	Hot
Kalt	Cold

Two Most Important Phrases

Ich spreche kaum Deutsch and ***Sprechen sie Englisch?***—
'I hardly speak any German' and 'Do you speak English?'
Let's face it, unless you arrive with some good prior
knowledge of German, you will have to rely on your English
a great deal during the first stages of your German experience.
These two phrases will help you along that path.

RESOURCE GUIDE

EMERGENCIES AND HEALTH
Emergency Numbers
- Police   110
- Fire department   112
- Ambulance services   115
- Poison treatment central office   (0761) 19-240

Hospitals
Leading hospitals in Germany include:
- Albertinen-Krankenhaus, Hamburg
- Universitäts-Krankenhaus, Hamburg-Eppendorf
- Kerckhoff Klinik, Bad Nauheim
- Deutsches Herzzentrum, Berlin
- Universitätsklinikum Benjamin Franklin, Berlin
- Universitätsklinikum Charitè, Berlin
- Universitätsklinikum Carl Gustav Carus, Dresden
- Vinzenzkrankenhaus, Hanover
- Klinikum der Johann Wolgang Goethe-Universität, Frankfurt
- Universitätsklinikums Tübingen
- Universitätsklinikums Ulm
- Dr. von Ehrenwall'sche Klinik

In Germany, you don't often get the chance to choose your hospital. In an emergency, you'll be taken to the nearest hospital with the facilities to accommodate you. For non-pressing or elective treatment, you'll usually need a transfer from your primary care provider, who will make the decision as to the hospital, often based on knowing and trusting a particular specialist at the hospital in question.

The exception to this rule of thumb is private clinics. However, at these institutions, you have to pay yourself. That means they are effectively limited to those with private insurance coverage or very deep pockets.

Lost and Found
Almost every town or city in Germany, from the very small to the very large, has a 'Lost and Found' office. You can look

up the number for your local office in the phone book under *Fundbüro*. In small towns, this office is frequently found in the town hall building, while in bigger localities, it will have its own sizeable premises in some other government facility. Also, in bigger cities, the public transport system will maintain its own *Fundbüro* for objects lost on buses and trains.

HOME AND FAMILY
Relocation Services

Over the last decade or so, an extensive network of relocation services has sprung up in Germany. These services, which range in size from a few consultants to a staff of 30 or more, attend to the nuts and bolts of settling in Germany—or moving back to your own country. They offer advice on a wide range of practical matters, such as where to buy furniture or how to arrange to have your home painted.

These agencies will also help you manoeuvre your way through the bureaucratic red tape that newcomers to Germany have to deal with. Some of the companies even have someone go to government offices, sit in waiting rooms and pick up forms for you, then help you fill them out at home. You thus save trips for everything except those procedures which require you to appear in person before some civil servant.

Relocation services are still a growing field in Germany, with many practitioners. Here's a short list of those which operate throughout the country along with their websites.

- Helga Thomas Relocation Partner
  website: http://www.relocationpartner.de
- RE/MAX Relocation Europe
  website: http://www.Europe-relocation.com
- Relocation Management and Service
  website: http://www.reloc.com
- Relocation Services und Beratung
  website: http://www.rsb-relocation.de
- Crown Relocations
  website: http://www.crownrelo.com

HOTELS

Every German town of any size has a good store of hotels and pensions at varying price levels. You can always book in advance at a DER office, frequently located in the central train station of a city.

However, should you arrive in a city without a booking, don't panic. Most larger cities maintain a hotel booking desk at the central train station or airport. They will ask what you're willing to pay, then make calls or check their computers to see what hotels still have free rooms. But this system runs into serious bottlenecks during a major trade fair (i.e. Cebit in Hanover or the Frankfurt Book Fair) or big events such as Munich's Oktoberfest.

ENTERTAINMENT & LEISURE
Bookshops

Germans still like to refer to themselves as a *Kulturvolk* (People of Culture), and the number and size of their bookstores would seem to indicate that this term still carries a lot of validity. The list below barely scratches the surface, but it includes some of the best book outlets in the Federal Republic.

Berlin

- **Kiepert** (near Ernst-Reuter Platz)
  Has a large store of maps, old books, art books and paperbacks in German and original language, including many in English.

Cologne

- **Buchhandlung Walther Koenig** (Breite Strasse 93)
  Two adjoining bookshops, with a large number of English volumes each. One store has second-hand books and remainders, the other new editions.

Frankfurt am Main

- **British Bookshop** (Börsenstrasse 17, near the Stock Exchange)
  A friendly and informed staff and a large stock of books, mainly but not exclusively in English. The window features

notices regarding various activities and job opportunities in the Anglophone community.

- **Hugendubel** (Steinweg 12, just off the Hauptwache) Frankfurt's largest bookstore has one floor devoted entirely to foreign-language material, mainly English.
- **Sussman's** (Zeil 127, An der Katherinenkirche) A small, pleasant shop devoted to books, newspapers and periodicals in foreign languages. The well-informed staff is quite helpful.
- **Die Wendeltreppe** (Brückenstrasse 34, Sachsenahusen). Specialises in detective and mystery literature. Mostly in German, but there is a tidy English collection. Topping off the ambience are spiders, cobwebs, handcuffs and instruments of torture—only for display, of course.

Hamburg

- **Frensche International** (Landsbank Galerie, Gerhart-Hautpmann-Platz) A good place for foreign-language volumes and editions.
- **Thalia Buchhaus** (two stores: on Spitalstrasse near the Hauptbahnhof and on the Grosse Bleichen near the Jungfernstieg) Large general bookstores with a fair sampling of English-language materials.

Munich

- **Fremde Welten** (Müllerstrasse 43) A non-profit shop that turns its earnings over to good causes in developing countries. Offers books in German and foreign languages (including English).
- **International Bookshop** A good selection of foreign-language books purveyed in a friendly, helpful atmosphere.
- The **Hugendubel** chain operates at least five outlets throughout Munich. The largest, with the biggest selection of books in English and other foreign tongues, is at Marienplatz 22. Not far away at Karlpatz is the newest branch, also quite large, with a pleasant café.

TRANSPORT AND COMMUNICATIONS
City and Country Dialing Codes

Germany's country code is 49. For city codes, include a '0' if calling within Germany; drop it if calling from another country.

Codes for Some Major Cities

- Berlin   030
- Cologne   0221
- Dortmund   0231
- Dresden   0351
- Dusseldorf   0211
- Frankfurt   069
- Hamburg   040
- Hanover   0511
- Leipzig   034
- Munich   089
- Stuttgart   0711

MEDIA
Newspapers

Germany's biggest newspaper is the *Bild Zeitung*, printed in various local editions throughout the country. (*Bild Berlin*, for instance, highlights local Berlin news mixed in with the same stories and features *Bild* readers in other cities get.) It is considered rather low-brow, and the accuracy or fairness of its stories is often challenged. It is, however, turned out in easy-to-read German for those still mastering the language. The *Berliner Zeitung*, or BZ, is similar to the *Bild* in many respects.

Much more respectable publications—those read and written by opinion-makers in Germany—include *Die Zeit*, a Hamburg weekly; the *Frankfurt Allgemeine Zeitung* (FAZ); the *Süddeutsche Zeitung* of Munich; Hamburg's *Die Welt*; the *Frankfurter Rundschau*; and the *Handelsblatt* out of Dusseldorf, the most widely read business and financial publication. Some of these publications put out a Sunday edition, but there's still no real Sunday newspaper of note here.

Magazines

Among the deluge of glossy German news magazines, the best are the formidable *Der Spiegel*, *Der Stern* and *Focus*. Many of the others (and many they are) serve up a curious mix of interesting articles, cheap fluff and gossip, and nude photos.

English-language publications readily available in much of Germany include the Paris-based *International Herald Tribune* (owned by the New York Times Company). Printed in Frankfurt, the 'Trib' is as readily available in big cities as any German sheet. Other Anglophone papers easy to get here include the major British newspapers, such as *Times*, *Guardian* and the *Daily Telegraph*, plus American mainstays *The Wall Street Journal* and USA Today, along with magazines like the *Economist* and European editions of *Time* and *Newsweek*.

Television

The German TV landscape is still dominated by the government-funded stations. These include the two large national networks (ARD and ZDF) as well as a group of so-called 'third channels', connected to a particular state, such as Bavaria, North Rhine-Westphalia or Hesse; the smaller states combine their resources to form regional third channels, such as Southwest Television, North German Television and Central German Television. The third channels have traditionally been known for their more challenging programming, though of late even these stations have bent their principles a bit to squeeze in broadly-popular shows. But in two areas, the third channels have certainly remained true to their original charters: the presentation of more local news and reports on local communities and personalities.

Perhaps the best news about these stations is that they restrict commercials to limited blocks of time and don't interrupt programmes for a word from the sponsor. The score or more of private stations pepper their broadcasts with commercials.

MANAGING YOUR MONEY
Taxes

Basic tax questions or problems can be handled cost-free at the local *Finanzamt*, or Tax Office. Every large town or county has its own *Finanzamt*, and one of their mandates is to provide confused taxpayers with assistance. But be forewarned: You'll invariably face long queues and long waits, and the advice they'll give you will be minimal and typically more favorable to the tax collector. For all but the simplest of tax brackets, you're best advised to find a good tax consultant (*see page 257*).

Banking

Private banking customers face the option of three types of banks in Germany, though the once clear distinctions between these three types have become hazy over the last few decades.

Nevertheless, differences still exist amongst the three: large commercial banks; the *Sparkassen*, or full-service savings banks; and the *Kreditgenossenshaft*, or credit co-operatives. Members of the last type tend to be the smallest of the three, with their offices being located in the neighbourhoods of towns and cities in the area.

The large commercial banks, dominated by the Big Three (Deutsche Bank, Commerzbank and Dresdner) had the reputation of attending more to the needs of big clients than the more focused needs of small customers. But in recent years, they've introduced more and more programmes for private customers to entice them away from the *Sparkassen*, which had traditionally been regarded as much friendlier and more beneficial to the small customer. However, a number of the large commercial banks have in recent years seen the advantages of this trend and have opened their own full-service direct banks. Some good examples here are Deutsche Bank's Bank 24, Commerz Bank's ComDirect and Vereinsbank's Advance Bank.

Many locals with small accounts and small problems still trust their business to the local *Sparkassen* (whose individual name will precede this term with the town name) or the local *Raiffensbank*, the traditional *Kreditgenossenshaft* base.

Other small clients like the service and solid offers of *Bausparkassen* (building societies), such as Wüstenrot, or banks run by large retail chains—mail-order companies, such as Quelle Bank. The environmentally conscious sometimes put their money in the Ökobank, which theoretically invests only in environmentally friendly projects.

LANGUAGE

There's no dearth of opportunities for learning German within Germany. Probably the cheapest way is to enroll in a course at the *Volkshochschule* in your area. The *Volkshochschulen* form a network of adult education schools throughout Germany. The advantage of these schools is that they are cheap; the downside includes large class sizes and teachers of widely varying levels of commitment to actual teaching. If you're lucky, these classes can be quite rewarding; if you're unlucky, you won't get much out of them.

Private Schools

Private-language school chains with branches throughout Germany include Berlitz, Inlingua and Linguarama. Consult your telephone directory for the one closest to you.

Many students complain that they don't really get their money's worth at the large-chain schools. One complaint is that teachers disappear suddenly, perhaps due to the fact that there's a lot of job-hopping in this field. Small private-language schools are there in abundance, and they're usually stronger in the area of staff retention. The best thing might be to ask others who have taken language courses for their recommendations.

Goethe-Institut

The most reliable option is to go to one of the Goethe-Instituts. It's also, however, probably the most expensive option. But you'll almost always get your money's worth there. The Goethe-Institut maintains 16 full operations within Germany itself, with another 126 in 77 foreign countries. For detailed information, visit ther website at: http://www.goethe.de.

FURTHER READING

THE CULTURAL MINEFIELDS

Facts About Germany. Societäts-Verlag. Frankfurt am Main.
- A yearly survey of key facts regarding Germany. This thick volume gives short but valuable synopses of history, culture, economy, government, education, transport, industry and leisure activities. Looks at the country as a whole as well as the 16 individual states comprising the new Germany.

These Strange German Ways. Susan Stern. Bonn: Atlantic-Brücke 1994.
- A short but informative guide to the foibles, customs and daily doings of German society. Quite interesting to note is where Stern's judgements agree and disagree with those rendered in this work.

GERMANY AND THE GERMANS— A GENERAL VIEW

Europe and German Unification. Renata Fritsch-Bournoyel. New York and Oxford: Berg, 1992.
- Like Marsh's book below, this volume examines the ramifications of a new, larger, more powerful Germany in a Europe trying to define its own new, larger, perhaps more powerful identity.

The Germans, Gordon A. Craig. London: Penguin 1991.
- A noted historian, Craig here serves up an absorbing account of German society and the German people, supported by a broad historical outlook.

Germany and Europe: The Crisis of Unity. David Marsh. London: Mandarin Paperbacks, 1995.
- A leading British journalist stationed in Germany, Marsh offers a thoughtful look at the changes wrought by German

unification and how these will effect the nation's role in a uniting Europe.

Germany and the Germans. John Ardagh. London: Penguin Books 1991.
- A thoughtful look at the Germans and their country, updated to take in the first shocks of unification.

In Europe's Name. Timothy Garton Ash. New York: Vintage 1984.
- Ash combines a deep knowledge of Germany's history with a broad perspective on the current European scene to analyse the present situation in a transformed Germany within a transformed Europe.

Meet United Germany Handbook 1992/93. Susan Stern (ed). Frankfurt am Main: Frankfurt Allgemeine Zeitung Information Services and Atlantik-Brücke, 1992.
- Chock full of key facts and practical information that will help you get through the early stages of your German stay.

Meet United Germany: Perspectives. Susan Stern (ed).
- Produced by the same publisher, this one is a series of informative essays which allow you a better grasp of how diverse sectors of German society function.

The New Germany: A Human Geography. Alun Jones. Chichester: John Wiley & Sons, 1994.
- Similar to Diem's book right below, except that this opus doesn't set as close a focus on individual regions as does Diem's book. Still, packed with informative material, charts, diagrams and figures upon figures.

The New Germany: Land, People, Economy. Aubrey Diem. Kitchener Ontario: Aljon Print-Craft Ltd, 1993.
- A valuable general resource book. Filled with charts, maps and figures, this work offers a quick background and updated look at Germany's regions.

BUSINESS

Doing Business in Germany. Price Waterhouse, 1998. (Available at your nearest Price Waterhouse office.)

- A quick but nourishing survey of the nuts and bolts of doing business in Germany. Especially strong on giving good overviews of taxation, investment, exporting, auditing and accounting.

EuroManagers and Martians: The Business Culture of Europe's Trading Nations. Richard Hill. Brussels: Europublications, 1994.

- A quick but informative survey of the differing business cultures in the major EU countries. Has an especially rich section on Germany and the prevailing business mentality hereabouts.

Riding The Waves of Culture. Fons Trompenaars. Irwin Professional Publishing, 1994.

- Like Hill's book, this work concentrates on various types of business cultures. Trompenaars, however, doesn't restrict himself to the EU nations, and presents many valuable insights into the German business mentality.

Succeed in Business: Germany. Richard Lord. Singapore: Times Editions, 1998.

- A compact, handy guide by the author of this volume, which delves into all aspects of successfully doing business in Germany. This is a useful guide for all, whether you're an expat executive taking a post in a German company or an entrepreneur opening a business of your own.

LEARNING THE LANGUAGE

It's been some time since I had to learn German, so I was unsure what learning-German texts captured the state of the art at the moment. The following were recommended by salespeople at English language book shops here in Germany.

- *German in Three Months.* Hugo Press Suffolk 1990.

- *Teach Yourself German: A Complete Course For Beginners*. Hodder 1989.
- *German For Business*. Hugo Press Suffolk 1992.
- *Guide To German Idioms*. Passport Books 1994.

HISTORY

A Concise History of Germany. Mary Fulbrook. Cambridge University Press, 1991.
- A compact survey of the most important episodes of German history, this slender volume gives you a quick but informative look at the course of events up to the unification of the two German states.

Germany 1866–1945, Gordon A. Craig. Oxford University Press, 1984.
- A classic text that offers a firm footing in understanding how modern Germany came into existence—and then almost went out of existence. Excellent scholarship, though some may find it a little tough slogging through at times.

Germany Divided: From The Wall To Reunification. A. James McAdams. Princeton NJ: Princeton University Press, 1993.
- A quite readable, scholarly look at a most recent chapter in the German chronicle. This one will give you a good grounding in understanding the current problems of a united Germany.

The Rise and Fall of the Third Reich. William L. Shirer. New York: Fawcett Crest, 1992.
- This is the 34th printing of the classic examination of the Nazi regime. Shirer was a journalist posted in Germany during the regime's early period, so he was able to observe first-hand how the system functioned. A frothy mix of solid reportage, painstaking research and personal experiences. Even if you can't make it through the book's gargantuan length, you can dip in at various points to get a fascinating insight into the operations of Germany's darkest age.

FOOD

The Gourmet's Companion: German Menu Guide and Translator.
Bernard Rivkin. John Wiley & Sons, 1991.

- A rather helpful guide until your German is up to par and/or your knowledge of German food gets you what you want in a German restaurant. In addition to helping you survive in a German restaurant, this primer contains a grab bag of useful hints on shopping for food and drink.

ABOUT THE AUTHOR

A US citizen, Richard Lord has lived and worked in Britain, the United States, France and, for 18 years, in Germany. After taking his MA in English from Boston College, Lord worked as a freelance journalist specialising in film and theatre criticism, and as the associate editor of *CHOMP*, a food and dining monthly.

His theatre criticism expanded into a broad range of theatre activities including writing, acting and directing. He has had quite a few of his plays and sketches staged professionally in Boston, London and in Germany. Two of his plays were broadcast by BBC World Service, the second of which, *The Boys At City Hall*, was a BBC Highlight of the Month in 1989. In the early 1990s, he was a co-founder of two English speaking theatres performing pub theatre in the Frankfurt area.

Lord also taught English, Drama and Film at Boston College and English and Creative Writing for the University of Maryland—European Division. In recent years, he taught business and technical English for the German electronics company AEG and financial English for the Deutsche Bundesbank. In the 1990s, he wrote on the Frankfurt dining scene and a wide range of other topics for *Main City*, the *Frankfurter Allgemeine*'s English-language magazine.

His previously published works include a volume of poems about Berlin, *Beyond Walls: Berlin Views* (Amberse Press, 1988), *Succeed in Business: Germany* (Times Editions, 1998), *Countries of the World: Germany* (Gareth Stevens Publishing, 1999) and the English translation of *Thirty Years of German-Israeli Relations* (Tribüne Verlag, 1995). He's currently working in Singapore as a writer, editor and performer.

INDEX

Titles in the CULTURESHOCK! series:

Argentina	Hong Kong	Paris
Australia	Hungary	Philippines
Austria	India	Portugal
Bahrain	Indonesia	San Francisco
Barcelona	Iran	Saudi Arabia
Beijing	Ireland	Scotland
Belgium	Israel	Sri Lanka
Bolivia	Italy	Shanghai
Borneo	Jakarta	Singapore
Brazil	Japan	South Africa
Britain	Korea	Spain
Cambodia	Laos	Sweden
Canada	London	Switzerland
Chicago	Malaysia	Syria
Chile	Mauritius	Taiwan
China	Mexico	Thailand
Costa Rica	Morocco	Tokyo
Cuba	Moscow	Turkey
Czech Republic	Munich	Ukraine
Denmark	Myanmar	United Arab
Ecuador	Nepal	Emirates
Egypt	Netherlands	USA
Finland	New York	Vancouver
France	New Zealand	Venezuela
Germany	Norway	Vietnam
Greece	Pakistan	

For more information about any of these titles, please contact any of our Marshall Cavendish offices around the world (listed on page ii) or visit our website at:

www.marshallcavendish.com/genref